Gandhi's Vision of Social Transformation

Gandhi's Vision of Social Transformation

Malabika Pande

RAWAT PUBLICATIONS

Jaipur • New Delhi • Bangalore • Hyderabad • Guwahati

ISBN 81-316-0374-1

Published by
Prem Rawat for **Rawat Publications**
Satyam Apts, Sector 3, Jawahar Nagar, Jaipur 302 004 (India)
Phone: 0141 265 1748 / 7006 Fax: 0141 265 1748
E-mail: info@rawatbooks.com
Website: www.rawatbooks.com

New Delhi Office
4858/24, Ansari Road, Daryaganj, New Delhi 110 002
Phone: 011 2326 3290

Also at *Bangalore, Hyderabad* and *Guwahati*

Typeset by Rawat Computers, Jaipur
Printed at Chaman Enterprises, New Delhi

I dedicate this book,
which is a humble effort to study Gandhi
as I understood him, to my grandfather
Shri Suhrid Chandra Choudhury
who reminded me of Gandhi in many ways.

Contents

	Preface	ix
	Introduction	1
1	Evolution of Gandhi's Social and Economic Ideas	13
2	Vision of the Ideal Society	55
3	Perception of the Indian Social Structure	80
4	Issues in Social Change	109
5	Instruments of Social Change	159
6	Theory of Social Change and Contemporary Relevance	206
	Bibliography	239
	Index	246

Preface

I can enumerate only in bare outline the considerable debts of gratitude accumulated during the course of my study of the subject and the preparation of this work, which began its journey as a thesis for the DPhil degree of the University of Allahabad.

My supervisor, the late Dr Uma Rao, formerly of the Department of Medieval and Modern History, University of Allahabad, and fellow of the Indian Institute of Advanced Study, Shimla, not only suggested the topic, but gave me constant inspiration, encouragement and guidance at all stages of the work. Despite her onerous academic commitments, Dr Rao ungrudgingly invested time and energy in the fruition of my efforts. Her detailed critiques of the earlier drafts of my thesis were invaluable to my endeavours to make this study comprehensive and coherent. Her indefatigable and perfectionist zeal in the pursuit of her academic and other responsibilities also set a personal example.

The Department of Medieval and Modern History, University of Allahabad, provided me with a secure base and the essential academic facilities for undertaking the study. Professor C.B. Tripathi, the former head of the department, gave me steady support and valuable advice in the crucial initial stages of this work. The late Professor Radhey Shyam, head of the department after Prof. Tripathi, was graciously helpful as the study progressed. The librarian and staff of the university library were generously cooperative with the venture as were other academic and administrative functionaries and staff of the university.

The Indian Council of Historical Research (ICHR) awarded me a research fellowship from July 1985, which enabled me to pursue this study with a sense of confidence, in addition to sustaining my enterprise morally and materially. Professor Irfan Habib, chairman, ICHR, took expeditious personal action on all my requests for the resolution of procedural holdups at the university level to ensure the regular availability of the fellowship grants. Dr Raj Kumar, senior research officer, ICHR, was courteous, helpful and efficient in administering all aspects of the fellowship, and patiently bore with the inevitable delay in the completion of the thesis. It is doubtful if this thesis would have materialized without the generosity of the ICHR.

The Govind Ballabh Pant Social Science Institute, Allahabad, gave me ready access to its impressive library. Professor A.D. Pant, the former director of the institute, took a keen interest in the progress of my work, and my discussions with him were of great value in clarifying a number of conceptual issues. Professor L.R. Singh, professor of geography at the institute, also proffered significant help in extending the academic facilities of the institute in the final stages of the work.

The Nehru Memorial Museum and Library, New Delhi, was of great significance to my exploration of documentary material and Gandhian authorities. Its director, the late Professor Ravinder Kumar, was instrumental in this. Prof. Kumar's own writings on Gandhi's movements and the social history of modern India are full of insights that are highly relevant to this study.

The Institute of Gandhian and Peace Studies (or Gandhi Bhawan), University of Allahabad, proved to be of considerable help in my work. Former directors Professor J.S. Mathur and Professor Banwari Lal Sharma and the staff of Gandhi Bhawan allowed me to consult their library. Gandhi Bhawan also gave me the opportunity to observe and participate in its programmes and projects, which may be described as Gandhism in action.

I must also acknowledge my gratitude to my colleagues in the Department of History, Faculty of Social Sciences, Banaras Hindu University, Varanasi, for their help and advice on various occasions. The central library of the Banaras Hindu University has excellent material for research work, which was very useful to me.

I have profited immensely from my discussions with the late Deoki Nandan Pande of Almora, freedom fighter and Gandhian social activist, and with Professor Gyanendra Pandey, Dr David Hardiman and Gautam Bhadra. The late Professor Amar Nath Kakkar of the Department of Defence and Strategic Studies, University of Allahabad, gave me gentle encouragement and advice through the most trying stages of this work, and I shall always cherish his words to me. To my deep regret, he was tragically taken away from us in the prime of his life, before my work assumed final shape as a thesis. My friends, Ranjana Kakkar, Rajul Mathur and Nisha Srivastava, have given me immeasurable moral and intellectual support in this effort. Dr Asha Seth and the late Dr Indu Varma were very helpful in the concluding phases of my work. My aunt, Preeta, sister-in-law, Jaishree, and cousins, Jaya and Adity, offered me warm hospitality during my various visits to New Delhi to consult the Nehru Memorial Museum and Library, and also gave me food for thought through lay perspectives on the subject. Rakesh Kumar Shukla efficiently performed the crucial task of typing the drafts of this work at the different stages of its metamorphosis from a dissertation to a book.

This venture could not have been undertaken without strong encouragement and support from my parents-in-law, Kusum and the late Jiwan Chandra Pande, my parents, Sabita and the late Suchit Chandra Choudhury, my son-in-law, Vivek, my daughter, Suparna, and my husband, Vinaya.

I gratefully acknowledge the contribution of all these individuals and institutions, and of countless others who have not been named only on account of constraints of space, in the making of this study. Nevertheless, I alone am responsible for the manifold shortcomings in this work.

Malabika Pande

Introduction

The sheer volume of the interpretative works of Mohandas Karamchand Gandhi (1869–1948) is matched by the bewildering variety of assessments of his ideas and his contributions by different scholars, ranging from the reverentially eulogistic to the irrationally hostile. A number of factors may be held responsible for the apparent absence of critical coherence or balance in much of such literature.

In the first place, the vast body of Gandhi's writings (including letters) and speeches as well as the sheer magnitude of his political and social work render it difficult to seek the crucial foci of his thoughts. Secondly, Gandhi's evaluation of contemporary reality, his prescriptions for India's problems and even his developmental objectives for the country underwent steady evolution with time, as a result of which it is not always easy to keep track of the temporal context of his views while analysing them. Finally, Gandhi's critique of British imperialism, his action programmes for attaining swaraj and his blueprint for the liberated India challenged the assumptions and purposes of all shades of contemporary political opinion in India (including conservative, liberal, socialist and Marxist nationalists, 'loyalists' and communalists), thereby generating critical reactions that have had a persistent effect on the standpoints of various analysts.

In recent years, however, the shrillness of the polemics on Gandhi has tended to lessen, while scholarly appraisals of his life and work have converged towards a narrower spectrum of viewpoints. The perspective of distance in time on his social, economic and political ideas and programmes, the intractable problems besetting the industrialization oriented mixed economy variant of liberal democracy in India after independence and the very crisis of survival facing the world due to the ecological excesses of human beings have brought forth more objective – and positive – appraisals of what Gandhi stood and worked for.

In these exercises, Gandhian thought has been placed in the crucible of comprehensive analyses. Yet, by and large, one can agree with Ravinder Kumar that "there has been no attempt to see the social structure of India through his eyes".[1] The major issues of change perceived by Gandhi as confronting Indian society and the theory of social change articulated or implicit in his writings have also not received specific attention.

This work endeavours to bridge some of these gaps by searching for the issues and theory of social change in Gandhi's writings during the period, 1909–39. The starting point of the study – 1909 – marks the wide dissemination of *Hind Swaraj* (a booklet first published in Gujarati in 1908), which was the earliest comprehensive, though concise, statement of Gandhi's social ideals with special reference to India. The years, 1936–39, are generally regarded as the period in which the Gandhian ideology and social programme were projected in a final form, which is why 1939 has been taken as the terminal year for the work.

Most scholarly appraisals of Gandhi, critical as well as approbatory, are predicated on the view that he was a pragmatic and not a systematic theorist and suggest that the eclectic character and moral temper of his thought inevitably imbued it with ambiguities and logical inconsistencies. However, many of these analyses tend towards an a-historical approach to Gandhi's ideas and seem to overlook the fact that (as pointed out earlier) they evolved with the growing enrichment of his assessment of Indian social reality as a result of his deepening interaction with the people and with popular culture, traditions and institutions, in the course of the social, economic and political movements, which he initiated or in which he participated. There are, of course, several honourable exceptions and most of them have been referred to in this body of work at the relevant places. Among these, we may include one book[2] and two edited volumes[3] by the eminent international Gandhian scholar, Anthony Parel.

The problem, essentially, is that Gandhi was not given to detailed theoretical expostulations per se or to justifications of his programme of action. He was also quick to concede errors in his approach and prescriptions. Nevertheless, he has indicated at different places in his voluminous writings the conceptual basis of his ideas and programme and given reasoned explanations for changes in his views, where such changes occurred. It is therefore possible to reconstruct Gandhi's social (as indeed his economic or political) thought as a holistic system, with definite premises and logically derived conclusions on the specifics of social structure and the imperative of social change in the special context of India.

This work is an effort in this direction and seeks to apply for the purpose the historical methodology of analysis to the corpus of Gandhi's writings (including letters) and speeches, now available in print in full[4] and in several general or purposive selections.[5] To this end, standard works on social structure and social change, authoritative volumes on Gandhi, his ideology and his movements, and a host of relevant secondary work, all indicated in the Bibliography at the end, have been consulted. The book is arranged thematically in five chapters, and the conclusions from the study are spelt out in Chapter 6.

Chapter 1 (Evolution of Gandhi's Social and Economic Ideas) seeks to identify the traditional and non-traditional influences (Indian as well as non-Indian) that moulded Gandhi's thinking on social questions and on the principles of truth, ahimsa, satyagraha, bread labour and trusteeship, and to trace the evolution of his perceptions and prescriptions in these areas over the period covered by the study.

Chapter 2 (Vision of the Ideal Society) attempts an analysis of Gandhi's views on the elements and objects of an ideal social order and refers in this regard to his critique of modern industrial civilization, interpretation of the pristine principles underlying the traditional social order of India and the conception of swaraj and the social norms and values it sought to encapsulate.

Chapter 3 (Perception of the Indian Social Structure) is directed at Gandhi's appraisal of Indian society as he saw it, his evaluation of its basic dysfunctionalities (arising from what he saw as the perversions it had undergone both in the course of historical development and the impact of British rule) and his views on the extent to which India's social and cultural heritage was relevant to modern imperatives.

Chapter 4 (Issues in Social Change) endeavours a review of Gandhi's assessment of the crucial areas of national life as well as the retrogressive features of the social landscape, including caste rigidities, untouchability, degradation of women, communalist tendencies, elitism and deprecation of manual labour, which called for reform, if Indian society was to move towards the ideal social order.

Chapter 5 (Instruments of Social Change) explores Gandhi's ideas on efficacious modalities for the transformation of Indian society (such as satyagraha, restructured education, swadeshi, decentralized production and trusteeship) and highlights the significance he assigned in this regard to the role of the state as well as to the emancipation of unprivileged sections of society, such as untouchables and women.

Chapter 6 (Theory of Social Change and Contemporary Relevance) ventures to delineate, on the basis of the study, the salient features of the issues and theory of social change articulated in Gandhi's writings and the structure and functions of the non-violent state envisaged by him, and makes an assessment of the contemporary relevance of his ideas.

It would be appropriate at this juncture to briefly conceptualize our approach to the problem of social change. Change and persistence are as fundamental facts of our being as they are in nature. As we change, society changes, and from ancient times, two large questions have puzzled philosophers and historians – the questions of social statics and social dynamics – what society is and how it changes. Both these are difficult to analyse and many complex facts are involved. Gandhi's copious writings have in their own way dealt with both these questions, addressing the malaise affecting contemporary society and the values necessary for stability on the one hand, and the essential requisites for reshaping future society on the other. Due to the complex nature of the issues involved, it would be appropriate to begin with a working definition of social change.

According to the *International Encyclopaedia of the Social Sciences*, "Social change is the significant alteration of social structures (that is, of patterns of social action and interaction), including consequences and manifestations of such structures embodied in norms (rules of conduct), values, and cultural products and symbols."[6] This is a comprehensive definition because it covers small scale change such as the gradual development of a leadership role in a small task oriented group; cyclical patterns of change such as the succession of centralization and decentralization in administrative organizations; and revolutionary change such as the overthrow of the government. It includes short term change in occupational structures; both growth and decline in membership and size of social units; continuous processes such as specialization and bureaucratization; and discontinuous processes such as particular technical or social interventions.

A historical perception of social change is suggested by Richard Bierstedt. "Permanence and change," he writes, "being and becoming each of these has been emphasized by different philosophers in the western tradition as more pervasive and more important than the other .... The generations pass one after another in response to inexorable biological process and in passing alter the character of human societies. Nothing social remains the same, nothing social abides .... The tempo of change itself is different in different periods and in different societies and even in different parts of the same society."[7]

Kuppuswamy offers a more precise definition: "Social change may be defined as the process in which is discernible significant alteration in the structure and functioning of a particular social system. The term 'change' itself is wholly neutral. It only implies that there is some difference through time in the object under study. When we speak of social change, we simply assert that there is some change in social behaviour, social structure and social and cultural values. We do not indicate the direction in which the change takes place. When we speak of social change as a process, we imply ideas of continuity and persistence."[8]

However, the concept of social change has many analytical facets, as it is an object of study, and indeed a crucial concern, in almost the entire range of social sciences – anthropology, economics, history, political science, sociology and social work, among others. Each discipline has, in fact, developed its own perspectives on social change. Moreover, as Haferkamp and Smelser state: "Change is such an evident feature of social reality that any social-scientific theory, whatever its conceptual starting point, must sooner or later address it. At the same time, it is essential to note that the ways social change has been identified have varied greatly in the history of thought. Furthermore, conceptions of change appear to have mirrored the historical realities of different epochs in large degrees."[9]

The theories and disputes about social change need not detain us further, as Haferkamp and Smelser, Eisenstadt[10] and Piotr Sztompka[11] have competently explained the treatment of social change across time from the 18th century, and across the disciplines of social science.

Expositions of social change generally tended to go hand in hand with explorations of modernity, but critiques of modernism have necessarily influenced the conceptions of the subject. A comparatively recent approach to social change is that related to postmodernism. Postmodernist questions began to be raised from the 1960s, but were properly articulated as an academic subject only in the 1980s and 1990s. More than a theory of social change, postmodernism implies a new way of looking at contemporary civilization, particularly western civilization, raising questions about the nature and direction of present day societies.[12] Postmodernism marks a paradigm shift where authority in general is rejected and scepticism becomes the defining cultural characteristic.[13] The debate over postmodernism has stimulated a reappraisal of modernity as a social-cultural phenomenon. The emerging social order, whether conceived of as 'post' or 'high' modern, is characterized above all by new modes of information and communication, which, in turn, have wide ramifications.

Postmodern thought crystallized as a philosophical reaction against the intellectual and social constructions of modernity. It was brought into sharper focus when the issues of imperialism, exploitation and violence perpetrated by hegemonic powers in the name of order, progress and civilization emerged in the 1960s. The momentum has been kept up since by the negative fallout of various other mega projects of modernity. The newest provocations are the looming global crises facing mankind – food, energy and global warming, to name a few.

Postmodernist theory questions the validity of grand or meta narratives (or, universal theories) such as Marxism, sovereignty and progress, all subsumed under the doctrine of modernity. The clear suggestion is that mankind is only partially in control of its destiny and that culture will always resist being controlled in the manner the grand narrative theorists like to believe is possible. Without a discernible pattern in history, it is said, we have no justification for proclaiming the truth of any grand narrative.[14]

Among the postmodernist writers, the most notable are Foucault, Lyotard and Boudrillard. All of them question the tall claims about the Enlightenment, especially the "absolute" elements of rationalism, exact science, individualism and the "cult of progress". For Lyotard, industrialization and the demands it makes on workers become an outlet for "libidinal energies" – almost an excuse for their expression, rather than a class consciousness of exploitation and suffering. Behind this view lies the idea that we are not simply rational beings awaiting the moment of enlightenment in order to throw off our socioeconomic chains.[15] We are much more complicated and unpredictable creatures than that – neither totally in control of our own natures, nor totally controllable by others.

For Boudrillard, the Marxist conception of nature as something to be tamed and harnessed to the forces of production represents the Enlightenment creed at its most questionable. He believes there is an obsession with production in Marxist thought that distorts social relations and that is no less market oriented in its way than capitalism. For that reason alone, Marxism cannot be considered a liberating social theory. For similar reasons, Boudrillard is critical of political economy as a theory. He says political economy dictates that both nature and mankind must be dominated and exploited in the name of production – in fact, both nature and mankind are, since the Enlightenment, subordinated to the process of production, as if this were an end in itself.[16]

Sovereignty, another important aspect of modernity, is hotly debated by postmodernists. R.B.J. Walker rejects the idea of there being any 'essence' to sovereignty holding over time. This is no more true of 'sovereign' identity than it is of personal identity. He emphasizes the contingent, historically specific nature of political sovereignty instead in a bid to recognize the possibility of new articulations in this area, such as dual or shared sovereignty. Sovereignty, he believes, is a narrative whose time has passed and we cannot continue to rely on modernist categories of spatial expansion to resolve geopolitical problems. He wants to replace the grand narrative of sovereignty with a combination of world and local politics, aware that such a possibility goes against the grain of our standard assumptions about sovereign identity.[17]

Other postmodernist commentators have pointed out the imperialist assumptions that are so often embedded in modernist notions of political sovereignty as, for instance, in the case of the original inhabitants of North America, Australia and South Africa. They find that sovereignty does not seem to apply to them retrospectively, but only to those who have taken over their territory in an act of colonialist expansion. Sovereignty here is a means of oppression and only some radical adjustment to the way the concept works can address the oppression.[18] In this context, it would be relevant to remember that pluralism and difference are popular postmodernist concepts.

Another fault of modernity, as observed by postmodernists, is its obsession with order and planning and its inability to cope with spontaneity.[19] As a result, "the human being is being displaced, decentred" and what the future holds is anybody's guess.[20]

The postmodern debate is indeed forcing many to form judgements, both analytical and philosophical, on modernity itself. Is it leading to progress or some kind of nihilism?[21] Many ethical questions are being raised as opposed to totally rational, commercial and objective criteria. The value of myth, religion and 'ancient wisdom' is being seriously debated.

Many Indian scholars and writers have also been exploring the prospects of an alternative modernity and there has been a focus on Gandhi's life and work in this context. The most notable among them is Ashis Nandy, whose two early publications (of 1980 and 1983) began a widespread reappraisal of Gandhi.[22] In other early contributions of this kind, we may include some of the papers presented at a seminar on *Hind Swaraj* and published as a volume edited by Nageshwar Prasad (1985).[23] An important intervention, almost a decade later (1993), was Makrand Paranjpe's "neo-Gandhian interrogation" of modernity.[24]

Gandhi as a postmodernist has been seriously considered by Lloyd I. Rudolph in a recent work.[25] Rudolph asserts that by writing *Hind Swaraj*, Gandhi "helped to inaugurate the postmodern era by critiquing and rejecting 'modern civilization' and by articulating a civilizational alternative to it. Gandhi was a practitioner and an activist as well as a theorist."[26] Rudolph believes that Gandhi anticipates a good deal of postmodern thinking by taking the view that, at best, humans can know partial and contingent truths; he is postmodern, too, in his hermeneutics as regards the *Bhagvad Gita* and in his relationship to vegetarianism.[27]

Further proof of Gandhi's postmodernism, says Rudolph, was his notion of development, which was contextual for he "started with the village and the villager, with local autonomy and employment, with work in small scale industries, crafts and agriculture and thus challenged modernity's emphasis on physical capital and its efficiency when deployed in Fordist mass production lines".[28] Moreover, the scope and potential in civil society were exemplified by Gandhi through his concepts of satyagraha and sarvodaya, practice of which could achieve the common good in spite of the state or even in opposition to the state.

Lloyd is convinced that "Gandhi also anticipated postmodern discourses on war and violence, ... on gender, ... on the professions, ... on food, ... on difference, ... on cooperation, social capital and love. His postmodern voice and pursuit of truth in action sought to chart a course away from a failing modernity."[289]

The preceding discussion on social change, and the conceptual differences about it, is to clarify the object of this study – the issues and theory of social change as perceived by Gandhi. It must be admitted at the outset that Gandhi's prescriptions for social change are peculiar to him and difficult to classify exclusively under any specific concepts or theory. Indeed, he made no attempt to theorize formally on the subject, but put his thoughts down in writing at random as his perceptions clarified and changed. The effort in this study is to examine the different aspects of the social issues raised by Gandhi and then seek a coherent pattern of thinking on the important subject of social change.

Notes

1. Ravinder Kumar, *Essays in the Social History of Modern India* (New Delhi: Oxford University Press, 1983), p. 51.
2. Anthony J. Parel, *Gandhi's Philosophy and the Quest for Harmony* (Cambridge: Cambridge University Press, 2006).
3. Anthony J. Parel, ed., *Gandhi, Hind Swaraj and Other Writings* (Cambridge: Cambridge University Press, 1997) and *Gandhi, Freedom and Self-Rule* (New York and Oxford: Lexington Books, 2000).
4. *The Collected Works of Mahatma Gandhi* (New Delhi: Government of India, Publications Division, and Ahmedabad: Navajivan Trust, Volumes 1–100, 1960–94). *The Collected Works* are referred to hereinafter as *CWMG*.
5. These include Shriman Narayan, ed., *The Selected Works of Mahatma Gandhi* (Ahmedabad: Navajivan Publishing House, Volumes 1–6, 1968), referred to hereinafter as *SWMG*.

6. David L. Sills, ed., *International Encyclopedia of the Social Sciences* (New York: The Macmillan Company and The Free Press, Volumes 13–14, 1972), p. 365.
7. Robert Bierstedt, *The Social Order* (Bombay: Tata McGraw Hill, 1970), pp. 509–10.
8. B. Kuppuswamy, *Social Change in India* (Sahibabad: Vikas Publishing House, 2nd Edition, 1979), p. 19.
9. Hans Haferkamp and Neil J. Smelser, eds, *Social Change and Modernity* (Berkeley: University of California Press, 1992), Introduction, pp. 1–2.
10. Samuel N. Eisenstadt, *Tradition, Change, and Modernity* (New York: John Wiley, 1973).
11. Piotr Sztompka, *The Sociology of Social Change* (Oxford: Blackwell, 1993).
12. David Lyon, *Post Modernity* (New Delhi: Viva Books, 2002), pp. 10–11.
13. Stuart Sim, *Post-Marxism: An Intellectual History* (New York: Routledge, 2000), p. 105.
14. Ibid., p. 107.
15. Ibid.
16. Ibid., p. 114.
17. Ibid., p. 121.
18. Ibid.
19. Ibid., p. 123.
20. Lyon, *Post Modernity*, p. 110.
21. Ibid., pp. 23, 91.
22. Ashis Nandy, *At the Edge of Psychology: Essays in Politics and Culture* (Delhi: Oxford University Press, 1980), and *The Intimate Enemy: Loss and Recovery of Self under Colonialism* (Delhi: Oxford University Press, 1983).
23. Nageshwar Prasad, ed., *Hind Swaraj: A Fresh Look* (New Delhi: Gandhi Peace Foundation, 1985). Notable papers in this collection include those of P.V. Pillai ('*Hind Swaraj* in the Light of Heidegger's Critique of Modernity') and Indira Rothermund ('*Hind Swaraj* and the Idea of Democracy').
24. Makarand Paranjape, *Decolonization and Development:* Hind Svaraj *Revisioned* (New Delhi: Sage Publications, 1993).

25. Lloyd I. Rudolph, 'Postmodern Gandhi', in *Postmodern Gandhi and Other Essays, Gandhi in the World and at Home*, eds., Lloyd I. Rudolph and Susanne Hoeber Rudolph (New Delhi: Oxford University Press, 2008).
26. Rudolph and Rudolph, *Postmodern Gandhi*, p. 3.
27. Ibid., p. 10-11.
28. Ibid., p. 27.
29. Ibid., pp. 36-7.

CHAPTER 1

Evolution of Gandhi's Social and Economic Ideas

It is always interesting to try and find out what could have led a great personality to think and act as he or she did. Thought processes do not evolve in a vacuum, they are nurtured in an environment that provides the stimulus. Fortunately, for our purpose, there is a lot of material on this aspect where Gandhi is concerned. One of the most important sources is his autobiography, which he called *An Autobiography, or The Story of My Experiments with Truth.*[1] It is not a pure biography, but rather a record of the different stages of his intellectual and spiritual development up to middle age.

Gandhi's social ideas owed much to his religious background. He believed that a man without religion was a man without roots and that religion was the basis on which all life structure had to be erected, if life were to be real.[2] A.L. Basham thinks that certain elements in the religious life of 19th century Hinduism may have prepared the ground for some of Gandhi's ideas.[3] It is a profitable line to pursue and Gandhi's writings yield much valuable material to study the development of his personality and values.

Gandhi was born on 2 October 1869 in the princely state of Porbandar in Kathiawar, Gujarat. He spent his childhood and boyhood partly in Porbandar and partly in Rajkot state, where his father and grandfather were prime ministers to the native princes. Both were well known for their loyalty to the ruler and their high sense of honour.[4] They belonged to the Vaishya class of Modh Baniyas. Gandhi's father had little religious training, but frequently visited temples and listened to religious discourses. Gandhi was deeply influenced by his mother. To quote his words, "The outstanding impression my mother has left on my memory is that of saintliness. She was deeply religious – she would not think of taking her meals without her daily prayers."[5]

The rich cultural tradition of Kathiawar must also have played an important part in shaping Gandhi's mental outlook. "The culture of Kathiawar," writes Pyarelal Nayyar, Gandhi's personal secretary, who has written extensively about the Mahatma's life, "is saturated with the Krishna legend."[6] Gandhi's grandfather, Ota Gandhi, belonged to the Vallabhacharya sect of Vaishnavism, which believes in the Krishna Bhakti doctrine of love and surrender to God, personified by Lord Krishna, which makes him accessible to all, regardless of social standing or cultural background. Putali Ba, Gandhi's mother, descended from the Pranami or Satpranami sect, whose 18th century founder, Prannath, attempted to unify Islam and Hinduism in a supreme God. Followers of Prannath were forbidden addictive drugs, tobacco, wine, meat and extramarital relations.[7] Jainism was also strong in Gujarat and its influence was felt everywhere and on all occasions.[8] Gandhi attributes his religious tolerance to the influence of his parents. They would visit, he writes, the temple of Shiva, Rama and Vishnu with their children. Jain monks would visit his father frequently and would go out of their way to accept food from his family, though they were non-Jains. His father also had Parsi and Muslim friends, who would talk to him about their own faiths and he would listen to them always with respect and often with interest.[9]

Two dramatic plays based on Hindu mythological characters left a deep impression on Gandhi as a boy. The first was *Shravana Pitribhakta Nataka*, a play about the devotion of a son to his parents. One picture he recalled vividly was of Shravan Kumar carrying his blind parents in baskets hung from his shoulders and taking them on a pilgrimage.[10] The inspiration gathered from the story of Shravan later found expression in the zealous service Gandhi rendered his father as a nurse during his last illness and in his nursing propensities, which were so much in evidence in South Africa.

The other play was the story of Harishchandra, who was the king of Ayodhya in ancient times and suffered great hardships on account of a pledge he had given, to the extent of selling himself, his wife and son in bondage. Gandhi writes that it 'captured' his heart. To follow truth and to go through the kind of ordeals Harishchandra went through was the ideal inspired in him. "I literally believed," he writes, "in the story of Harishchandra. The thought of it often made me weep ... both Harishchandra and Shravan are living realities for me, and I am sure I should be moved as before if I were to read these plays again."[11] This deep impact of devotion to truth is perhaps responsible for Gandhi's honesty of speech in his early school days and in later life.

Another childhood influence on Gandhi was that of his nurse, Rambha. He describes himself as a timid boy who was afraid of ghosts and spirits. All his prayers and visits to temples could not cure him of this fear. As a remedy for this fear, Rambha suggested the repetition of the Ramanama (the recitation of the name of Rama). "I had more faith in her than in her remedy," he writes, "and so at a tender age, I began repeating Ramanama to cure my fear of ghosts and spirits .... I think it is the seed sown by that good woman Rambha that today, Ramanama is an infallible remedy for me."[12]

Gandhi's well known faith in the Ramanama and his tremendous love for Tulsidas' *Ramcharitmanas* (or *Ramayana*, the *Story of Rama*) had another basis. This was the reading of the *Ramayana* before his father by Ladha Mahraj of Bileshwar, a great devotee of Rama. He was reputed to have cured himself of leprosy by applying *bilwa* (*bel*) leaves, which had been discarded after being offered to the image of Shiva at the Bileshwar temple, and by the regular repetition of Ramanama. This story left a deep impression on Gandhi. And Ladha Maharaj's narration of the text in a melodious voice and his moving explanation of the verses kept Gandhi spellbound. "That laid the foundation of my deep devotion to the *Ramayana*. Today I regard the *Ramayana* of Tulsidas as the greatest book in all devotional literature,"[13] he writes.

All these factors made Gandhi an intensely religious person, but without any dogma or rigidity. He defined religion as "service of the helpless" for he believed that God manifests himself to us in the form of the stricken and the helpless. He did not care for outward ceremony and his approach to Hinduism can be said to be that of a universalist. About Hinduism, he said, "My Hinduism is all inclusive. It is not anti-Mussalman, anti-Christian or anti any other religion. But it is pro-Muslim, pro-Christian and pro every other living faith in the world. To me, Hinduism is but one branch from the same parent trunk, whose roots and whose quality we judge only by the collective strength and quality of the different branches put together, and if I take care of the Hindu branch on which I am sitting and which sustains me, surely I am taking care also of the sister branches. If the Hindu branch is poisoned, the poison is likely to spread to others. If that branch withers, the parent will be the weaker for its withering."[14]

Of all the religio-philosophical strains of Hinduism, Gandhi acknowledged his deepest admiration for the Vaishnavite tradition. He said he clung to the Vaishnavite faith because it inculcated universal love and, therefore, brotherhood; it laid the greatest emphasis on meticulous observance of truth and non-violence and affirmed unselfish devotion to God.

Gandhi attached the greatest importance to the spiritual aspect of human nature because he recognized the underlying unity of all sentient beings – the essential oneness of the universe.[15] He believed that it was from experiments in the spiritual field that he derived such power as he possessed for working in the political field. The driving force in his life was the desire for self-realization. "What I want to achieve," he says, "what I have been striving and pining to achieve these 30 years is self-realization, to see God face to face, to attain 'moksha'.[16] I live and move and have my being in pursuit of this goal."[17]

The only path to this goal was that of renunciation and, accordingly, he based his life and work on this principle. His favourite quote in relation to this was the first verse of the *Ishopanishad*:

Isavasyamidam sarvam/yatkin' cya
Jagatyam jagat/tena tyaktena
Bhunjitha/ma gridaha kasyasviddhanam.

He translates it thus: "All this that we see in this great universe is pervaded by God, renounce it and enjoy it, Do not covet anybody's wealth or possession."

This verse epitomized Hinduism for him and he felt that if by some mischance, all the scriptures of Hinduism were reduced to ashes except this one, Hinduism would still live forever.[18] His doctrine of trusteeship was derived from his faith in the principle of renunciation. He believed that if zamindars, monied men and all those who have possessions would treat themselves as trustees and perform the act of renunciation as he had described, this world would indeed be a blessed place to live in.[19]

It would be convenient for our purpose to consider the major elements in his ideology – truth, ahimsa, satyagraha, equality – individually and study their likely origins and evolution. This is important for our purpose because these concepts form the basis of the social reconstruction Gandhi had in mind. Through the propagation of these ideas, he aimed at producing a new consciousness, which he hoped would ultimately move the whole world.[20]

Truth

Of all the moral principles, Gandhi placed truth as the first and foremost. He called it "the sovereign principle", which included numerous other principles. It did not merely imply truthfulness in speech, but in thought also "and not only the relative truth of our conception, but the absolute truth, the eternal principle, that is God".[21] He equated God with truth, as he says, "I worship God as truth only. I have not yet found him, but I am seeking after him. I am prepared to sacrifice the things dearest to me in pursuit of this quest .... Often in my progress, I have had faint glimpses of the absolute truth, God, and daily the conviction is growing upon me that the above is real and all else is unreal."[22]

Gandhi's conception of truth has obviously not the common meaning attributed to it for there were divine and philosophical dimensions to it. It can perhaps be said that the predominant factor in moulding his vision of truth was his deep attachment to the epic, *Ramcharitmanas,* written by Tulsidas and his faith in the Ramanama. A.L. Basham has offered some very cogent arguments in this regard. "One of the commonest ejaculations of popular north Indian Vaishnavism," he says, "is Rama *naam sach hai* (the name of Rama is true, or is truth, since modern Indian *sach,* like the Sanskrit satya, may be either an adjective or a noun). Here we have already the possible source of the Gandhian emphasis on truth, and of the special and unwestern usage of the word in Gandhi's speeches and writings. The implication of the phrase for the believer is not simply that God exists; it must also connote that the essence (*naam,* literally name) of divinity is ultimate reality and that God carries out his promises without swerving and expects his followers to do likewise. The use of the word *sach* with this extended connotation can also be found in the Hindu *Ramayana* of Tulsidas ...."[23] For instance, Dashrath carried out his promise of granting a boon to his wife, Kaikeyi, at the cost of his life and his family's happiness. The ideal of sticking to the truth, the word, shines bright and it is not at all improbable that it was imprinted on young Gandhi's mind as an exemplary ideal.

During a brief period in his youth, for about three years, Gandhi led a kind of double life in which he staged a mild revolt against parental authority in secret. His native honesty and sincerity prevented a final fall.[24]

As Gandhi's interests widened and he became more concerned with the question of truth, gradually, he was able to transcend these early aberrations. His meditations and search led him to one important conclusion. "One thing took deep root in me," he says, "the conviction that morality is the basis of all things, and that truth is the substance of all morality. Truth became my sole objective. It began to grow in magnitude every day, and my definition of it has been ever widening."[25]

Another moral precept, that of repaying the smallest service with the utmost generosity, which became his guiding principle, was, he says, derived from a Gujarati didactic stanza by Shamal Bhatt. It "gripped" his heart and mind. Gandhi quotes what were to him "wonderful lines":

For a bowl of water give a goodly meal;
For a kindly greeting bow thou down with zeal;
For a simple penny pay thou back with gold;
If thy life be rescued, life do not withhold.
Thus the words and actions of the wise reward,
Every little service tenfold they reward,
But the truly noble know all men as one,
And return with gladness good for evil done.[26]

That such ideas left a deep impression on Gandhi is evident from his lifelong conduct towards the underprivileged and outcastes of India, who performed hard labour and menial tasks for the comfort of the rest of society even when they did not receive any sympathy or civility in return.

As we have said, Gandhi equated truth with God, with the ultimate reality that pervaded the entire universe. He thus had a unifying view of life and could look at life in totality. He found all the parts interdependent and realized that good reciprocity was necessary for their smooth functioning. In a letter to Horace Alexander, he wrote, "We needlessly divide life into watertight compartments, religious and other. Whereas if a man has true religion in him, it must show in every detail of life .... The slightest irregularity in sanitary, social and political life is a sign of spiritual poverty. It is a sign of inattention, neglect of duty. Anyway, the ashram life is based upon this conception of fundamental unity."[27] This unifying view of life was one of the ideas which evolved with Gandhi's deeper and deeper pursuit of the concept of truth. A detailed discussion of this follows later.

An appropriate way to conclude this section on the evolution of Gandhi's concept of truth would be to quote his own estimate in this regard. In reply to a correspondent, he wrote,

"... I represent no new truths. I endeavour to follow and represent truth, as I know it. I do claim to throw a new light on many an old truth."[28]

The reflection of Gandhi's concept of truth in his social action is found in his persistent emphasis on the purity of means to attain desired ends. His propagation of the methods of non-violence, civil resistance and honourable cooperation exemplify this. His message for revolutionizing the social order with these means was relevant not only to India, but the whole world.[29] Gandhi's conception of truth as God and the universal reality stands as a refreshing challenge and alternative before the world.

Ahimsa

For Gandhi, non-violence was a principle second in importance only to truth. Indeed, it sometimes seemed to precede it. Gandhi affirmed that non-violence was the first article of his faith and also the last article of his creed.[30] Undoubtedly, he owed this attitude, in the first instance, to the cultural influences of his childhood. Mention has been made before of the influence of Vaishnavism and Jainism in Gujarat. Gandhi has himself written that the opposition to and abhorrence of meat eating that existed in Gujarat among the Jains and Vaishnavas were to be seen nowhere else in India or outside in such strength. These were the traditions in which he was born and bred.[31] They were, perhaps, partly responsible for his compassion for the weak and helpless and for his love of non-violence as a social and political instrument.

The compositions of Gujarati poets such as Narasinha Mehta and Shamal Bhatt, who belonged to the Bhakti tradition, had a great influence on Gandhi. Mention has been made before of a poem by Bhatt. Proponents of the Bhakti tradition were lay preachers, mostly non-Brahmins, whose style of communication was through devotional hymns in the indigenous languages. They were itinerant preachers and brought the message of brotherly love and good conduct and they deprecated ritualism. Renunciation and non-violence were also popular themes. They preached intense devotion to a personal God, who would generally be an avatar of Vishnu, like Krishna and Rama. Bhakti preachers were very popular and had a positive influence on the day to day life of the Hindus.

One event early in life made Gandhi realize powerfully the value of an act of pure non-violence. When he was about 15, he once stole a bit of gold to repay a debt incurred by his brother. After this, his conscience gave him no peace and he resolved to make a clean breast of things to his father. As he could not muster the courage to speak to his father, he wrote out a confession and, in the note, he asked for adequate punishment for himself, requesting his father not to punish himself for his son's offence. He also pledged never to steal in the future. He writes that he was trembling as he handed the note to his father. His father was bedridden those days, but he sat up to read the note, and as he read it, tears rolled down his cheeks. He then tore up the note and lay down. Gandhi writes, "I also cried. I could see my father's agony. If I were a painter, I could draw a picture of the whole scene today. It is still so vivid in my mind. Those pearl drops of love cleansed my heart, and washed my sin away. Only he who has experienced such love can know what it is."[32]

Gandhi has described this incident as an object lesson in ahimsa and he believed that when such ahimsa becomes all embracing, it transforms everything it touches. There is then no limit to its power. Like his concept of truth, Gandhi's concept of ahimsa also had a wide meaning – it included the "largest love" and "largest charity". About the immediate impact of the episode, he writes that day he learnt the value of a clean confession and the sublime forgiveness it could evoke in a person not given to a particularly peaceful disposition. The social dimension of the feeling this incident evoked in him was his precept of hating the sin and not the sinner; realization of the need for patience and perseverance in implementing social reform programmes; and finally, willingness to forgive and overlook the misdeeds of those who offended him.

Gandhi's faith in ahimsa was strengthened greatly on account of his religious contacts in England, where he went in 1888 to train as a barrister. With two theosophist friends, who were also brothers, he read the *Bhagvad Gita* for the first time in

Sir Edwin Arnold's English translation (*The Song Celestial*). Some verses of the *Gita* made "a deep impression" on his mind,[33] this one in particular:

If one ponders on the objects of the sense,
there springs attraction, from attraction
grows desire, desire flames to fierce passion,
passion breeds recklessness, then the memory
all betrayed lets noble purpose go, and saps
the mind, Till purpose, mind and man are
all undone.[34]

Gandhi probably learnt the lessons of self-restraint from such study. In the company of his theosophist friends, he also read *The Light of Asia*, a long poem on the life of the Buddha by Sir Edwin Arnold. He writes that he read this with even greater interest than he did the *Bhagvad Gita* and he found it hard to "leave off". Madame Blavatsky's *Key to Theosophy* stimulated him to read books on Hinduism and disabused him of the notion fostered by the missionaries that Hinduism was rife with superstition.

About the same time, a Christian acquaintance introduced him to the *Bible*. He was not impressed by the Old Testament. But the New Testament "produced a different impression", he writes, "especially the Sermon on the Mount which went straight to my heart".[35] He quotes the verses he liked best:

But I say unto you, ye resist not evil:
but whosoever shall smite thee on thy
right cheek, turn to him the other also,
and if any man take away thy coat
let him have thy cloak too.

In this, the message of non-violence is clear. Gandhi writes that these verses reminded him of Shamal Batt's poem, which has been quoted before. Gandhi was thus receiving the influences of different religious texts and must have tried to fuse them into one basic tenet. Renunciation, dharma or the duty of one's calling, compassion and non-violence are elements that are clearly manifest in his actions and writings later.

In the spiritual field, there was another person who deeply influenced Gandhi – Rajchandra Mehta. A businessman by profession, Mehta was widely known for his great learning and knowledge of the scriptures. He was a poet, too. From him, Gandhi learnt the lesson of religious tolerance for Mehta had made it a practice to study and understand the excellence of each faith and explain it to the followers of that faith.[36]

Apart from religious sources, one major influence on Gandhi's moral and intellectual evolution was the writings of Leo Tolstoy. Much before he made his acquaintance through correspondence, Gandhi read Tolstoy's *The Kingdom of God is within You* in South Africa, which, to use his own words, "overwhelmed" him. He writes that he was greatly impressed by the thought, morality and truthfulness of the book.[37]

As Tolstoy's beliefs very nearly approached his own, Gandhi later summarized them in his weekly journal, *Indian Opinion*, which he published in South Africa. Briefly, Tolstoy denounces the accumulation of wealth by men and the wielding of political power because it led to many evils and participation in fighting or war. More positively, he writes that evil must never be returned with evil, but with goodness. Man is born to do his duty to his creator and should, therefore, pay more attention to his duties than to his rights. Lastly, he says agriculture is the true occupation of man, so it is contrary to divine law to establish large cities and factories which enslave the poor and the helpless.[38] Tolstoy's ideas did two things for Gandhi: On the one hand, they reaffirmed and echoed ideas that were forming in his own mind, and on the other, they guided his thoughts to their logical conclusion.

During this time, the 1890s in South Africa, Gandhi's religious quest continued. He sought to increase his knowledge of his own religion and read Rajchandra's *Dharma Vichar*, translations of the *Upanishads* brought out by the Theosophical Society, and Max Mueller's book, *India – What Can It Teach Us*. All this, he stated, enhanced his regard for Hinduism and its "beauties" began to grow on him. He also read standard works on Islam and its founder and on Judaism. He made an intensive study of Tolstoy's books, too. As a result of the catholicity of his reading, he writes, "I began to realize more and more the infinite possibilities of universal love ...; the study stimulated self-introspection and fostered in me the habit of putting into practice whatever appealed to me in my studies."[39]

Gandhi's belief in ahimsa was linked to his belief in the fundamental unity of the universe. All living beings, he writes, were tarred with the same brush and were children of one and the same creator and, as such, the divine powers within them were infinite. Therefore, "to slight a single human being is to slight those divine powers, and thus to harm not only that being, but with him the whole world."[40]

Gandhi's concept of ahimsa evolved through confrontations with situations giving rise to moral dilemmas. For instance, Gandhi had to explain his concept in the context of war and to explain his own participation in the First World War. "When two nations are fighting," he wrote, "the duty of a votary of ahimsa is to stop the war. He who is not equal to that duty, he who has no power of resisting war, he who is not qualified to resist war, may take part in war, and yet wholeheartedly try to free himself, his nation and the world from war."[41] He knew that some destruction of non-human life was inevitable. Much as he abhorred violence, on one occasion, he permitted the killing of an ailing calf, which was in terrible agony, and on another, the destruction of several dogs, which were a menace to the factory premises in Ahmedabad. This raised a great controversy in the country, but Gandhi remained calm and defended his action: "My defence of the destruction of the dogs is no doubt partly utilitarian and a concession to and an admission of our weakness. But destruction of suffering animals is defended on the highest ground of religion."[42]

From all this, it is not difficult to conclude that for Gandhi, ahimsa or the concept of non-violence was multidimensional. It involved not only the act of abstaining as far as possible from doing physical injury to living beings, but also actively caring for and loving them irrespective of their behaviour towards oneself and others. Gandhi's struggle to create a harmonious and egalitarian society is based on this concept. His use of the concept of ahimsa as a weapon in the struggle for independence has the elements of suffering, self-sacrifice and universal goodwill inherent in it.

Satyagraha

Gandhi explained the meaning of satyagraha as an increasing awareness of dharma or truth and this awareness, he says, first came to him in 1887. In that year, his caste of Modh Baniyas threatened to excommunicate him if he went to England for, according to custom, travelling overseas meant losing one's caste. His reaction was that they were welcome to do so, but he would certainly go to England. "My satyagraha was born on that day," he says. Thus, his first satyagraha was directed against the elders of his caste whom he respected as much as his father.[43] The satyagraha with the government was only a part of this satyagraha.

The root of Gandhi's satyagraha is self-restraint. Its foundation was laid when he promised his mother that he would not touch "wine, woman and meat" during his stay in England. He had to face innumerable difficulties during his initial days there and "practically had to starve" on account of his vow to abstain from eating meat. This caused some irritation, but soon, "the strict observance of the vow produced an inward relish distinctly more healthy, delicate and permanent".[44] Meanwhile, he had joined the Vegetarian Society in England and became a convinced vegetarian. His own experiments in dietetics taught him that the real seat of taste was not the tongue, but the mind.

The habit of self-restraint affected him in another manner as well. During the first few months of his stay in England, which he describes as "the period of infatuation", he spent a lot of time, energy and money on trying to copy English manners. But soon he realized his mistake and cut down heavily on his expenses. He became a serious student and led an extremely simple and frugal life. About this transformation, he writes, "The change harmonized my inward and outward life. It was also more in keeping with the means of my family. My life was certainly more truthful and my soul knew no bounds of joy."[45]

The element of self-restraint in Gandhi's concept of satyagraha is particularly significant. He was convinced that before one could lead others and try to shape social and political events, one must learn to control and discipline oneself. Only such a person was equipped to influence others and persuade them to accept his guidance.[46] It was because of this capacity for self-restraint that Gandhi could hold back the masses from indulging in wanton destruction in the many movements that he led. The value of self-restraint as a social virtue became evident to him in the course of the struggle of Indians for self-respect, which he led in South Africa.

Gandhi's technique of satyagraha truly evolved in South Africa in response to what he perceived as a life of utter degradation imposed on the conservative and almost illiterate emigrant Indians there. He had several nasty experiences himself within the first few days of his arrival on account of the colour of his skin. He saw that his background and status were of no consequence there – only the colour of the skin mattered. What grieved him more was to see the resignation and helplessness of the Indians about their untenable position. This state of affairs seemed intolerable to him and he immediately set about remedying the situation. His first step was to call a meeting of all the Indians in Pretoria and to present to them a picture of their condition in the Transvaal. This small beginning led to the formation of an association to make representations to the authorities about the hardships faced by the Indian settlers, and he accepted the post of secretary and all the major responsibilities connected with it.

He realized that before the Indians could demand political and other civic rights, they had to unite and improve their negative image in South Africa. He made them conscious of this fact and helped them in various ways to better their condition. Constraints of space forbid the tracing of all the developments in South Africa, so only a few significant facts are mentioned here in order to highlight their importance for Gandhi's personal growth.

Gandhi at the charkha at Sabarmati Ashram in 1925. The charkha (spinning wheel) became a symbol of national unity

The crux of the conflict was the number of legal disabilities imposed on the Indians in the Transvaal. Gandhi summed them up as follows: By the amended law of 1886, all Indians would have to pay a poll tax of £3 as fee for entry into the Transvaal. They could not own land, except in locations set apart for them, and even this was sought to be made difficult. They had no franchise. Indians, like other coloured people, could not walk on public footpaths and could not move out of doors after 9 pm without a permit.

One event in the life of Gandhi while in South Africa proved to have revolutionary significance for the evolution of his technique of satyagraha. In the middle of 1896, he returned to India to fetch his family. He utilized this visit to publicize the grievances of the Indians in South Africa through speeches and a pamphlet he wrote known as the *Green Pamphlet*[47] because of its green cover. The leading newspapers gave wide coverage to this and the Reuters news agency sent a cabled despatch to England, from where it reached South Africa. It was a distorted summary of his speeches and aroused great public indignation among the Europeans there. Gandhi was hurriedly recalled by his employers in South Africa. On his landing there, he was nearly lynched by a European mob, but his life was saved by the heroic intervention of the wife of the superintendent of police who happened to be passing by.[48]

Gandhi gave his version of the events in an interview to a reporter of a Durban newspaper, in which he fully vindicated his stand in India and explained why it was his imperative duty to do what he had done. He talks of the ordeal as a most valuable experience because he came out of it much stronger. He says, "Whenever I think of that day, I feel that God was preparing me for the practice of satyagraha."[49] He gave evidence of his self-restraint when he refused to prosecute his assailants on the grounds that it was not their fault, but that of their leaders who had incited them. This gesture was widely appreciated by the European authorities. Harry Escombe, the attorney general, said to him, "I do not hesitate to say not only that you have come to a right decision in the matter, but you will render further service to your community by your self-restraint."[50]

Gandhi recorded many events in his life in South Africa which he regarded in retrospect as progressive developments in the path of satyagraha. The underlying principle in them, he writes, was the element of satyagraha, or the insistence on truth. This often had social consequences. One such occasion presented itself to the Indians at the outbreak of the Boer War in 1899. Gandhi realized that as British subjects, enjoying the benefits of British citizenship in South Africa, the Indians should volunteer on the British side, just as all the leading Europeans were doing on both sides, the British and the Dutch. One of the main charges against the Indian settlers was that their only purpose was "money grubbing" and they were merely "a dead weight upon the British". Gandhi pointed out to the Indians that this was a golden opportunity to disprove this charge and earn the respect of the European rulers. The result was that after some persuasion, many Indians agreed and, on acceptance by the British authorities, they formed the Indian Ambulance Corps and rendered valuable service during the war. Their exemplary work was mentioned in the dispatches of General Buller and war medals were conferred on them.[51]

Gandhi says that he learnt several lessons from this episode. Indians rose in the estimation of the Europeans as was evident from the English newspapers. This was because in spite of being ill-treated, they came forward to fulfil their obligations as British citizens. Indians of all creeds and communities worked harmoniously in the ambulance corps, even indentured labourers were allowed to join. Another revelation was that the European soldiers treated the Indians in the ambulance corps not with contempt, but as fellow workers. Finally, he writes that he gained a valuable insight into human nature: "We should not despise any man, however humble or insignificant looking he might be. Secondly, no matter how timid a man is, he is capable of the loftiest heroism when he is put to the test."[52]

A significant stage in Gandhi's life came in 1903 as a result of his deep study of theosophical literature and the *Bhagvad Gita*. He and his friends had formed a Seekers' Club, where such books were read and discussed. The *Gita*, he writes, became to him "an infallible guide of conduct ...; words like *aparigraha* (non-possession) and *samabhava* (equability) gripped me".[53] He felt the urge to renounce all his belongings because an aspirant to truth could not have personal possessions, for this would hinder the goal of self-realization or attaining oneness with the universe, which was the ultimate truth.

This state of mind was closely followed by a radical transformation in his mode of living. He attributed this to the reading of John Ruskin's *Unto This Last*, in which he found some of his deepest convictions reflected and which so moved him that he determined to change his lifestyle in accordance with the ideals of the book. He later translated it into Gujarati, calling it *Sarvodaya* (*The Welfare of All*). Gandhi summarized Ruskin's teachings as follows:

1. The good of the individual is contained in the good of all.
2. A lawyer's work has the same value as a barber's in as much as all have the same right to earn their livelihood from their work.

3. A life of labour, that is, the life of the tiller of the soil and the handicraftsman, is the life worth living.[54]

Gandhi writes that he was aware of the first two principles, but the third had never occurred to him. He records that he rose at dawn, ready to put these principles to practice. This was also the time that his journal, *Indian Opinion*, was incurring heavy losses and was in danger of being closed down; only heroic measures could save it. A scheme suggested itself to Gandhi after he read *Unto This Last*.

Fortune smiled on Gandhi for he was able to translate his plan into action quite soon. In 1904, he set up a colony near Phoenix Station, some miles from Durban, on the northern coastline. He called the settlement Phoenix. This was a novel experiment, fraught, as he says, "with momentous consequences". An incident at the very beginning of his life at Phoenix taught him the lesson of self-reliance and augured well for the future. The night before the day of publication of the journal, the printing machine got jammed and, despite the best efforts of the engineer, would not work. Motivated by Gandhi, the workers plied the hand wheel all night, working in relay batches, and a considerable amount of work was done. But some still remained. At 7 am the next morning, Gandhi suggested that the machine be tried again – it worked the moment he touched it. The result was that the copies were dispatched in time. He writes that for him, the failure of the printing machine had come as a test for all of them and its working in the nick of time as the fruit of honest and earnest labour.[55]

Having tasted success as a result of hard labour, the workers were enthused, at times, to deliberately give up the use of the machine and work only with hand power. There is no doubt that the success born of self-reliance and unflinching effort must have given them a sense of moral uplift. It is easy to perceive here the preoccupation of Gandhi with the spiritual aspect of labour and the influence of Ruskin on his mind.

Celibacy

An important turning point in Gandhi's life came during the time of the Boer War in 1906, when he organized the Indian

Ambulance Corps. The corps' work was to nurse the wounded Zulu prisoners of war, which the white people were not willing to do. The corps had to undertake long arduous marches carrying the wounded and put up with a lot of physical hardship. It was while doing this work that the spiritual turmoil Gandhi had experienced for the last few years reached its culmination and he realized that complete self-restraint is the necessary basis of all action. He made two important decisions. First, an aspirant to a life devoted exclusively to service must lead a life of celibacy. Second, he must accept poverty as a constant companion through his life. He cannot take up any occupation that would prevent him or make him shrink from undertaking the lowliest of duties or the largest of risks.[56] Thus, Gandhi became a celibate and renounced most of his personal possessions.

Civil Disobedience

Henry David Thoreau, an American philosopher, was another influence on Gandhi, one who helped him further evolve his concept of satyagraha in both social and political terms. Though Thoreau's views were articulated in the context of political dissent in his essay, *On the Duty of Civil Disobedience*, the message of protest against the injustice and inequality prevailing in organized society was loud and clear. Thoreau preached and practised the right to obey one's conscience and against the habit of being blindly governed by respect for authority.[57] Gandhi also interpreted these views in social terms and disapproved of submission to social regimentation of any kind. He postulated it as a duty to protest against social norms and traditions that went against one's conscience. His fight against the rigidity of the caste system, untouchability and women's degradation are cases in point.

Tolstoy Farm

As the struggle for civil rights in South Africa gained momentum and hundreds of Indians in the provinces of Transvaal and Natal began to fill the jails of South Africa, Gandhi was faced with the acute problem of maintaining and caring for their families. Though they belonged to different communities and faiths, Gandhi realized that it was important, from his point of view, to have them stay at one place. Meanwhile, news of the crisis had reached India. R.J. Tata, the well-known industrialist, sent a generous donation of Rs 25,000 to Gandhi. With this help, Gandhi thought of a radical solution to his problem, which would exemplify some of his unique views on social planning. The scheme was that the families should become members of a "cooperative commonwealth", in which there would be no scope for fraud or injustice; public funds would be largely saved; and they would be trained to live a simple life in harmony with nature and with other Indians belonging to diverse regions and creeds.[58]

This scheme came to be actualized soon because a close friend, Herman Kallenbach, a German architect, purchased 1,100 acres of land near Johannesburg and gave the use of it to the *satyagrahis* (those offering satyagraha) free of rent or charge. Gandhi named the settlement, which was set up in May 1910, Tolstoy Farm. Tolstoy Farm taught Gandhi many lessons of life such as harmonious living, an ascetic lifestyle and egalitarian principles.

Tolstoy Farm may be described as Gandhi's first ashram for he ran it along almost ascetic lines. It marked an important stage in his development. It embodied his ideas on social harmony and equality. There were no servants even for the most menial jobs and most of the construction work was undertaken by the residents themselves. He personally supervised the work of sanitation to ensure cleanliness; he learnt all about the use of human manure. Gandhi also made strict rules for casual visits by inmates with an eye on economy and healthy living.

For Gandhi himself, the experience of life on Tolstoy Farm was a kind of revelation. Simplicity was made its hallmark and this was responsible, he felt, for a saving of at least Rs 2–3 lakh of public money. The settlers, though belonging to different backgrounds, learnt to look upon one another as members of the same family. Gandhi undertook a number of experiments in food reform and natural treatment of diseases. He also performed arduous labour and often walked up to 40 miles a day. In a sentence, it could be said that self-restraint was the foundation of life on Tolstoy Farm.

Gandhi believed that the experiment had endowed him with a great deal of moral and spiritual strength and served as a good training ground for dealing with the situation that arose during the course of the final campaign in South Africa in 1913.[59] Gandhi felt that without the experience of life on Tolstoy Farm, the *satyagrahis* would not have been able to undergo the rigours of the last phase of their struggle in South Africa, including sentences in prison with hard labour. Though Tolstoy Farm was never in the limelight, Gandhi found that it attracted a great deal of public sympathy. The reason was, he analysed, that the other Indians in South Africa had had a visible demonstration of the capacity for suffering in those committed to a public cause.[60] This public confidence, he discovered, was a great asset to the movement when it was organized afresh on a large scale in 1913. Even the authorities regarded the *satyagrahis* with such respect that the magistrates did not think it necessary to ask them for bail.

Equality of the Sexes

Another lesson taught by life on Tolstoy Farm and the satyagraha movement was that of equality of the sexes. This equality was later reflected in the ashram life organized in India, where no distinction was made in the work done by men and women and in the struggle for independence and women's participation in it. The participation of women in significant numbers was a very important feature of the satyagraha movement in South Africa. The immediate provocation was the judgement pronounced by Justice Searle of the Cape Supreme Court on 13 March 1913. According to it, marriages performed according to Indian rites were not to be recognized and all marriages had to be registered in South African courts. At one stroke, Gandhi writes, the wives of all Indians married in India were declared "prostitutes" or "concubines".[61] The Indian community was outraged and immediately decided that "an invading army composed mainly of women and some men should cross from Natal into Transvaal and vice versa with the purpose of defying the immigration law".[62] It was also thought prudent that to ensure arrest, the identities of the people crossing thus should not be disclosed as some were well-known names. The Phoenix party included Gandhi's wife, Kasturba. On 23 September 1913, they were arrested, tried and sentenced to three months' imprisonment with hard labour. The Transvaal 'sisters' were also arrested for the same term. "These events stirred the heart of the Indians not only in South Africa, but also in the motherland to its very depth,"[63] wrote Gandhi.

Gandhi writes very highly of the bravery of the Indian women who participated in the satyagraha struggle in South Africa. They were harassed in prison. Valiamma, a young girl of 18, died soon after her release from prison, where she had fallen sick. Her death made her a heroine among the Indians in South Africa. Other women, too, rendered exemplary sacrifice and service. Gandhi was deeply impressed by the courage displayed by the women, particularly because almost all of them were illiterate and ignorant of legal technicalities. They had acted, he believed, out of sheer patriotism and faith in his leadership. "They knew," he writes, "that a mortal blow was being aimed at the Indians' honour, and their going to jail was a cry of agony and prayer offered from the bottom of their heart ... Such 'heart prayer' is always acceptable to God."[64]

Gandhi found that the immediate and spontaneous consequence of the arrest of the women *satyagrahis* was that thousands of Indian miners working in the mines in Natal struck work simultaneously. Although they had been unhappy with some inequitable laws imposed on them, the role played by the women served as a catalyst for their action. As a result of the strike, the Indian labourers were thrown out of their houses by their white employers. They then applied to Gandhi for help. Gandhi could not refuse and he went to meet them. The manner in which Gandhi handled this crisis and its outcome was to leave a deep impact on his social and political philosophy. He camped with the Indians in the open and, contrary to his fears, was ably helped by the trader class with provisions. Many volunteers came forward to help in looking after the needs of the miners.[65]

Gandhi realized that this state of affairs could not continue indefinitely as the crowd continued to swell to about 5,000. The only solution that appeared to him was to take this "army" into Transvaal and secure them in prison. The mode of transport had to be on foot and rations would necessarily be very meagre so as to last the journey. All the conditions were accepted by the men and the march began on 28 October 1913. Although most of the men were uneducated, Gandhi found that he was able to enforce rules of discipline regarding sanitation and other things by setting an example himself. He concluded, "Where the leader himself becomes a servant, there are no rival claimants for leadership."[66] These two ideas – that social and political consciousness can exist without literacy and formal education and that leadership can be effectively exercised in a given situation through personal example – proved to be invaluable guides for Gandhi for future action.

The traders, including a big European firm, again rendered valuable help to the marchers till they reached Charlestown safely. This was the border station for crossing into the Transvaal. At the end of the heroic struggle, the chief demands of the Indian *satyagrahis* were met, among which were the validation of Indian marriages, abolition of the £3 tax on ex-indentured labourers and the domicile certificates of the Indians in Natal being considered valid for entry into the Union of South Africa.[67]

About his 21 years in South Africa, Gandhi writes in retrospect that it was where he realized his "vocation in life",[68] which may be summarized as raising the consciousness of the people about self-respect and constructive collective action. The social idea that he reaped was that of equality, whether between the sexes, between races, or between the lowly and the elevated. Gandhi, though previously shy, diffident and conscious of his recent failure as a lawyer in India, was able to shake the poor immigrant Indians out of their stupor and, through persistent effort, make them a socially and politically active community. He was convinced that had the Indians not offered satyagraha, they would have been hounded out of South Africa; their victory "more or less served as a shield for Indian emigrants in other parts of the British Empire".

We may conclude this analysis of satyagraha in Gandhi's own words: "I will consider myself amply repaid if I have in these pages demonstrated with some success that satyagraha is a priceless and matchless weapon, and that those who wield it are strangers to disappointment or defeat."[69]

It was through the exercise of his method of satyagraha, involving self-sacrifice and self-suffering, and standing steadfast in the face of adversity, that Gandhi was able to modify the social outlook of the Indians in South Africa. In place of a common feeling of helplessness, he evoked a consciousness of organized strength in them. They began to regard themselves as self-respecting individuals, rather than as social outcastes.

Impact of Hindu Religious Philosophy

We may now turn to an examination of the effect of Gandhi's religious philosophy on his social thinking and activities. Some modern writers on Gandhi have criticized him for his frequent use of the Hindu religious idiom, which, in their view, had communal consequences. However, a close analysis of his style and work presents quite a different picture. Gandhi often said that all the great religious works, such as the *Ramayana*, the *Mahabharata*, the *Koran*, the *Bible* and the *Zend Avesta*, depicted the eternal war between good and evil and they all showed different paths to the same goal of self-realization. He believed that every religion was perfect from the point of view of its followers and imperfect from that of the followers of other faiths and, examined from an independent point of view, every religion was both perfect and imperfect.[70]

Despite his deep faith in the efficacy of the Ramanama, which has been explained before, his conception of Rama was an allegorical one. In a letter to a friend called Raojibhai Patel, he explains this: "Be clear in your mind who this Rama is. He is unconditioned, formless. Armed with the countless virtues that belong to the godly nature, he destroys Ravana representing a host of monstrous ideas. He practised penance for 12 years to earn his strength."[71] As such, Rama represented for Gandhi the highest morality.

An example of his distinctive interpretation of religious terms can be cited from a letter he wrote to a well-known exponent of the Hindu faith called Santoji Maharaj. He says that yajna,[72] *daan*[73] and *tapas*[74] are obligatory duties, but the manner of performing them cannot be the same for all ages. Of his own time, he writes that the supreme yajna was the plying of the spinning wheel, which would give employment to millions and stop costly imports of cloth. The right gift or *daan* was to dedicate one's all – body, intellect and possessions – to the service of the country. And, likewise, the right *tapas* consisted of burning with agony at the suffering of countless untouchables and others who were starving for want of food or because of famines. He believed that anyone who performed these three important duties would certainly become purified.[75]

It can be forcefully argued that Gandhi's use of the religious idiom was for the purpose of highlighting transcendental and perennial human values and not to impose the Hindu view of life on his countrymen. This is not an appropriate place to enter into the details of this argument, but it can be pointed out that to attribute communal consequences to such an approach would be to ignore the autonomous political, economic and imperialist factors that contributed to the polarization of communal forces.

One aspect of Gandhi's religious perception was of crucial importance in moulding his mental makeup – this was the Jain doctrine of *anekantavada*. In its original form, this means that a proposition might at the same time be true and false from two relative points of view.[76] Gandhi has asserted that he was an *anekantavadi* and that it was the most important thing he had learnt from Jain philosophy. His favourite way of proving this doctrine was the story of the seven blind men who tried to describe an elephant by feeling its different parts and gave quite different opinions. He tried to follow this doctrine of *anekantavada* and it was due to this that he learnt, he says, to judge a Muslim from his own standpoint and a Christian from his. In other words, this doctrine taught Gandhi the value of religious tolerance and social harmony as every question or issue could be looked at from different points of view. This explains his constant emphasis on the need for mutual understanding and adjustment.

One may also conclude that it was as a result of Gandhi's being an *anekantavadi* that he developed the ability to make compromises where there was no question of sacrifice of principle. This was an important reason for his success in life. He was not rigid in his stand, but quite willing to listen to the other side and negotiate whenever no loss of dignity was implied. This won him the hearts of the people. He regarded this spirit as an essential part of satyagraha.[77]

There are many well-known examples of this ability in him to compromise when surrender of principles by either party was not involved. The long satyagraha campaign for the entry of untouchables into the Guruvayur temple in south India ended peacefully when Gandhi found a solution that satisfied both parties. While, on the one hand, the untouchables were allowed common entry on equal terms with other Hindus, a short time was kept apart exclusively for the small section of highly orthodox Hindus who had resolved to challenge the common entry of "touchables and untouchables" into the temple with physical force, if necessary. Another famous instance is the Gandhi-Irwin Pact of 1931, which led to the withdrawal of the civil disobedience movement in its first phase and the participation of Gandhi in the Second Round Table Conference. Such examples can be found in plenty throughout his career in both the social and political fields.

Impact of Western Civilization

The evolution of Gandhi's social and economic philosophy was also the result of his disillusionment with the western way of life. After his initial infatuation with English manners in England, he gave up the quest for external traits and gave in to his own predilections for a religious quest. He was helped in this by some of his acquaintances and he learnt the fundamentals of the major religions. He saw through the "tinsel and glitter" of modern civilization and turned away from it. Consciously then, he started on the journey of spiritual discovery and self-realization. He began to search deep into Indian culture and tradition and found in them elements of great value. This helped him formulate the social and economic policies that he propagated all his life in India.

Gandhi compares the two civilizations, eastern and western, and writes that the latter was based on two fallacious maxims – "might is right" and "survival of the fittest". This was not enough for the full development of the human personality, he says, as the strength derived from the 'heart' was much greater than that derived from following these two maxims. He described the strength derived from the heart as "heart strength" or, in Ruskin's words, "social affections". To Gandhi, the difference between the two civilizations was that "western civilization is destructive, eastern civilization is constructive. Western civilization is centrifugal, eastern civilization is centripetal." "I believe also," he said, "that western civilization is without a goal, eastern civilization has always had a goal before it .... I think western civilization also represents tremendous activity, eastern civilization represents contemplativeness."[78] This assertion of the values of eastern civilization is perhaps a search for self-realization, for finding the roots to uphold the values that were being formulated in his mind. He was not blind to the shortcomings or the dangers of misuse of some eastern values. For instance, he realized that contemplation could be interpreted to mean idleness and to justify an unwillingness to surmount obstacles.

Gandhi was not dogmatic and saw benefits in western civilization. He thought a healthy intermingling of the two cultures would be best and, when that happened, the eastern civilization, he felt, would become quickened in its pace with the "western spirit". Eastern civilization would become predominant, he believed, because it had a goal – the goal of attaining oneness with the Supreme Being. He concluded that the two forces were undoubtedly opposing forces, but perhaps both had a place in nature's plan.[79]

Gandhi's views on the nature of western civilization are expressed in a little booklet he wrote in 1909, called *Hind Swaraj*. He was influenced by Edward Carpenter's *Civilization: Its Cause and Cure*. Gandhi found no morality or religion in western civilization and both these were essential elements in the structure of any society Gandhi supported or promoted. He had little use for materialistic achievements or materialistic goals, his creed centred on the human and the spiritual.

It was for these reasons that Gandhi believed that western civilization was based on a foundation of sand and would not endure like eastern civilization. He writes, "This civilization is such that one has only to be patient and it will be self-destroyed."[80] But, he says, it was not like an "incurable disease", which had no remedy. If there were people with foresight and enterprise, they could stop its march in a materialistic direction and give it a more human and spiritual content, which would also stabilize it. It was due to his concern for a spiritual content in civilization that Gandhi consistently put forward his ideas on swadeshi, untouchability, bread labour and trusteeship, all of which had at their base the concept of oneness of all life.

Influence of Indian Social Philosophy

As far as Indian social philosophy was concerned, Gandhi found the concept of *svadharma*, based on the traditional Hindu varna system, most remarkable. It seems that his views were derived mainly from the *Bhagvad Gita*, which he regarded as his "guide in life". He gave his own interpretation of the *Gita* in a book called *Anasaktiyoga*, written in 1929 in the sylvan surroundings of Kumaon where he had gone to recuperate. A passage is quoted from this in illustration of his belief in the concept of *svadharma* (literally, 'one's own way'):

> *Better one's own duty bereft of merit, than*
> *another's well-performed, better is death in the*
> *discharge of one's duty; another's fight is fraught with danger.*

He adds in explanation, "Before God, the work of man will be judged by the spirit in which it is done, not by the nature of the work, which makes no difference whatever. Whoever acts in a spirit of dedication fits himself for salvation."[81] Gandhi's stress on the concept of *svadharma* is probably related to his deep sympathy for the untouchables of India, whose work of scavenging was held in contempt by the majority who branded them as outcastes. He decried this attitude for he understood the value of their work and appreciated that they were doing their duty and being true to their calling. Gandhi held work or labour as a value in itself and, therefore, all work was laudable for him. To set an example, he undertook the work of scavenging himself in his immediate neighbourhood and all his followers emulated him. Through this means, he hoped to remove the stigma attached to the work of the untouchables. This philosophy of work done in a spirit of dedication, or of work as a value, was perhaps derived mainly from the writings of Ruskin and formed an essential element of Gandhi's social thought.

Gandhi believed in the ideal form of *varnavyavastha* (the system of varnas), in which there was no notion of superiority or inferiority between the castes or of untouchability, all of which, he thought, were later accretions. He was convinced that all men are born equal and that it is unmanly for any person to claim superiority over a fellow being.[82] But he did believe that varnas were based on hereditary occupations, which had no hierarchy. There were, he thought, sound social and economic reasons for the occupational division. He defined varnas as universal occupations: "Varnas are four, to mark four universal occupations, that is, imparting knowledge, defending the defenceless, carrying out agriculture and commerce, and performing service through physical labour."[83] It was to the credit of the Hindu religion, he believed, that it alone recognized the varnas as the "law of our being" and made use of it in regulating social relations and conduct.[84] As individuals would not have to worry about their future, which was cut out for them, they could in fact devote their leisure hours to self-improvement and their efforts towards self-realization. Although he knew that this form of *varnadharma* was only an ideal, he felt that it was a necessary ideal because no nation and no individual could possibly live without proper ideals. But such an ideal could never find place in a democratic structure embodying individual freedom. Gandhi was possibly expressing his views in the context of the modern exploitative system in which greed and muscle power determined social roles and status.

Gandhi had no illusions about the existing caste structure in India, which he knew was a travesty of the original that had only defined men's hereditary callings.[85] He felt that the abuse of the law of varna had resulted in innumerable castes with unnecessary and harmful restrictions on intermarriage and inter-dining. The law of varna, he writes, "... has nothing to do with these restrictions".[86] The restrictions arose later, initially to impose self-restraint and hygiene, but finally became instruments of exploitation, he believed.

Marriage and Varna

On the subject of interreligious and inter-caste marriage, Gandhi's views underwent radical evolution from one polar extreme to the other. Till the early 1920s, he regarded such marriages as contrary to dharma and he found several practical objections to such unions,[87] but by April 1928, he had a very different opinion. He writes that caste should not be a consideration in marriage; what was important for both partners was a sense of belonging to the same nation.[88] In 1931, he went further and saw "no moral objection" to even interreligious marriage as long as each party was free to observe his or her own religion.[89] He says the progeny of such unions should be brought up in the faith of their father because of "sound religious and philosophic reasons".[90] Gandhi does not specify these reasons, but it is easy to find in his view reflections of the patrilineal and patriarchical tradition to which he belonged. As a bulwark against provincialism and caste exclusiveness, he began advocating in 1933 interprovincial and inter-communal marriages among educated people.[91]

As a result of his intellectual development, his ideas on *varnadharma* changed profoundly in later years. He came around to believe that all Hindus should now be classified in the fourth varna, as Shudra. This would at one stroke level down all distinctions of high and low. This should not, of course, prevent anybody from attaining divine or any other knowledge, he writes, but it did mean that all must live by their labour and all become entitled, therefore, to nothing more than simple maintenance.[92] This view was a corollary of his belief in the doctrine of 'bread labour', which he acquired from reading the *Bhagvad Gita* and the *Bible*.[93] The excesses of the caste system in India made him a severe opponent of it and he began to feel that it should be destroyed. The best way of doing this, he thought, was for reformers to begin the practice with themselves and, where necessary, take the consequences of the ensuing social boycott.[94]

To those who defended the cruel custom of untouchability on the basis of the Hindu law of karma, Gandhi responded in his own style and gave his interpretation of this law in the following words: "My karma does not compel me to throw stones at a sinner. Religion is made to uplift and not to keep a man crushed under the weight of his karma. It is a prostitution of the grand doctrine of karma to consign a man of lowly birth to perdition. Ram felt himself privileged to be honoured by a fisherman. The Hindu religion is replete with illustrations of great men lifting their unfortunate brethren from their miseries. Will not the modern Hindus copy their own great men and once and for all rub out the blot of untouchability that so defiles Hinduism?"[95]

The issue of untouchability, which is related to the construction of an egalitarian society, became a major, if not the most important, social issue in his thought. A detailed discussion of this issue follows in a later chapter.

Gandhi's Perception of Women

The social conditions for women in India at the time when Gandhi grew up were extremely backward. Though the custom of purdah (codes and dress enabling the seclusion of women) was not prevalent in Gujarat, girls seldom received any education and free mixing of the sexes socially was not encouraged. Boys and girls were married at a very early age and joint patriarchical families were the rule. Young people, therefore, had no independent lives. British civilization had made no inroads inside the homes of the middle class to which Gandhi belonged. His perception of women could well have been influenced by this negative setting, but for the fact that his mother left a very deep and contrary impression on him. Her intense religiosity left an abiding mark. Gandhi's mother visited the Vaishnava temple every day and, according to him, took "the hardest vows without flinching".

One vivid recollection that Gandhi records was of the time his mother, during the monsoon, vowed not to partake of food without seeing the sun. He and the other children in the family would wait eagerly for the sun to appear and hurry to inform their mother about it, but often, it would disappear before she could see it. "That does not matter," she would say cheerfully, writes Gandhi. "God did not want me to eat today."[96] This stoic attitude can also be found in Gandhi's personality. He remembers his mother as a woman with strong common sense, well informed about matters of state and widely respected by the women in her circle. She kept herself abreast of affairs of state and used to be highly regarded for her intelligence by the ladies of the local princely family. As a child, Gandhi recalls, he would accompany her and listen to the "many lively discussions she had with the widowed mother of the Thakor Saheb".[97]

Under the care of such a mother, it may be assumed that his earliest impressions of womanhood and women's position in society were positive. Yet his relations with his wife in the first 20 years of their married life were not particularly happy for he would try to dominate her and she would not submit willingly. About this period of his life, he writes, "It was a time when I thought that the wife was the object of her husband's lust, born to do her husband's behest, rather than a helpmate, a comrade and a partner in the husband's joys and sorrows."[98]

Gandhi's estimation of women's abilities was considerably enhanced by the activities of the suffragettes in England around the year, 1906.[99] Another factor that contributed to his high regard for women was his experience of the participation of women in the final phase of the satyagraha struggle in South Africa. One incident may be cited by way of illustration: During the course of the long march by some 3,000 Indian labourers across the Natal-Transvaal border, there were many women with babies in their arms. One child died due to exposure, another fell into a stream while crossing and was drowned. There was no mourning for them and he recalls that one woman said, "We must not pine for the dead who will not come back to us for all our sorrow. It is the living for whom we must work."[100] Gandhi was deeply influenced by the quiet heroism and strong practical sense of these women, most of whom were illiterate.

Gandhi's ideas on the education of women came from his experiences in England and South Africa. Most of the women with whom Gandhi came in contact during his three year sojourn in England left a positive impression on him. He found them educated and liberal in their thinking and leading unrestricted lives like many young men of the time. Soon after his return to India, he went to live in South Africa and what he saw there of Indian women contrasted sharply with his British experience. The Indian women in South Africa were in a deplorable condition as, in addition to being poor and uneducated, they were absolute aliens in that country. They were totally dependent on the men, the majority of whom were in an equally hapless position. Thus, the two experiences – one in which education was seen to have liberated minds and broken down constrictive social norms and the other where lack of education added to the miseries of an already distressing situation – left an abiding impression on him. As early as 1910, Gandhi spoke of equal opportunities of education for both boys and girls. On Tolstoy Farm, he and his co-workers taught both and there was no distinction in the curricula he prescribed for them. He writes that they met freely and, though he had some bad experiences, he would not, for that reason, debar coeducation. He would only advice "extra caution".[101]

In short, it can be said that Gandhi's concept of women's place in society owed much to childhood influences and later associations in England and South Africa, though he did not remain wholly unaffected by the social milieu of his early life. As a result of these later experiences, he became sanguine about women's capabilities and their capacity to play a positive role in society. He became a champion of their liberty and equality. A detailed discussion will follow in a later chapter.

Public Service

A very important aspect of Gandhi's thought, which had significant social consequences, was the norms he set for a 'public worker'. These were formulated according to his high moral standards without which, he felt, there could be no wholesome public life. He set the example in 1899 in the following manner.

In recognition of his public service in South Africa, the Indian community there bestowed on him many costly gifts, including diamonds, silver and a heavy gold chain for his wife. This weighed him down with a sense of guilt as he had declared previously that such work was done without remuneration. Moreover, he was preparing himself and his family for a life of selfless service and he had publicly exhorted people to conquer their infatuation for jewellery. Keeping all this in mind, he decided not to keep these gifts as personal possessions, despite the protestations of his wife. He created a trust of the gifts to benefit the community and appointed some leading Indians as its trustees. He was definitely of the opinion that a public worker should accept no costly gifts.[102]

Gandhi lays down another important guideline for public service. This is that a public worker should not take upon himself too many burdens, but should devote himself to a few chosen fields. This would lead to the best results, he feels. In a letter to a friend, he expresses this view, "Surely God has not laid on us the burden of ending all that suffering (of the world). If he has, then he has also taught us the secret of carrying it, and it is that from cut of the heap of suffering, we should pick up one clod of earth. If we resolve to do all we can to end that suffering and firmly refuse to take up any other task, we shall have carried the load of the entire hill."[103]

Gandhi's Economic Ideas

Gandhi's economic views were largely moulded by the evolution of his social and moral ideas. He often emphasized the total view of life – that a man could attain his fullest expression only through the integrated development of himself and his environment.[104] This had necessarily to include an appropriate economic milieu. His own view of economics was: "Economics that hurts the moral well-being of an individual or nation is immoral and therefore sinful."[105] It is obvious from this that he was fully committed to the building of a society based on social and economic justice.

It may be reasonable to assert that the sources of his socio-economic views were partly the result of his spiritual and intellectual evolution and partly the result of his understanding of Tolstoy's and Ruskin's works. From Ruskin, he imbibed the value of labour and the significance of agricultural effort, which was further bolstered by his own experience of setting up Phoenix and Tolstoy Farm.

From Tolstoy, he acquired the notion that men should not accumulate wealth in this world, and that agriculture is the true occupation of man because it alone can ensure social and economic justice for all. Gandhi's lack of enthusiasm for large cities and factories also came from his admiration for Tolstoy, who held that large cities and factories were the means through which a few could wallow in riches by exploiting the helplessness and poverty of the many.

The reflection of these influences can be observed in his economic prescriptions for India. Gandhi never constructed a systematic theory of economics, but his economic beliefs can be gleaned from what he wrote and said on various occasions. Only their evolutionary aspect has been considered in this chapter. A more elaborate discussion is attempted later.

Gandhi expressed some of his socioeconomic views in *Hind Swaraj*. He condemned the large scale use of machinery for mass production of goods because it dehumanized man and led to the amassing of riches by a few through various means of exploitation. A good economic system for India, in his opinion, meant not the use of inanimate machines, but an effort to make the "crores of living machines inhabiting it" into "intelligent machines" and ensuring that for the necessaries of life and other needs, cities depended on villages rather than on mass produced goods. For this purpose, village arts and crafts had to be revived to be able to produce marketable goods and volunteers from the cities had to go to the nearest villages to assure markets.[106]

In the formulation of his social and economic ideas, Gandhi was also influenced by Marx's philosophy. He knew well that social justice was incomplete without economic justice. In fact, he often quoted the communist maxim: "From each according to his ability to each according to his need."[107]

However, due to his belief in the oneness of all life, Gandhi's concept of socialism is quite different from the orthodox formulation and he himself points out the difference. According to him, western socialism was based on a conception of the "essential selfishness of human nature", while he believed that the essential difference between man and brute lay in the fact that the former could respond to the call of the spirit in him and rise above the passions he owns in common with the brute. This capacity in man is therefore superior to selfishness and violence, which belong to brute nature and not to the immortal spirit of man. He argued that our socialism or communism should be based on non-violence and on the harmonious cooperation of labour and capital and the landlord and tenant.[108] The relationship must be of mutual trust, not a reflection of conflicting interests.

Doctrine of Bread Labour

A very important aspect of Gandhi's social plan is his doctrine of 'bread labour', which, he says, he owed to the reading of the *Bhagvad Gita* and the *Bible*. He quotes Verses 12, 13 and 14 from Chapter III of the *Gita* in this context:

> *Brahma created his people with the*
> *duty of sacrifice laid upon them*
> *and said: 'By this do you flourish.*
> *Let it be the fulfiller of all your*
> *desires. 'He who eats without performing*
> *This sacrifice eats stolen bread.*[109]

And from the *Bible*, Gandhi quotes these lines:

> *Earn thy bread by the sweat of thy brow.*

Gandhi interprets the injunction about 'sacrifice' in the *Gita* and 'sweat' in the *Bible* as bread labour. He writes with the fervent hope of an idealist: "If all laboured for their bread and no more, then there would be enough food and enough leisure for all. Then there would be no cry of overpopulation, no disease, and no such misery as we see around."[110]

For Gandhi, bread labour essentially meant manual labour as relating to agriculture or the handicrafts and cottage industries. In the context of India's development, he considered the work of spinning (next to agriculture) as the ideal kind of bread labour because it ensured work and food for all. Gandhi asserted that bread labour did not include intellectual labour such as teaching, practice of medicine and writing. He writes: "Mere mental, that is, intellectual, labour is for the soul and is its own satisfaction. It should never demand payment. In the ideal state, doctors, lawyers and the like will work solely for the benefit of society, not for self."[111] For their livelihood, intellectuals should also perform adequate manual labour.

If the law of bread labour was followed by all, he believed, there would be "a silent revolution in the structure of society. Man's triumph will consist in substituting the struggle for existence with the struggle for mutual service. The law of the brute will be replaced by the law of man."[112] A discussion and critique of the concept of bread labour follows in a later chapter.

Principle of Trusteeship

Closely related to the above doctrine was Gandhi's principle of trusteeship, according to which the wealthy should hold their superfluous wealth in trust for the poor. This principle evolved in Gandhi's mind as a result of his spiritual development, which he owed partly to his deep involvement with and the study of theosophical literature and the *Bhagvad Gita*. His familiarity with the maxims of equity in western legal tradition also made him aware of the implications of the principle of trusteeship. On an individual plane, he realized that those who sought to attain God through social service, even if they controlled vast possessions, should not regard any of it as their own. They should rather hold their possessions in trust for the benefit of those less privileged than themselves.[113]

On the social plane, this principle implied that the wealthy could not justly claim their possessions to be theirs entirely. The reason was that they could not accumulate their wealth without the labour and cooperation of workers and the poorer sections of society. Hence, they were logically and morally bound to share their wealth in a fair measure with their workers and the poor. But instead of ensuring this through legislation, Gandhi wanted wealthy people to voluntarily surrender part of their wealth and hold it in trust for those working for them. Adoption of this doctrine on an individual and national scale was, he believed, the only way to form an egalitarian and non-violent society. He defines trusteeship in simple terms: "The rich man will be left in possession of his wealth of which he will use what he reasonably requires for his personal needs and will act as a trustee for the remainder to be used for society."[114]

Gandhi did not believe in inherited wealth for he was of the view that a trustee has no heir but the public. He did not favour compulsion in the surrender of riches because he believed that forcible dispossession of the wealthy would deny to society the talents of people who could create national wealth.[115] His method was to persuade the wealthy to act as trustees, failing which satyagraha could be adopted. But by the 1940s, he had come to believe that state legislation would be necessary to ensure compliance with the principle of trusteeship.[116] A more detailed discussion of this principle is attempted in Chapters 2 and 3.

In short, one may say that the sources of Gandhi's social ideas could be traced to the culture in which he was born and bred. They were certainly stimulated and clarified by his contact with the west and his experiences in South Africa. In fact, he often said that he never stopped learning. Introspection and experiment played a major part in the evolution of his social ideas. Even though, till the end, Gandhi maintained that the ideas expressed by him in *Hind Swaraj* as far back as 1909 still held good, in actual fact, he made many compromises over the years mainly because he was a pragmatist and believed in making compromises without sacrificing fundamental principles. Thus, a study of the sources and evolution of Gandhi's social ideas is a survey of the complexities that go to mould a man's ideas. In it are the cultural influences imbibed unconsciously, the impact of other minds, the experimentation with ideas and ideals, the adjustments and compromises and, above all, the lessons learnt from experience.

Notes

1. *CWMG*, Volume 39, pp. 1–402.
2. Ibid., Volume 84, p. 441.
3. A.L. Basham, 'Traditional Influences on the Thought of Mahatma Gandhi', in *Essays on Gandhi Politics*, ed., Ravinder Kumar (Oxford: Clarendon Press, 1971), p. 17.
4. *CWMG*, Volume 39, pp. 8–9.
5. Ibid.
6. Pyarelal Nayyar, *Mahatma Gandhi: The Early Phase* (Ahmedabad: Navajivan Publishing House, 1965), p. 117.
7. Ibid., pp. 179, 124.
8. *CWMG*, Volume 39, p. 22.
9. Ibid., p. 32.
10. Ibid., p. 10.
11. Ibid., p. 11.
12. Ibid., p. 31.
13. Ibid., p. 32.
14. *CWMG*, Volume 52, p. 72.
15. *CWMG*, Volume 64, p. 259.
16. Literally, 'liberation', freedom from the phenomenal cycle of birth and death.
17. *CWMG*, Volume 39, p. 3.
18. Ibid.
19. *CWMG*, Volume 39, p. 260.
20. *CWMG*, Volume 28, p. 187.
21. *CWMG*, Volume 39, p. 4.
22. Ibid.
23. Basham, 'Traditional Influences', pp. 24–5.
24. *CWMG*, Volume 39, p. 20.
25. Ibid., pp. 33–4.
26. Ibid., p. 34.
27. *CWMG*, Volume 36, p. 449.
28. *CWMG*, Volume 21, p. 14.
29. *CWMG*, Volume 28, p. 187.

30. *CWMG*, Volume 23, p. 114.
31. *CWMG*, Volume 39, p. 22.
32. Ibid., pp. 27, 28.
33. Ibid., p. 60.
34. Gita, Chapter II , verses 62-63 from Arnolds' *The Song Celestial or Bhagvad Gita*.
35. *CWMG*, Volume 39, p. 60.
36. *CWMG*, Volume 32, p. 13.
37. *CWMG*, Volume 39, p. 114.
38. *CWMG*, Volume 5, p. 57.
39. *CWMG*, Volume 39, p. 131.
40. Ibid., pp. 220–1.
41. Ibid., p. 279.
42. *CWMG*, Volume 32, p. 71
43. *CWMG*, Volume 28, p. 412.
44. Ibid., Volume 39, pp. 52–3.
45. Ibid., p. 50.
46. *CWMG*, Volume 29, p. 83.
47. Ibid., p. 44.
48. Ibid., p. 52.
49. Ibid., p. 55.
50. *CWMG*, Volume 29, p. 56.
51. Ibid., p. 67.
52. Ibid., p. 68.
53. *CWMG*, Volume 39, p. 212.
54. Ibid.
55. Ibid., 243.
56. *CWMG*, Volume 29, p. 83.
57. *CWMG*, Volume 7, p. 218.
58. *CWMG*, Volume 29, p. 188.
59. Ibid, p. 207.
60. Ibid.
61. Ibid., p. 221.
62. Ibid., p. 225.

63. Ibid., p. 226.
64. Ibid., p. 227.
65. Ibid., pp. 228–31.
66. Ibid., p. 235.
67. Ibid., p. 266.
68. Ibid., p. 268.
69. Ibid., p. 269.
70. *CWMG*, Volume 32, p. 13.
71. *CWMG*, Volume 12, p. 377.
72. Sacrifice.
73. Gift-giving, charity.
74. Austerity.
75. *CWMG*, Volume 24, p. 93.
76. Basham, 'Traditional Influences', p. 26.
77. *CWMG*, Volume 39, p. 122.
78. *CWMG*, Volume 8, p. 244.
79. Ibid.
80. Ibid., p. 21.
81. One's own duty.
82. *CWMG*, Volume 41, p. 108.
83. *CWMG*, Volume 35, p. 3.
84. *CWMG*, Volume 46, p. 303.
85. Ibid.
86. *CWMG*, Volume 29, p. 411.
87. *CWMG*, Volume 46, p. 303.
88. *CWMG*, Volume 30, pp. 229–30.
89. *CWMG*, Volume 36, p. 200.
90. *CWMG*, Volume 46, p. 303.
91. *CWMG*, Volume 56, p. 236.
92. *CWMG*, Volume 54, p. 25.
93. This has been discussed in Chapter VI, in the section on 'Basic Issues in Social Change'.
94. *CWMG*, Volume 62, p. 122.
95. *CWMG*, Volume 21, p. 175.

96. *CWMG*, Volume 39, pp. 8–9.
97. Ibid., p. 9.
98. Ibid., p. 222.
99. *CWMG*, Volume 6, p. 30.
100. *CWMG*, Volume 29, pp. 237–8.
101. Ibid., p. 195.
102. *CWMG*, Volume 39, p. 179.
103. *CWMG*, Volume 30, p. 361.
104. *CWMG*, Volume 68, p. 200.
105. *Young India*, 13 October 1921, p. 325.
106. *CWMG*, Volume 60, p. 256.
107. *SWMG*, Volume 6, p. 340.
108. *CWMG*, Volume 58, p. 248.
109. *CWMG*, Volume 61, pp. 211–2.
110. Ibid.
111. Ibid.
112. Ibid.
113. *CWMG*, Volume 39, p. 212.
114. *CWMG*, Volume 72, p. 400.
115. Ibid., p. 100.
116. *CWMG*, Volume 76, pp. 9–10.

CHAPTER 2

Vision of the Ideal Society

In this chapter, the discussion focuses first on the elements that Gandhi thought contributed towards the making of an ideal society, second on his continually evolving concept of swaraj followed by his conceptualization of Ram Rajya, democracy, the republic, citizenship and education, and third on his views on the legal and medical professions and on industrialization.

Gandhi's vision of the ideal society is that of a non-violent and democratic social order in which there is a just balance between individual freedom and social responsibility. He has a very high regard for the place of ideals in human life. Without ideals, he says, life can have no meaning because there would be no goals towards which human endeavour can be directed. His supreme ideal, as has been mentioned earlier, is self-realization, or knowing God and merging in him.[1] But this, he admits, is not possible entirely as long as man exists in the flesh and remains subject to its desires. What is possible for him is to lead a life and help construct a society (for man is a social being) that will help him come closest to the supreme goal.

Apart from the influence of his upbringing and education, Gandhi's conception of the ideal society is in a large measure the result of his distaste for the modern civilization of the west. His views on this subject are set forth in the booklet he wrote, *Hind Swaraj*. As noted earlier, he clearly states in his introduction to the book that his negative ideas on modern civilization are not original, but acquired from the writings of several great writers and thinkers.[2] Another factor that moulded Gandhi's vision of the ideal society was his love for the simple life. This arose in the first instance from his own roots in the small towns of Porbandar and Rajkot in Kathiawar. Later, his reading, though selective and generally restricted to theological and philosophical works, affected him deeply. The Phoenix Trust Deed[3] is a very significant document for it contains a model of the type of society he wished to create for humanity. Among the objectives of the settlers on Phoenix Farm were: to order one's life so as to earn a living through handicrafts and agriculture without the aid of machinery; to promote better understanding between peoples; to live a pure life and thereby set an example for others; to try and promote the ideals of Ruskin and Tolstoy; to introduce vernacular education; to propagate the philosophy of 'nature treatment' in the medical field; to train for social service; and finally to conduct a journal for the advancement of these ideas.[4]

As mentioned earlier, Gandhi was critical of industrial civilization not only because it led to severe and wasteful competition for goods and markets leading to colonization of weaker nations and exploitation of the countryside, but also because it led to displacement of manual labour and growing unemployment. In contrast was Indian civilization in which there was "no system of life corroding competition". Each followed his own occupation or trade and charged a regulation wage.[5] On balance, Gandhi finds that the tendency of Indian civilization "is to elevate the moral being", while "that of western civilization is to propagate immorality".[6] This rather harsh condemnation of the west may be viewed in the background of his deep faith in a supreme creator and the necessity of spirituality in a civilization, both of which he found lacking in his experience of western life.

Another element in Gandhi's thinking is very significant for his conceptualization of an ideal society. This is the doctrine of bread labour. It has already been discussed in relation to its emergence; here, we propose to examine his belief that it would, if implemented, create an ideal social order. In broad terms, bread labour means that one should eat only after doing adequate labour to earn it. Gandhi is positive that bread labour meant manual labour alone and not intellectual labour. His logic is: "The needs of the body must be supplied by the body."[7] He also feels that in any society, there are many individuals who can work physically or mentally to an extent that is more than is required to sustain themselves. The products of their surplus labour capacity should, according to Gandhi's principle, be devoted to the common good. If this principle were followed, he asserts, there would be "no rich and no poor, none high and none low, no touchable and no untouchable".[8] He believes that it is the wide gulf between manual and intellectual labour that is the cause of poverty and inequality in society. If each of us, he writes, performed only enough physical labour for our bread, even that, though short of the ideal, would go a long way in producing a just society – our wants would be reduced and our lives would be simplified and each would "derive the greatest relish from the production of his labour".[9] In his ideal state, those doing intellectual labour, such as doctors, lawyers and teachers, should not expect payment because such work is done for its own satisfaction and not for the self, according to him.

Gandhi gave high honour to labour per se. He seems to have been extremely anxious that those engaged in physical labour should not be looked down upon and their place should be considered equal to those engaged in intellectual pursuits. His anxiety in this regard has led him into the rather absurd position of expecting professionals to do enough physical labour for their bread and then follow their intellectual pursuits in the manner of art for art's sake.

It was not that Gandhi held intellectual labour in low esteem. He even says at one place that he would allow those with greater intellect to earn more. But he believed that all should perform manual labour, irrespective of their professions, so that the load of physical labour was not borne unfairly by some and a sense of identification was created with the hardships of others. That is the crux of his argument – that those engaged in intellectual or higher pursuits should not consider themselves superior, that the law of the brute, or the struggle for existence, should be replaced by the law of man, or the struggle for mutual service. However laudable this ideal, it was obviously not practical, which is why there are contradictions in Gandhi's argument. He asserts that professionals should not expect payment for their work, but at the same time, he was willing to allow those with greater intellect to earn more. The pragmatic in Gandhi had been overwhelmed by the idealist in pursuit of an egalitarian, just society.

For Gandhi, his emphasis on village uplift and a return to the villages meant a definite voluntary recognition of the duty of bread labour and all it connoted. He launched a movement to rid village life of poverty and disease through a programme of economic and social revival. The All India Village Industries Association (AIVIA) was, in his own words, "an experiment in willing bread labour". It required the involvement of those used to an urban and sedentary life in the hard life of the villages. Groups of city dwellers would go periodically to live and work among people in rural areas. Moreover, the city dwellers would be persuaded to use products manufactured in the villages to help improve the villagers' economic status. Goods of daily use that could not be produced in villages would be manufactured in the cities and sold in the villages.[10]

Gandhi's ideas are strewn all over his collected works and have to be gleaned from there. The shifts and changes in some beliefs and the strengthening of others are most interesting in the context of his experiences and his growing understanding of social situations. There are, however, some basic principles that do not alter as, for instance, truth and non-violence or his exposition of the value of means in any struggle for ends.

Gandhi places the greatest importance on the means that are employed to attain a goal. He believes that only fair means can produce a fair end and, to prove his point, he offers the following analogy: "The means may be likened to a seed, the end to a tree; and there is just the same inviolable connection between the means and the end as there is between the seed and the tree ... we reap exactly as we sow."[11] In Gandhi's ideal society, satyagraha is particularly stressed as a means (which he describes as "love force" or "soul force"). This force, he writes, is indestructible and the force of arms is powerless when matched against the force of love or the soul. He admits that there was no historical evidence of any nation having risen through the use of this force, but this fact did not trouble him because he regarded history as merely a sensational chronicling of kings and emperors, and not of efforts directed toward promoting individual and corporate happiness. He finds "the greatest and most unimpeachable evidence of the success of this force ... in the fact that in spite of the wars of the world, it still lives on".[12] Hence his emphasis on satyagraha as a means of social change. Using the logic of satyagraha, Gandhi regards it as a superstition to believe that an act of a majority binds a minority. He writes that many examples could be given in which majorities have been known to be in the wrong and minorities in the right. To quote him: "All reforms owe their origin to the initiation of minorities in opposition to majorities."[13]

Another advantage that Gandhi discerns in satyagraha is that it is not an esoteric weapon to be used by people specially endowed to use it; he believes firmly that it is an instrument that can be used by all, old and young, male and female, independent of physical strength. Those who use it would have no fear for they would have given up the fear of death. Evidently, in Gandhi's ideal society, only the weapon of satyagraha would be used to obtain rights or to undo wrongs. The only requirement for becoming a passive resister, he writes, is "control over the mind and, when that is attained, man is free like the king of the forest and his very glance withers the enemy".[14] Moreover, passive resistance, in his opinion, is a double edged sword, it can be used anyhow and it blessed him who used it and him against whom it was used.

The other significant component in the making of Gandhi's ideal society is the existence of a band of dedicated volunteers, who are committed to satyagraha, or passive resistance, as the means to usher in social change. Gandhi lays down four necessary conditions for such a band. They must observe "perfect chastity, adopt poverty, follow truth and cultivate fearlessness".[15] He believes that a person who is unchaste loses stamina and becomes emasculated and cowardly. Chastity is one of the greatest disciplines without which the mind cannot attain the requisite firmness. Poverty was necessary as only one who is used to it can suffer the consequences of passive resistance cheerfully. Truth was like the shield and sword of the *satyagrahi*, for, without the courage of his convictions, he would bow down before social pressures. The element of fearlessness was an indispensable factor because only one who was totally fearless could challenge social evils.

It seems that Gandhi was aware that in spite of his claim to the contrary that anyone could become a *satyagrahi*, the qualities required for passive resistance were not easy to cultivate, for he asked the readers of *Hind Swaraj* to not be put off by passive resistance on account of the injunctions he had laid down.

In the context of a discussion on satyagraha as the means for creating Gandhi's ideal society, something must be said about his views on the pace of social change. The social revolution he planned could not be the result of sudden and violent measures, but of a planned and comprehensive scheme of evolution. This aspect of satyagraha, which is now widely recognized, has been highlighted by Professor Ramashray Roy. Though Roy discusses satyagraha in the political context, the argument would hold good in the social sphere, too, where satyagraha is used as the 'means' for achieving the 'end' of social justice. Roy is of the view that when satyagraha is used as a political weapon, it leads to the "disclosure of truth" or "conflict resolution".[16] In a dispute, the various contestants express their relative perceptions of the truth. There is a moral tussle that may go on for some time, but the absolute truth has to emerge soon. The party with the greatest moral strength, exemplified by its capacity to sacrifice, will be victorious. To quote his words, "Since satyagraha is a dialectic process, which makes explicit the possibilities that lie in the womb of a particular situation, it follows that the possibilities, to be real, must ripen gradually to maturity. The pace of maturation cannot be forced."[17]

It is in this sense that Gandhi puts so much emphasis on gradual, peaceful, non-violent change. He believed that a new social order could not be forced; if change was brought through force, it would be a remedy worse than the disease. Gandhi did not wish to slacken the pace of change, but it had to be an organic growth, not a violent superimposition. The organic growth itself was to result in a thoroughgoing, radical social reordering.[18]

Here it would be interesting to counterpose this view with the Marxist argument that states that man cannot be liberated from his predicament without a revolutionary change in the economic order, followed by a restructuring of the social and political system. Opposed to this is Gandhi's view, which emphasizes moral and individual change as the precursor to social and economic change.

The concept of justice forms an important element in Gandhi's view of the ideal society. His definition makes it clear: "Pure justice is that which is inspired by fellow feeling and compassion. We in India call it the eastern or ancient way of justice ... where such an arrangement exists, there is hardly any need for a third party or an arbitrator."[19] He considers that action alone to be just which does not harm either party to a dispute. This view sprang from his supreme belief in the oneness of all life – that there is divinity in each individual and, hence, justice should not be such as to harm any individual.

This conviction is reflected in Gandhi's concept of social equality. His idea was that while all are equal in society, while each has a right to equal opportunity, all do not have the same capacity. Some would inherently have the capacity to earn more and others less. He would allow a man of intellect to earn more.[20] Though this view of differential equality of men expresses a very plausible argument, Gandhi appears to miss one dimension of social life – that individual capacity is itself determined by the structural inequalities in society. On the other hand, it can be said that Gandhi's view is a concession to the modern state with its imperfect social arrangements and does not belong to his conception of the ideal society where, as a result of the operation of the principle of bread labour and trusteeship, there would be equal distribution of wealth and not just equitable distribution. This is confirmed by his views on the subject of economic equality.

Gandhi quotes Marx on the concept of economic equality: "From each according to his ability to each according to his need .... If a single man demanded as much as a man with a wife and four children, that would be a violation of economic equality."[21] Gandhi upholds this ideal, but does not recommend force to implement it because his creed is non-violence. He formulated his doctrine of trusteeship to resolve this dilemma. The rich, he asserts, should behave as trustees for their surplus wealth and use it for the common good. This is their public duty and they ought to renounce their wealth voluntarily. Though absolute trusteeship, he was aware, was an abstraction like Euclid's definition of a point, and equally unattainable, "if we strive for it", he says, "we shall be able to go further in realizing a state of equality on earth than by any other method".[22] This was the only way in which a just and non-violent society could be established. He believed that if wealthy people did not heed his advice, the consequences would be formidable. The poverty stricken masses would rise from their stupor and plunge the country into utter chaos.

Gandhi's advice regarding the voluntary abdication of riches was treated with ridicule by many of his contemporaries. Despite this, he would not countenance confiscation of property because he believed that would prove counterproductive. Moreover, the nation would be denied the talents of those who could create wealth for it. The remedy, he says, was the sovereign one – "non-violent non-cooperation and civil disobedience as the right and infallible means".[23] Greater discussion on this subject follows in Chapter 4.

It is now time to discuss Gandhi's concept of swaraj, which was important for the formulation of his views on the ideal society. At one stage, he identified swaraj with Ram Rajya, or the idyllic society in Hindu terms. He defined the concept in several ways, ranging from "self-rule" to "total independence" of the nation. His thinking evolved substantially over a period of years during the struggle for independence. He writes in *Hind Swaraj*, "It is swaraj when we learn to rule ourselves. It is therefore in the palm of our hands."[24] Here it is obvious that he means that the moment we become conscious of our innate dignity, of a self higher than the external self, we become free, and to protect this freedom, he writes, we should willingly sacrifice even our lives. At the spiritual level, he finds swaraj synonymous with moksha, or salvation.[25]

Gandhi and Umar Shobani coming down the staircase of a mosque on Grant Road in Mumbai in 1919

Special Supplement.

The Bombay Chronicle

THE CRORE EXCEEDED

Headlines in Bombay Chronicle about Gandhi's successful drive to collect Rs 1 crore for the Tilak Swaraj Fund in 1921

In the December 1920 issue of *Young India*, Gandhi conceives of swaraj as the attribute of an independent nation. In sum, he says, swaraj is the state when a nation is free to make a choice between good and evil.[26] At the purely social level, Gandhi's discussion of swaraj revolves mainly round the need for emancipating the nation from the dead weight of unworthy traditions and building up a new consciousness on the noble elements of its heritage, such as mutual tolerance and community life. For this purpose, it is necessary, he observes, that Hindus discard the error of untouchability, Muslims and Hindus give up mutual enmity and accept "heart friendship" as an eternal factor of national life, all Indians adopt the charkha as the only universal means of attaining India's economic salvation, and, finally, all accept that India's freedom lies only through non-violence and no other method.

In the foregoing passage, we observe some of the chief characteristics of Gandhi's ideal society. Harmony and cooperation marked its social organization, while simplicity and lack of competition prevailed in the economic sphere. He believed that only a definite, intelligent and free adoption of the entire programme he outlined could lead to the attainment of the substance of swaraj.[27]

Gandhi's thinking on swaraj evolved further under the pressure of the national struggle for independence. He had to frame the ideology keeping the nation and her people in mind. In 1936, he wrote a passage on this subject, which is relevant for our study. As was his habit, he used an analogy to explain his viewpoint and compared swaraj to a square. At one end, he placed complete political independence and at the opposite end, full economic independence. At the third end was moral and social uplift, which he sums up as non-violent behaviour, and at the opposite end, dharma or truth. This truth, he says, was religion in the highest sense of the term. It included Hinduism, Islam and Christianity, but was superior to all of them. Elaborating further, he says that the truth was the ultimate reality which pervaded everything and survived death and destruction. In this conception of swaraj, there is indeed a picture of an ideal society where the highest moral standards are maintained in every sphere.[28]

Another picture of swaraj emerges when Gandhi compares swaraj with Ram Rajya. He draws an image of a pure, idyllic society in which both the government and the governed are led by the highest motives. To quote him: "We call a state Ram Rajya when both the ruler and his subjects are straightforward, when both are pure in heart, when both are inclined towards self-sacrifice, when both exercise restraint and self-control while enjoying worldly pleasures, and when the relationship between the two is as good as that between a father and a son. It is because we have forgotten this that we talk of democracy or the government of the people."[29]

It may now be concluded that for Gandhi, the starting point of thinking on swaraj is moral purification at both the individual and national level. He writes that from the beginning, his endeavour was to increase the "soul force" of the people, by self-purification and *tapasya*, or self-denial. He believed that it was as a result of this that good quality persons were elected to the municipal boards, et cetera, after the commencement of the Non-Cooperation Movement. But he knew well that the path was a difficult one and there were many pitfalls ahead, so he never tried to look too far ahead. He liked to say: "The distant scene I do not care to see, one step enough for me."[30]

Gandhi's projection of the ideal society underwent considerable transformation over the decades he spanned. In the early years, it was a nebulous picture of an altruistic society. Afterwards, as a result of his own experiences and experiments, there began to emerge the firm outlines of a society that he painstakingly planned and hoped to create. Gandhi has given his attention to all its aspects – political, social and economic. In the 1920s, while visualizing the ideal society, he represents individuals as conscientious citizens, who are able to transcend religious, caste and class barriers. The government is shown as a self-righteous body, which performs its duties only with a view to the common good.[31] In the 1930s, Gandhi developed a more concrete programme and set it before the country as the goal toward which national endeavour had to be directed. The self-contained village is his ideal, built as it is on the firm foundation of the concept of non-violence. This is highlighted when he writes: "Rural economy, as I have conceived it, eschews exploitation altogether and exploitation is the essence of violence. You have, therefore, to be rural minded before you can be non-violent, and to be rural minded, you have to have faith in the spinning wheel."[32] The spinning wheel, or charkha, signified for him simple technology, which he considered indispensable for a harmonious and contented society.

In emphasizing a return to village life, Gandhi makes it very clear that he does not at all mean the villages of the past or of the present, which wallowed in ignorance and squalor. He clarified his view further in a letter to Jawaharlal Nehru in October 1945: "My ideal village will contain intelligent human beings. They will not live in dirt and darkness as animals. Men and women will be free and able to hold their own against anyone in the world. There will be neither plague nor cholera, nor smallpox; no one will be idle, no one will wallow in luxury. Everyone will have to contribute his quota of manual labour .... It is possible to envisage railways, post and telegraph ... and the like ....[33]

From the manner in which Gandhi uses the term, 'village', to refer to his ideal society, it is obvious that it is in reality a euphemism for a whole philosophy of life, his very own creation.

Let us now look at the plan he envisaged for the ideal village or community or society. Gandhi's purpose is to make each individual's life more wholesome and rewarding. "An ideal village," he says, "will be so constructed as to lend itself to perfect sanitation. It will have cottages with sufficient light and ventilation, built of a material obtainable within a radius of five miles of it. The cottages will have courtyards enabling householders to plant vegetables for domestic use and to house their cattle. The village lanes and streets will be free of all avoidable dust. It will have wells according to its needs and accessible to all. It will have houses of worship for all; also a common meeting place, a village common for grazing its cattle, a cooperative dairy, primary and secondary schools in which industrial education will be the central fact, and will have panchayats for settling disputes. It will produce its own grains, vegetables and fruit, and its own khadi. This is roughly my idea of a model village."[34]

It is obvious from this passage that self-sufficiency is the motto of Gandhi's ideal society, at least for basic necessities such as food and clothing. Moreover, its people cooperate willingly in several activities to make their community life clean and wholesome. Extravagance is avoided in every field. The systems of justice and education are made rational and socially productive. So, in his ideal village, people labour for self-sufficiency, cooperate with one another and respect each other's religious beliefs and live a life that is altogether healthy. There is no violent competition or conflict and each individual is given a sense of participation and belonging.

Gandhi did not think that such a village was impossible to realize. All that was necessary, he writes, was a band of committed village workers, who were willing to give "intelligent guidance" to the village people. They did not have to be highly educated people, but responsible and sympathetic citizens of the country. They would teach the ignorant villagers the value of mutual cooperation and voluntary labour for the common good. With such help, he is convinced, the village income, as distinguished from the individual income, would double.[35] Though assistance from the government would be invaluable in the sphere of village reconstruction, much could be achieved even without it, he believed, with self-help and self-reliance.

Gandhi was actually very apprehensive about arming the government with too much power even in what purported to be a welfare state. He believed that the citizens in such a state pay for their dependence with a proportionate loss of their liberty. It is because of this that he greatly admires Henry David Thoreau, a champion of civil rights in the United States of America. Gandhi echoes him when he writes, "I look upon an increase of the power of the state with the greatest fear because, although while apparently doing good by minimizing exploitation, it does the greatest harm to mankind by destroying individuality, which lies at the root of all progress."[36] If we take the argument to the social sphere, we find that Gandhi stresses cooperation and equality. He appears to be apprehensive about the use of power anywhere, which might prove dangerous for egalitarian growth and individual initiative.

Gandhi's political ideas, too, with regard to the ideal society, advance much further over the years from the position he assumes in *Hind Swaraj*, wherein he cherishes an enlightened anarchy. He is a firm believer in the value of public opinion for good government. But its evaluation should be done differently, he asserts. "In my Ram Rajya, however, public opinion cannot be measured by counting of heads or raising of hands. I would not regard this as a measure of public opinion, the verdict of the *panch* should be regarded as the voice of God. Those who raise hands are not the *panch*. The rishis and the munis, after doing penance, came to the conclusion that public opinion is the opinion of people who practise penance and who have the good of the people at heart. That is the true meaning of democracy."[37] Therefore, in Gandhi's opinion, the best means of attaining the ends of social justice and harmony was by ascertaining the views of people who had, through hard work and sacrifice, proved their capabilities, rather than have each and every person voting on public issues, irrespective of their capacity for social judgement.

The concept of an ideal ruler was also envisaged by Gandhi. He was greatly concerned about the place of social conduct in the ideal society. The ruler's first duty, Gandhi felt, would be to ensure that his personal purity was never suspect and he must be willing to sacrifice everything for his reputation. In this context, Gandhi was deeply influenced by the example of Rama, the legendary hero of Hindu mythology. Rama honoured public opinion at great cost to himself. The conduct of the ruler had to be exemplary, reflecting the ideals of social justice and moral principles. "Even a dog", Gandhi writes, could not be harmed in that state because Rama felt that all living beings were part of himself. There would be no licentious conduct, no hypocrisy, no falsehood in such a state.[38]

Gandhi firmly believed that the private and public life of an individual must correspond closely and this was all the more important in the case of a ruler. The ruler had to set an example for his subjects. The ideal ruler or king was, in Gandhi's opinion, "a protector, a guardian and a trustee, the best servant, the servant of servants".[39] He should, moreover, subsist on the leavings of his subjects, sleep after making his subjects sleep, and live after enabling them to live. In expressing these idealistic notions, Gandhi was no doubt influenced by his study of ancient Hindu literature, particularly the *Manusmriti*, in which, among other things, the essential virtues of kings are defined. It has been observed about Gandhi that "his belief that private morality had public consequences reflects the emphasis in traditional Hindu thought on ethical as against institutional restraints. Traditional Hindu political thought, the *Dharmasastra* and the epics stress the importance of inner over external restraints on rulers, relying not upon countervailing institutions, but upon ethical commands to guarantee the public spirit of traditional kings. In practice, of course, countervailing institutions did act as irregular restraints."[40]

We shall now consider Gandhi's understanding of democracy. He has written so much that there are bound to be contradictions and variations in his writings. In one context, he could define democracy as the opinion of a few tested and proven men and women who had practised penance, while, in another context, he takes a less idealistic and more practical stance. He outlines the features of democracy thus: A dynamic democracy can grow only out of the meaningful relationships and spontaneous organization that spring up among people when they come together at the local level to solve their basic problems by cooperation among themselves. In such a community, achievement of self-sufficiency and security by neighbourly cooperation engenders a strong sense of local strength and solidarity, and the individual's sense of responsibility to the community and concern for its welfare are at its highest.[41]

This definition is indeed very different from the common meaning of democracy, which is characterized by universal adult suffrage and a parliamentary form of government. Gandhi's democracy underscores strong emotional bonds between the individuals of a locality who are guided by a public spirit and decide to cooperate in order to solve their common problems.

Gandhi's ideal of democracy is to be attained not through the conventional system of adult suffrage, but representative voting of the local communities. When these are organized as vibrant harmonious units, a vote for each person would be meaningless, he says. He explained this idea to Louis Fischer in 1942. He said that there were 700,000 villages in India and each would be organized according to the will of its citizens, all of them voting. Then there would be 700,000 votes and not 400 million. Each village, in other words, would have one vote. The villages would elect their district representatives and the district administrations would elect the provincial administration, and these, in turn, would elect a president who would be the national chief executive.[42]

Gandhi, it seems, recommended this system of indirect elections because he believed in the superior judgement of the *panch* or a "few good men" with proven ability in social affairs, rather than the indiscriminate use of the vote by each individual. Democracy, he thought, could not be forced upon people – the desire for it had to come from within. Gandhi did not think his system of voting undemocratic because he was of the view that it would give the people representatives who were tried and tested in the life of groups and would substitute the active participation of individuals for the present day passive expression of views. Villages, in his plan, are the "building blocks" of the democratic structure.[43] This scheme is further elaborated when he writes about the political organization of his "village republic", where he outlines what he believes would be a "perfect democracy": "The government of the village will be conducted by the panchayat of five persons annually elected by the adult villagers, male and female, possessing minimum prescribed qualifications. These will have all the authority and jurisdiction required since there will be no system of punishments in the accepted sense. This panchayat will be the legislature, judiciary and executive combined to operate for its year of office .... Here there is perfect democracy based upon individual freedom. The individual is the architect of his government. The law of non-violence rules him and his government. He and his village are able to defy the might of a world."[44]

Though Gandhi visualized the government of the ideal society as a non-coercive body, yet it was entrusted with comprehensive powers and it was to use its moral authority and persuasion to enforce its decisions. The only check on its authority was the force of public opinion or individual opinion expressed through the means of satyagraha.

Gandhi's view of citizenship is related to his conception of the ideal society. Though he had not made a systematic study of the subject, by inference, one can obtain it from his ideas on the theory of rights of individuals. Each right, according to him, had a corresponding duty, and all rights, whether in relation to the family, society or state, followed from the performance of the corresponding duties. The foremost duty, in his opinion, was to try to achieve the goal of self-realization – to seek identification of self with all life. The path was through social service with truth and non-violence as the means. By trying to claim rights without fulfilling the duties that preceded them, the rights would always escape our grasp and no real advance could be made with such rights.[45]

Against this background of his theory of rights, a true citizen, in Gandhi's opinion, was one who thought primarily of his duties towards society, rather than his rights in society. Such a citizen was confident that rights would automatically follow from the due performance of his duties. He would also know the remedy for any attack on his rights. The remedy was non-violent non-cooperation.

We shall now turn to an examination of some specifically social issues that Gandhi has considered in his formulation of an ideal society. The views expressed by him are not disowned later, but the emphasis changes according to his perception of the nation's needs.

Gandhi took a holistic view of education. He believed that one should be able to acquire self-restraint through education. He made a distinction between acquiring information and true education – acquiring information could help one earn one's living, but, because it could not build character, it could not fulfil the main purpose of human life, while true education enlightened one and pointed out one's path of duty. He said:

"Education, character and religion should be regarded as convertible terms. There is no true education which does not tend to produce character, and there is no true religion which does not determine character. Education should contemplate the whole life. Here, memorising and book learning is not education. I have no faith in the so-called system of education, which produces men of learning without the backbone of character."[46]

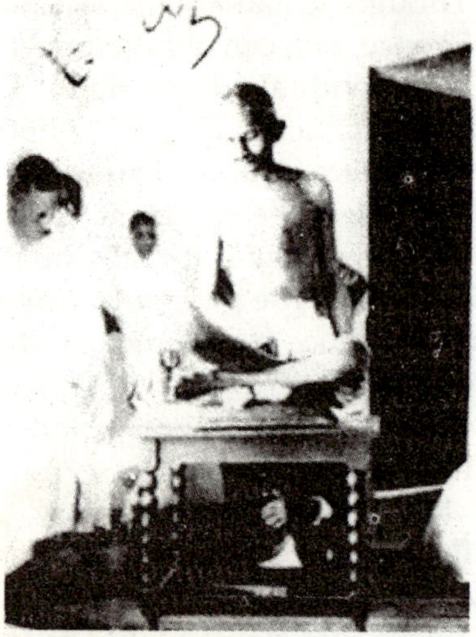

Gandhi being weighed during the 21 days' fast for Hindu–Muslim unity in Delhi in September 1924

Gandhi with textile workers at Darwen, Lancashire, in September 1931

Gandhi is severely critical of modern education as established by the British in India. This, he believed, has mentally "enslaved us". The Indians forgot their own great languages and wrote to each other in "faulty English". Their best thoughts were expressed in English and, therefore, never reached the masses. In *Hind Swaraj,* Gandhi expresses deep admiration for what he believed was the ancient education system of India. He stated that character building had first place in it and that was primary education, in his opinion. A building erected on such a foundation would last.[47] The ancient system of education had relevance to the life of the ordinary villager and provided stability in his life. Though Gandhi seemed to idolize the past, he stressed the necessity to continually make changes in our institutions and systems. He admired the Europeans for their ability to do this. His desire was that Indians should create a system of education that would lead to national resurgence in the social and cultural fields and make them aware of their great heritage.[48]

In a tentative scheme of education articulated by him in the early years, Gandhi laid great stress on language, which he saw as a medium of learning, as a medium of communication, and as a means to build mutual respect and goodwill. To quote his words: "We have to improve all our languages .... Those English books which are valuable, we should translate into the various Indian languages. We should abandon the pretension of learning many sciences. Religious, that is, ethical education, will occupy first place. Every cultured Indian will know in addition to his own provincial language, if a Hindu, Sanskrit; if a Mahomedan, Arabic; if a Parsee, Persian; and all, Hindi. Some Hindus should know Arabic and Persian; some Mahomedan and Parsis, Sanskrit, several northerners and westerners should learn Tamil. A universal language for India should be Hindi, with the option of writing it in Persian or Nagri characters. In order that the Hindus and Mahomedans may have closer relations, it is necessary to know both the characters. And, if we can do this, we can drive the English language out of the field in a short time. All this is necessary for us, slaves. Through our slavery, the nation has been enslaved and it will be free with our freedom.[49]

Gandhi's emphasis is on release from the stranglehold of the English language and related cultural phenomena and substituting in their place, Indian languages and cultural harmony. It is obvious that Gandhi is thinking both like a patriot and an educationist. In later years, his motivations are different and his schemes of education reflect his deep concern for the idle and downtrodden masses of the nation. The most significant of them was named by him as Basic Education – basic because it stood for the art of living.[50]

According to this scheme, which is discussed in detail in a later chapter, education of the young would be an important duty of the state; it would be free and compulsory during the primary stage from the age of seven to fourteen. Gandhi drew up a plan of self-supporting primary education, which would benefit both the child and society. This plan sprang out of his faith in non-violent values and the desire to evolve a truly democratic social order.

The central feature of the new plan was education of the child through a useful, productive craft – the application of the ideal of bread labour to education. The medium of instruction was to be the mother tongue and the education of all other subjects would be integrally related to the productive craft. Gandhi believed that training in a useful handicraft, when it was made the centre of education, would establish a purposive relationship between doing, learning and living and bring about the harmonious development of body, mind and soul.

Gandhi's critique of modern society also covered an appraisal of the legal and medical professions. It would be relevant for our purpose to consider his views on the subject. Gandhi, who was a trained lawyer himself, believed in the value of reconciliation and arbitration for the settlement of disputes, but was well aware that these values were generally ignored and corruption had crept into the practice of the legal profession.

In his ideal society, Gandhi would have lawyers give up their profession and take up a socially productive occupation like spinning or weaving. Lawyers should use their legal acumen to enlighten their countrymen on social and public issues. They should also resolve not to meddle in disputes, but persuade disputing parties to give up their quarrels and reach an amicable settlement,[51] which would rest on the wisdom of the elders or the *panches*.

Gandhi also demolishes the tall claims made by men of medicine about the value of their work. Instead of trying to attain the goal of serving humanity, he felt they served themselves by exploiting the weaknesses and credulity of people. He points out that most ailments were primarily the result of negligence or indulgence by individuals.

In his scheme of an ideal society, Gandhi would have doctors, like lawyers, give up their profession and teach people the way to develop healthy minds, which would automatically lead to their having healthy bodies. He would completely forbid vivisection, even if it meant checking the progress of medical science. As in the case of lawyers, he would persuade doctors to take up a socially productive occupation. If patients were to come to them for treatment, they ought to use their medical knowledge to explain to them the cause of their disease and advise them to remove the cause, rather than pamper them by giving them useless drugs.[52]

There is much in Gandhi's thought that awakens our admiration, but there are elements that are completely baffling. Surely Gandhi could not have believed that doctors would be able to keep their medical knowledge alive and up to date while busying themselves in some "socially productive" occupation. The early Jain influences were apparently very strong and are manifest in his argument that even at the risk of checking medical progress, he would oppose vivisection. But one has to take these arguments in the light of a dream of an ideal society which Gandhi cherished and knew to be difficult to achieve.

As mentioned earlier, Gandhi was an outspoken critic of the machine age that had begun to flower in the west and was beginning to find its roots in India as well. Mill owners, he was convinced, could never have the interests of the people at heart; they would always support governments that bolstered their interests. The nexus between the two was very close[53] and quite alien to the spirit of mutual goodwill and cooperation envisaged by Gandhi in his vision of a harmonious social structure and self-sufficient village.

In the ideal society, Gandhi would not order the destruction of mills already established, but he would implore the mill owners not to add to them. He would persuade them to "gradually contract their business". They can instead, he says, "establish in thousands of households the ancient and sacred handlooms and they can buy out the cloth that may thus be woven".[54] On the other hand, a movement like the Swadeshi Movement could be launched, he felt, and people would voluntarily cease to use machine made goods when their social consciousness was aroused.

In later years, Gandhi opposed mechanization on the more practical grounds of its unsuitability in a vast agricultural country like India. In a public speech in 1928, he says that the result of industrializing India would be like establishing the age of Ravana,[55] instead of the age of Rama.[56] "Where there were thirty crores of living machines," he says, "and cows and calves of great number, worshipping machines would be suicidal. In depopulated countries like the UK and USA, there may be a need for machines, but then they also resorted to robbery and plunder of other countries with the help of these machines."[57]

India, he asserts, could regain her riches and prosperity if she followed a natural course of development with the help of her vast lands, good climate and unlimited natural resources. It is for this reason that he propagated khadi. In *Hind Swaraj,* he says he regards all machinery, including electricity generators and printing presses, as evil.[58] Though this remained his ideal till the end, Gandhi made many concessions to the propagators of the machine age in later years and became, in fact, an avid supporter of the sewing machine. He even favoured the installation of electricity in villages and realized that some industries producing capital goods had come to stay. Only he would have them owned by the state.

Thus, it can be said that Gandhi's conception of the ideal society was primarily in moral terms, rather than in social or political terms. Self-restraint and self-reliance were the keys to the founding of his ideal society. Through the practice of these virtues, the individual could ultimately gain mastery of himself and learn to identify himself with all life. In this situation, he would not exploit his environment for his selfish aggrandizement, but establish a reciprocal relationship in which he would use the products of his environment without impoverishing it.

From this point of view, Gandhi's concept and practice of swadeshi assume great significance. It had at its basis harmonious social, political and economic interaction with the immediate neighbourhood as opposed to reliance on distant and remote cultures and places. By following the principle of swadeshi, the all round development of the human personality and society was possible. The manifestation of this belief was his ideal of the self-sufficient rural community.

Such a society could be created, Gandhi believed, provided one was convinced about the power of non-violence, the value of manual labour and the principle of trusteeship. Public spirited citizens holding these values would cooperate voluntarily and, with the help of simple technology, organize community life on harmonious lines.

Notes

1. *CWMG*, Volume 39, p. 3.
2. *CWMG*, Volume 10, p. 7.
3. *CWMG*, Volume 11, p. 320.
4. Ibid., pp. 321--2.
5. *CWMG*, Volume 10, p. 37.
6. Ibid., p. 38.
7. *CWMG*, Volume 61, p. 212.
8. Ibid.
9. Ibid.
10. This is discussed at greater length in Chapter V.
11. CWMG, Volume 10, p. 43.
12. Ibid., p. 48.

13. Ibid., p. 51.
14. Ibid.
15. Ibid., p. 52.
16. Ramashray Roy, *Self and Society: A Study in Gandhian Thought* (New Delhi: Sage Publications, 1985), p. 168.
17. Ibid., p. 169.
18. *CWMG*, Volume 58, p. 220.
19. *CWMG*, Volume 14, p. 234.
20. *SWMG*, Volume 6, p. 366.
21. M.K. Gandhi, *Economic and Industrial Life and Relations*, Volume I, p. 150.
22. *CWMG*, Volume 9. p. 318.
23. *CWMG*, Volume 72, p. 401.
24. *CWMG*, Volume 10, p. 39.
25. *CWMG*, Volume 19, p. 81.
26. Ibid.
27. *CWMG*, Volume 21, p. 459.
28. *CWMG*, Volume 64, pp. 191–2.
29. *CWMG*, Volume 35, pp. 489–90.
30. *CWMG*, Volume 32, p. 535.
31. *CWMG*, Volume 20, pp. 506–7.
32. Sarvodaya, *SWMG*, Volume 4, p. 36.
33. Pyarelal Nayyar, *Mahatma Gandhi: The Last Phase* (Ahmedabad: Navajivan Publishing House, 1956), p. 545.
34. *CWMG*, Volume 64, p. 217.
35. Ibid.
46. *CWMG*, Volume 59, p. 319.
36. *CWMG*, Volume 35, p. 490.
37. Ibid.
38. *CWMG*, Volume 42, p. 23; Volume 66, p. 390.
39. Lloyd I. Rudolph and Susanne Hoeber Rudolph, *The Modernity of Tradition* (Chicago: University of Chicago Press, 1967), p. 194.
41. Pyarelal Nayyar, The Last Phase, p. 581.
42. *CWMG*, Volume 76, p. 437.

43. Ramashray Roy, *Self and Society*, p. 165.
44. *CWMG*, Volume 76, pp. 308–9.
45. *CWMG*, Volume 69, p. 52.
46. *CWMG*, Volume 37, p. 362.
47. Ibid., p. 55.
48. *CWMG*, Volume 13, pp. 55–6.
49. Ibid., pp. 56–7.
50. *Harijan*, 11 May 1947, p. 145.
51. *CWMG*, Volume 10, p. 63.
52. Ibid.
53. Ibid., p. 58.
54. Ibid.
55. Demon king of Hindu mythology.
56. Divine king of Hindu mythology.
57. *CWMG*, Volume 35, p. 492.
58. Ibid.

CHAPTER 3

Perception of the Indian Social Structure

Gandhi's patriotism and admiration for the ancient traditions of India did not blind him to the many ills ripping the social fabric of the country. Through his experiences and a sense of empathy, he had identified the major social issues that needed to be addressed by all thinking members of the community in concert with the people. He was deeply distressed by the manifold divisions in the highly stratified society of India and by the general lack of education, which had given rise to an erroneous value system based on ignorance and superstition. Outlining this state of affairs in an article titled 'India's Sorry Plight', he wrote: "A patriot's first duty is to know the state of his country. Having done so, his next duty is to search for a remedy. This done, his third duty is to give effect to the remedy."[1]

In the backdrop of these pointed imperatives for "patriots", we may look at Gandhi's analyses and prescriptions on some of the main contours of the social landscape of his age.

Caste System

Gandhi believed that Hindu society in its pristine state – during the Vedic times – was based on Varnashramadharma, or the law of varna and *ashrama*. According to Gandhi, this was society's "predominant characteristic". This implied two things – that dharma or "social conduct" (as he termed it) varied, firstly, according to each class of society and, secondly, according to the four stages in the life of the individual. The former is called Varnadharma and the latter, Ashramadharma. Gandhi believed that this form of social classification was purely functional and did not have any hierarchical or iniquitous connotations. But the law of the *ashrama* was a "dead letter today",[2] he said.

Each of the varnas, which he referred to as social classes (while also using the term, castes, for them elsewhere), was determined by birth and to each was assigned a particular hereditary calling with no implication of superiority or inferiority. In this form, Gandhi did not consider varna to be a manmade institution, but "the law of life universally governing the human family". He believed that it provided the basis of an egalitarian society. One important attribute of varna, writes Gandhi, is that while it is determined by birth, it can be retained only by observing its obligations. One who fails to do so loses his title to that varna. On the other hand, a person, though born in one varna, but displaying the predominant characteristics of another, is regarded as belonging to the second varna.[3] There is ambiguity in this analysis because Gandhi talks of varna being determined by birth, even as he recognizes the possibility of a person being born in one varna and belonging to another by virtue of his qualities. What is important, perhaps, is his conviction that the social structure delineated in ancient times was true in conception and that the blemishes seen now were a result of faulty practice.

This pristine law, in Gandhi's opinion, fell into disrepute because it became distorted by rigidity in its observance by high class, orthodox Hindus. The four original varnas became subdivided into innumerable groups called jatis, or castes, and they began to represent gradations of high and low. Self-control, which was the hallmark of the original law, was now replaced by selfishness and exploitation.

"We have made ourselves the laughing stock of the world," says Gandhi. "No wonder that we have today amongst the Hindus a section,[4] which is bending its energies to a destruction of the institution, which, in their opinion, spells the ruin of the Hindus."[5] He was of the opinion that in the existing state of

Hindu society, there was only one varna left and that was the Shudra. This was because the Shudras were those who served and who were dependent upon others. "India is a dependency," wrote Gandhi, "therefore, every Indian is a Shudra. The cultivator does not own his land, the merchant his merchandise. There is hardly a Kshatriya or a Brahmin who possesses the virtues which the *Shastras* attribute to his varna."[6] The decay in the Varnadharma had corrupted the social structure and a rot seemed to have set in, which was all too visible in Hindu society.

Gandhi wrote extensively about the excrescences of the caste system as it operated in India. For the most part, it signified bondage and disgrace for those affected by it. It had led to the ultimate fragmentation of society, as there were rigid rules governing inter-dining and intermarriage even between members of a sub-caste. What dismayed him most was that these customs were common even among the intelligentsia in the country.

Gandhi had attended the annual Congress session held in Calcutta (now Kolkata) in 1901. There were many blocks of camps to house the thousands of delegates and volunteers. Observing the goings on there, he wrote with some exasperation: "Even here, I was face to face with untouchability in a fair measure. The Tamilian kitchen was far away from the rest. To the Tamil delegates, even the sight of others whilst they were dining meant pollution. So, a special kitchen had to be made for them in the college compound, walled in by wickerwork. It was full of smoke which choked you. It was a kitchen, dining room, washroom, all in one, a close safe with no outlet. To me, this looked like a travesty of Varnadharma. If, I said to myself, there was such untouchability between the delegates of the Congress, one could well imagine the extent to which it existed among the constituents."[7]

The caste segregation led to other ills such as dirty water collecting in pools in the camps and dirty latrines, with nobody willing to clean the filth, which was traditionally considered to be the work of scavengers. Gandhi perceived all caste divisions and the resultant ills as a distortion of the ideal of Varnadharma.

In 1917, when Gandhi was engaged in the campaign at Champaran, he was shocked by the caste consciousness of his lawyer friends. "Each of the *vakils*," he writes, "had a servant and a cook, and therefore a separate kitchen."[8] Under his persuasion, they agreed to dispense with their servants and amalgamate their kitchens. Besides the factors of simplicity and convenience, the change led to a great saving of time and energy. However, some changes were visible and Gandhi was happy that mixed public dinners were being arranged by people at various places.[9] He exhorted forward looking youths to destroy such caste traditions and challenge all irksome and irreligious restrictions on marriage and inter-dining.

Gandhi looked upon untouchability as a contemptible abnormal outgrowth in the Hindu social structure, which spelt inequality and exploitation. Even while in South Africa, Gandhi condemned it roundly. He felt that poetic justice was done in the cruel treatment Indians received at the hands of the whites there.[10] Gandhi believed that the class of untouchables arose as a result of the decline of the valued traditions of Hindu society. The four varnas forsook their traditional occupations and became engaged in worldly pursuits. Thus, the social and economic order degenerated. This, writes Gandhi, "gave rise, against the spirit of religion, to a fifth one and this came to be looked upon as a class of untouchables. Having created this fifth class, the four castes kept it in suppression and, in consequence, they themselves came to be suppressed and fell."[11]

Gandhi found that the supporters of untouchability defended the foul practice on the grounds of religion and cited scriptures in their favour, but he believed that everything passing in the name of religion was not of eternal value – some might not have any value at all. "This religion," he says, "if it can be called such, stinks in my nostrils. This certainly cannot be the Hindu religion. It was through the Hindu religion that I learnt to respect Christianity and Islam ..."[12] He went on to say that the Sanatana Dharma (literally 'the eternal way of life', used for Hinduism) would not be saved by defending every verse printed in the scriptures. It would be saved only by putting into action the principles enunciated in them – principles that were eternal.

Gandhi also found that education, whether indigenous or western, made little dent in the prevalence of the practice of untouchability. The educated were expected to have their mental horizons widened and to reject the institutionalization of inequality. But the educated in India were disappointingly insensitive and thoughtless. In the course of his campaign against untouchability, Gandhi attracted the bitter opposition of the Hindu pundits, who were respected as both priests and educators. It pained him to discover that even after five years of continuous propaganda against untouchability, there were enough learned people to support such an "immoral and evil custom".[13]

Even western education, which was looked upon as a liberating and emancipating influence, did not undermine the strength of the belief in the custom of untouchability. Those educated in the west felt no contradiction between the humanistic values taught by their education and the oppression they heaped on the untouchables. In 1933, at the height of his campaign against untouchability. Gandhi received letters from Trivandrum (now Thiruvananthapuram) from persons claiming to be MAs, BAs and lawyers, who, he observed, resorted "to sublimities of argument for defending the obviously indefensible".[14]

In Gandhi's view, the social structure in India had become so diseased that hypocritical and anomalous attitudes were to be found everywhere. On the one hand, he saw caste Hindus unwilling to associate with untouchables in any way, but on the other, they mingled freely with them in places such as factories, workshops and trains. And the caste Hindu deemed it a privilege to shake hands with Englishmen, even though untouchables were welcome in the latter's homes. Moreover, once the untouchables converted to Christianity, caste Hindus ceased to maltreat them,[15] though there were exceptions here, too.

The picture which emerges of the condition of untouchables in Gandhi's writings is extremely distressing. In Bhal district of Gujarat, the untouchables were reduced to a deplorable condition when they found most avenues of employment closed to them. They picked out undigested grain from the dung of cattle, washed, dried and ground them and made chapattis. Gandhi was aghast at the insensitivity of the caste Hindus who forced such degradation on them.[16] In western Rajasthan, he was informed, the Harijans had to take their drinking water from troughs kept for cattle, in which caste Hindus washed their clothes.[17]

Some of the untouchables who converted to Christianity were treated just as badly. A Malabar Christian wrote to Gandhi that the condition of his community was absolutely the same as that of Harijan Hindus: "… public institutions, roads, inns, rest houses, temples, churches, court houses, business houses, shops, streets and even taverns that are unapproachable by the one are exactly to the same extent unapproachable by the other. To both, caste men like Namboodiris are unseeable to this day. Allow us to add that we, being agricultural serfs mostly, have been and are dependent on the caste Hindus and Christian masters and that, owing to increasing poverty and fragmentation of land, we are day by day reduced to greater and greater economic plight."[18]

Gandhi observed that "this state of things is no doubt a disgrace to Hinduism, but it is no less so to Christianity, if not more so".[19] But at the same time, such instances made him all the more conscious of the extent of social degradation and the enormity of the task ahead.

Contrary to expectations, the plight of the untouchables was equally dismal in Punjab. Gandhi quotes from letters from the Adi Dharma Mandal of Jalandhar and the Balmic Ad Dharma Mandal of Lahore: "The high class proud Hindus of the Punjab province have degraded and lowered our position in society to an 'unbreakable' extent. They think themselves to be polluted if we happen to touch them. Our entry at public places and getting water from public wells and tanks is thought objectionable. Hindu washermen and barbers are not prepared to serve us in their respective occupations. We are not allowed to dine at Hindu hotels. We are not 'privileged' to use bands, palanquins on the occasions of our marriage celebrations. We are forced to carry the palanquins of Hindu brides at their marriage. If we happen to put on good clothes, it irritates them

.... Even the houses in which the (Harijans) live are not considered their property."[20]

On a visit to Almora in 1929, Gandhi was dismayed to find that even in such a beautiful place and among such hospitable people, the "evil custom" of untouchability prevailed. He discovered that there was no necessary connection between untouchability and a person's occupation. A class of cultivators, locally described as *shilpi,* were traditionally considered untouchable, although their occupation, even according to classical Hinduism, did not warrant such treatment. Another class of people, the Boras, suffered a similar fate. Neither the *shilpi* nor the Boras ate carrion or consumed liquor and they followed all the orthodox rules of sanitation, yet they were rejected by the "upper caste" Hindus. Gandhi also took note of the rigid custom of *chokha* (fastidious concern for purity at mealtimes), about which he wrote: "In Almora, the *chokha* – untouchability at the time of dining – has worked its insidious way even among castes and sub-castes till at last, every man makes himself an untouchable. This *chokha* exercises its evil sway even in national institutions like the Prem Vidyalaya."[21]

When Gandhi enquired about this, he was told that though the trustees did not believe in the custom, they tolerated it "so as not to scare the parents of the boys attending the institution".[22] In fact, Gandhi found untouchability being justified on the grounds of high ideals, custom and interpretation of ancient law.

Gandhi observed that in southern India, the rules of purity and pollution were followed with greater rigidity than in the north. A peculiar phenomenon there which did not escape his notice was that very often, the economic status of the untouchables was such as to make them indistinguishable from those who did not allow them into their fold. He writes particularly about the Ezhavas of Tamil Nadu, whose leaders he met while on a tour. He found that their economic status, educational qualifications and personal cleanliness were infinitely superior to that of a lot of Brahmins he had met all over India. Yet, they were treated as untouchables and denied entry to public roads, temples and public schools. Gandhi writes that while, on the one hand, they were denied access to civic amenities, on the other, they were liable to pay the same amount of civic taxes.[23] The consciousness of such double standards had led many of them, says Gandhi, to adopt the very extreme position of denying the existence of God.

In some parts of south India, there was an additional imposition on the untouchables – they were required to give warning of their approach so that high caste Hindus could leave in time and not have to see them. When Gandhi came to know of this, he made a public declaration: "I am a touchable by birth but an untouchable by choice .... I have endeavoured to qualify myself to represent not the upper ten even among the untouchables ... but my ambition is to represent and identify myself with as far as possible, the lowest strata of untouchables, namely, the 'invisibles' and 'unapproachables', whom I have always before my mind's eye wherever I go."[24]

The abhorrence of any kind of contact with the untouchables was so widespread that on one occasion, Gandhi was almost completely ostracized by society at large. He had permitted an untouchable family to join his Sabarmati Ashram within a few months of its coming into existence. About the public outcry against this action, Gandhi recalls: "All monetary help was stopped ... (then) came rumours of proposed social boycott. We were prepared for all this."[25] He had prepared to go with his companions to the untouchables' slums, where they would live and earn money through manual labour. At that time, "as if by heavenly intervention", he writes, "a big industrialist of Ahmedabad (whom he had met only once) donated a large sum of money to the ashram." It was enough to see the inmates through a year. This incident greatly strengthened Gandhi's confidence in his cause.

Through his extensive writings, Gandhi hoped to rouse the country's conscience against the crimes that were committed in the name of tradition and religion. The several statements on untouchability Gandhi made during his imprisonment in 1932 are of considerable importance in this regard. In his second statement, he drew a graphic picture of the state of the untouchables. "Socially, they were lepers," he said, "economically, they were worse than slaves, religiously, they were denied entrance to places that were miscalled 'houses of God'."[26] In these circumstances, he wondered over their powers of endurance and their unquestioning acceptance of the Hindu faith. He concluded that they were too downtrodden to rise in revolt against their oppressors.

Gandhi and Kasturba with Harijan children at Bhavnagar on 3 July 1934

Gandhi collecting money for the Harijan Fund on a railway platform in Bhavnagar in July 1934

The pragmatic streak in Gandhi enabled him to perceive yet another significant dimension of the practice of untouchability. This was in terms of the enormous scale of waste caused by it. The moral and mental growth of one-sixth of the population was deliberately stunted. "If an economist," writes Gandhi, "were to work out the figures of waste caused by the curse of untouchability, they would be staggering."[27] In 1918, at the Second Depressed Classes Mission Conference at Bijapur, Gandhi saw the irony of the situation when he saw that there were no untouchables at a meeting called for them. He declared that the organizers were wasting their time because it was evident that they had no genuine feeling for the untouchables. It is a principle in law, he said, that he who seeks justice should render it to others.[28]

It would be useful at this juncture to examine Gandhi's perceptions of the ongoing changes in social practices, particularly with regard to untouchability. In fact, they could largely be attributed to his own efforts. In 1924, he wrote, "The removal of untouchability has been brought within the range of possibility in the near future because of the incessant propaganda by the Congress Hindus. No doubt a great deal still remains to be done. It is not an easy feat to root out prejudices which have acquired an undeserved sanctity because of their age, but the barrier is breaking down."[29]

The untouchables themselves were making conscious efforts to improve their lot. In Kutch, many gave up eating meat and drinking liquor in an attempt to set high moral standards for themselves. At crowded meetings in Andhra Pradesh in 1929, Gandhi found that 'touchables' and untouchables mingled freely and sat together. He even asked the crowds if they had any objections and got stout denials in reply.[30] He noted in *Young India* that the suppressed classes were daily growing more and more restive and resentful of the terrible treatment meted them by the higher classes. He considered it a positive sign and was heartened to see this discontent, which he thought would be a prelude to progress.

Gandhi found that there were many Brahmins, too, who were working very hard for the uplift of the untouchables. Giving the example of Govind Krishna Gokhale, Gandhi writes,

"It is possible to make out a long list of Brahmins who have stood up for equality between man and man. To decry the Brahmins as a class is to deny ourselves the benefit of the selfless service for which many of them have specially fitted themselves. They stand in no need of certificates. Their service is its own reward."[31]

Thirteen students of Trichy National College in Tiruchirapalli wrote to Gandhi that they desired to work on welfare schemes for Harijans and children in their leisure hours. He was overjoyed and replied that if they simply visited Harijan habitations and made them feel that they were their brothers and sisters, they would find "the right word and right action".[32]

A piquant situation arose on one occasion. At the Jaipur Rajya Sammelan held on 25 December 1934, a khadi exhibition was held on the first floor of a building overlooking the main market centre. A Harijan boy was in charge of the sales there and he could be seen by the caste Hindus who were gathered below in the market centre. The latter were outraged by the fact that a Harijan sat at a level higher than them. They called a panchayat meeting and resolved that:

1. No one from the village should attend the khadi exhibition on pain of excommunication.
2. No one should send his girls to the local Kanya Pathshala, as it was connected with the Rajya Sammelan people.
3. No one should permit teachers of the Harijan Pathshala to enter his home.

But the winds of change were already gathering strength. Twenty-eight young men defied the panchayat's decision and participated in the Sammelan. They were asked to pay a fine of Re 1 each, but they refused to do so. Some 300–400 people dined together in the Sammelan kitchen, without any caste distinctions being observed. The orthodox raised the cry of 'Religion in Danger'. Gandhi wrote, "The fact that the *savarna* (upper caste) reformers have remained undaunted by the threat of the boycott must be regarded as a happy augury .... The reformers must proceed with their work with patient, silent determination, unaffected by anger or fear."[33]

The path of change was not altogether smooth and many took it for selfish ends. The state of Wadhawan in Gujarat decided to constitute an elected municipality, which was seemingly a progressive step, but a clause in its constitution required untouchable voters to elect a representative from the upper castes. Gandhi was outraged when he came to know of this. He asked the people to oppose this clause and, if it was not expunged, he advised them to boycott the elections.[34]

Since the elections of 1919, the power of the people, even if limited, began to be felt and, with this, the potential of the suppressed classes as a docile but powerful electorate began to emerge. The politicians were quick to notice this and a trend arose to woo them for political gains. Gandhi condemned this roundly and warned the Hindus against this tendency. "To remove untouchability," he wrote, "is a penance that caste Hindus owe to Hinduism and themselves. The purification required is not of untouchables, but of the so-called superior castes."[35] Gandhi's reaction and perception rested on humane grounds and an anxiety to regenerate a decaying social structure.

Faulty Education System

In Gandhi's opinion, the education system instituted by the British in India functioned as a major instrument for consolidating their hold over the country. A direct consequence of this was the strengthening and widening of the fissures in Indian society. He believed that the ancient system of education, though not very efficient, worked to provide the rudiments of learning to most people. But with the coming of the British, administrative concern shifted to cities and rural areas were left to fend for themselves. The result of this was a gross imbalance in the education structure and village institutions were either closed down or lagged miserably behind their city counterparts.[36] Education became almost non-existent in the villages, while the educated class of the cities drifted away with no perception of the problems of villagers. Education, thus, merely widened the rural–urban gulf and offered no values for the cohesion and advancement of society.

In Gandhi's view, a significant social dimension of the British system of education was that it tended to subdue the mental faculties of those receiving it. They lost their imaginative and creative abilities in an attempt to master the intricacies of a foreign language and foreign culture. Gandhi uses the word, "denationalized", for them and says that they were deluded into thinking that everything indigenous was bad and all things British were superior to their own. To quote him, "The result has been that we function like blotting paper before western civilization, instead of imbibing the best from it, we have become its superficial imitators."[37]

Of much greater concern and disadvantage for the cohesiveness and harmony of Indian society was the gulf which had been created between "us and the masses". As Gandhi put it, "We cannot explain to them in a language which they will understand even the elements of hygiene and public health, let alone politics. We have become the modern counterparts of the Brahmins of old days, in fact, we are worse, for the Brahmins didn't mean ill. They were the trustees of the nation's culture. We are not even that."[38]

Yet another social consequence of the system was the creation of a class of frustrated youth who were in the position of having fallen between two stools. Their education equipped them for posts in the administrative system, but there were not enough of these. On the other hand, says Gandhi, they were alienated from the traditional mainstream.[39] The social structure had not been able to absorb this element and place them in the natural position of providing enlightened leadership. A potent element of change was seen to have resulted in alienation and frustration.

Another adverse outcome of the education system was the creation of a further imbalance in society – this was between spouses and between the two sexes of the upper and middle classes. While the girls and wives of this class were left uneducated, the men often received western education, which made them feel closer to the ruling classes. Such a situation could only aggravate the pressures in a male dominated society. Gandhi received many letters from young men who felt they were incompatible with their uneducated spouses and he began to feel that "the gulf between husband and wife as far as social attainments were concerned was almost unbridgeable".[40] Some young men, he was aware, solved the problem by cruelly turning their wives out of their houses, while others used them as sexual objects without sharing their intellectual life with them. However, the prospect was not altogether bleak and there was a growing section with a quickened conscience; yet, the problem of marital relationships was serious, he wrote. Education, as it was being imparted to and imbibed by Indians, had created fissures and tensions in the social structure without offering a new value system that was principled and forward looking.

Communal Tension

Through his experiences in South Africa and India and on account of his commitment to nation building activities, Gandhi became keenly aware of the numerous points of intrastructural friction in Indian society. Wrangles over caste coexisted with wrangles over political and denominational affiliations. Gandhi was deeply troubled and wrote: "Today our democracy is choked by our internecine strife. We are torn by dissensions – dissensions between Hindus and Muslims, Brahmins and non-Brahmins, Congressmen and non-Congressmen. It is no easy task to evolve democracy out of this mobocracy. Let us not make confusion worse confounded by further introducing into it the virus of sectionalism and party spirit."[41]

A major constituent of the social fabric that exercised Gandhi's mind was the issue of Hindu–Muslim relations. He considered this the pivot of national harmony and progress. The fact that these relations were becoming strained disheartened him deeply. He wrote a great deal and tried to analyse the problem in depth. He believed that prior to the establishment of British rule, there was no special conflict between the Hindus and the Muslims, but there existed only particular localized misunderstandings with no systemic or institutional overtones. These latter were superimposed under British policies and minor differences were blown out of proportion. They then assumed mammoth dimensions. The two nation theory was fostered with the help of ambitious elements in both communities. At the level of the masses, there was perfect coexistence, Gandhi believed, for had that not been the case, the Hindus would not have flourished under Muslim sovereigns and Muslims under Hindu. "Each party recognized that mutual fighting was suicidal, and that neither party would abandon its religion by force of arms. Both parties, therefore, decided to live in peace,"[42] he wrote.

It was a historical fact that most Muslims were Hindu converts and, therefore, their ancestors were the same and they shared a common culture. Like most historians, Gandhi believed that India had the capacity for assimilation – it had absorbed many foreign races. A fusion of Hindu and Islamic culture had been taking place over several centuries. He argued, "In no part of the world are one nationality and one religion synonymous terms; nor has it ever been so in India."[43] He goes on to say that a difference that had taken place was that whereas previously, Hindu–Muslim differences were resolved through mutual compromise, they were now referred to the British rulers for settlement.[44]

Gandhi identified some points of conflict that had arisen to pull the social fabric of India to breaking point, as, for instance, the activities of the so-called cow protection societies. Though Gandhi was Hindu in his orientation and worshipped the cow, he had no hesitation in condemning these societies as they threatened to disrupt the harmony and cohesiveness of Indian society. In *Hind Swaraj*, he writes, "When the Hindus became insistent, the killing of cows increased. In my opinion, cow protection societies may be considered cow killing societies. It is a disgrace to us that we should need such societies. When we forgot how to protect cows, I suppose we needed such societies."[45] The only way to protect cows, he said, was to try and persuade Muslims to desist from slaughtering them. They could not deny the economic importance of cows in the Indian subcontinent. If they refused to listen, he advised the Hindus to stop trying to convince them and accept the situation. If the Hindus found the situation beyond their endurance, they should perform the ultimate sacrifice and lay down their own lives, rather than take Muslim lives. This, he was certain, would have a salutary effect.

Gandhi also saw that the Hindus were as much to blame for the destruction of cows as the Muslims. The Hindu owners of cows treated them cruelly and, in many instances, calves were deprived of their mothers' milk. He was shocked by the inhuman practice of *phooka*,[46] used to extract the last drop of milk from a cow. As the cow became barren soon, they were sold off to butchers. As far as the principle of non-killing was concerned, all Hindus could not be said to be its adherents as many ate meat. "It is therefore preposterous," Gandhi writes, "to suggest that the two cannot live together amicably because the Hindus believe in ahimsa and the Mahomedans do not. These thoughts are put into our minds by selfish and false religious teachers."[47] Gandhi understood that it was not compassion for animals that drove the Hindus to take up the issue of cow protection, but communal tension.

British historians, he felt, also had a role to play in the mutual animosity between the different religious groups. Very often, they presented a distorted picture of the culture of different peoples who also happened to be subject peoples and, due to their subtle presentation, readers were hypnotized into believing them. The grant of separate electorates to the Muslims in 1909 had exacerbated social and political tensions. The British rulers intended to use the Muslims to counterbalance the strength of the majority community. Gandhi saw through this game and tried to bring the two communities together through the national movement he launched in 1919. After a temporary truce, relations soured again in 1924, but Gandhi was not disheartened. He wrote in *Young India*: "In spite of the present strained relations between the two communities, both have gained. The awakening among the masses was a necessary part of the training. It is itself a tremendous gain. I would do nothing to put the people to sleep again. Our wisdom consists now in directing the awakening in the proper channel .... The storm is but the forerunner of the coming calm that comes from a consciousness of strength, not from the stupor of exhaustion and disappointment."[48]

A major factor in heightening the communal tension and disturbing the harmony was, Gandhi believed, the fiery campaigns launched by the Arya Samajists to reconvert people to Hinduism by a method called *shuddhi* (literally, purification). The *shuddhi* movement, in his opinion, had no rational basis for there was no such thing as conversion in Hinduism, as there was in Christianity and Islam. The concept of *shuddhi* aimed at reforming Hinduism along spiritual lines, but the current manifestation, he wrote, was simply an appeal to the individual's selfish instinct as he was sought to be bribed into conversion.[49]

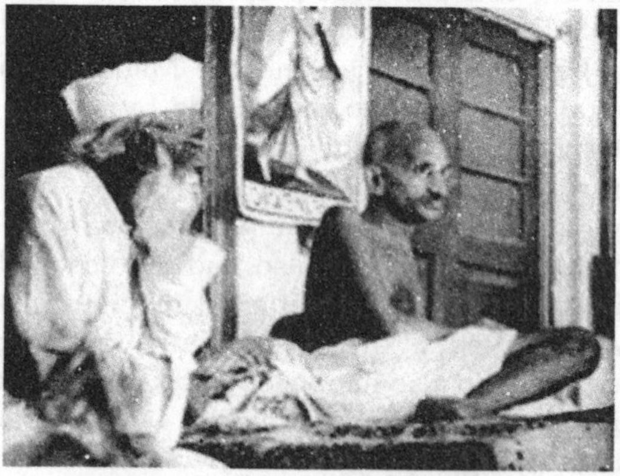

Gandhi with Abbas Tyabji in 1934

Miraben helping Gandhi repair his charkha in Wardha in 1936

In the context of the growing communal passions, Gandhi felt that the role of the press was highly questionable. The embers of inter-communal tension in society were fanned by mischievous propaganda in the press, particularly in the Punjab, where the two communities vied with each other in using abusive language and making scurrilous charges and counter-charges.[50] Mutual suspicion and prejudice, Gandhi believed, also had a part in embittering relations between Hindus and Muslims. The latter were sometimes deluded into thinking that they belonged to a race of conquerors, that the Hindus were their subjects, and that India was not their home. They suspected the Hindus of being cowards. This feeling was aggravated by the despicable behaviour of the Hindus towards the Harijans or untouchables. On the other hand, the Hindus, Gandhi believed, had certain misconceptions about Islam and its teachings and regarded its followers as *mleccha* or untouchables.[51]

Gandhi had personally experienced intolerance on the part of some influential Muslim scholars. They objected strongly to his citing the *Koran* in the context of non-violence on the grounds that he was not a Muslim. But Gandhi was not disheartened, he merely pointed out that truth was no man's monopoly and mutual respect and tolerance were the imperatives of civilized dialogue.[52]

However, in the midst of all the tension and strife, he found glimmerings of harmony. Gandhi witnessed a touching example in Mysore in July 1927. He received the address of the Gorakshana Mandali (Cow Protection Society), in which it was claimed that the majority of Muslims were with the Hindus on the question of prevention of cow slaughter. Mutual consideration, Gandhi felt, would prepare the ground for appropriate legislation to set at rest apprehensions and anxiety.[53]

A Civilization in Conflict

Though a Hindu, Gandhi was deeply attached to eclectic values and revered all faiths as representing perceptions of the supreme truth. He was proud of India's ancient heritage and, as such, he was acutely conscious of the glaring contrast presented by contemporary society. He was convinced that India's present decline was the result of her people's love for aping the west and concentration on increasing bodily comforts as opposed to spiritual uplift. His perception, in other words, was that Indian society had acquired a faulty value system and forsaken its own pure roots. Gandhi bemoaned the fact that India, which was once renowned for its divine knowledge and was the cradle of religions, was "becoming irreligious". He was not pointing at any particular religion, but at the fundamental morality that underlay all religions.[54] Religious superstition had taken the place of this fundamental morality and led to a lot of cruelty and rivalry among different sections of the people.

The so-called intelligentsia of the country was not fully committed to national development, according to Gandhi. He regretted the fact that practising lawyers, who had some influence on public opinion in India, restricted their political activity to the few leisure hours they got from their tennis and billiards. "I do not expect ... lawyers will bring us substantially near swaraj," he wrote, and further, "I want at least the public workers among them to be whole-timers and when that happy day comes, I promise a different outlook before the country."[55] In other words, one could say that Gandhi did not find the elements of modern civilization and social groups as lending cohesion or strength to the Indian social milieu.

Gandhi noted the "general degeneration" in the value system of Indian society with anxiety and concern. He wrote extensively about the fraud, hypocrisy and inequities he noted everywhere. The yawning gulf between the rich and poor came out even at social functions, where he saw the extravagant waste indulged in by the rich at the cost of the poor. "We make too much ostentation," he wrote, "rather than really enjoy ourselves, we make a show of enjoyment, instead of sincerely mourning, we make a show of mourning."[56]

Another effect of such lavish spending by the rich was that the poorer sections tried to emulate them to gain social recognition and ended up incurring ruinous debts.[57]

Gandhi noted that the poor contributed whatever they could spare for the national cause, whereas the rich "expect to gain everything by speeches and resolutions. They are keeping back a nation ready for sacrifice."[58] The elite in society are generally acknowledged to be the leaders of social conduct, which is emulated by the rest. But Gandhi saw the elite as poor initiators of social or political reform.

The religious leaders, he found, were no different from the social elites. They were sunk in ignorance and superstition. Of them, he wrote, "Our religious heads are always one sided in their thinking. There is no harmony between their words and deeds. Our non-violence is an unworthy thing. We see its utmost limit in refraining somehow from destroying bugs, mosquitoes and fleas, or from killing birds and animals. We do not care if these creatures suffer, nor even if we partly contribute to their suffering."[59]

The south of India, once famed for its culture and tradition, had not escaped the prevailing process of social degeneration. In Madras (now Chennai), he noted, in many places, the outward form of religion remained and the inner spirit had vanished. The Harijans in that region suffered more indignities than they did in almost any part of the country. He noted too that the Brahmins there were more sharply separated from the non-Brahmins than anywhere else. "And yet," he writes sarcastically, "no other region makes such abundant use of sacred ash, sandalwood paste and vermillion powder. No other part of the country has quite so many temples and is so generous in providing for their maintenance."[60]

As a result of this, on the one hand, the educated people were getting increasingly estranged from religion and becoming more cynical in consequence, and, on the other, total darkness and ignorance prevailed among the orthodox.

A renowned place of pilgrimage appeared to Gandhi as a microcosm of the social degradation that had befallen India. This was the Kumbh Mela in Hardwar in 1915. All that he noticed about the pilgrims was their "absent mindedness, hypocrisy and slovenliness than their piety. The swarm of sadhus, who had descended, seemed to have been born but to enjoy the good things of life."[61] Hypocrisy and opportunism went to such horrifying lengths that a fifth foot, cut off from a live calf, was grafted upon the shoulder of a cow for the express purpose of fleecing the ignorant of their money. "There was no Hindu," he writes, "but would be attracted by a five footed cow, and no Hindu but would lavish his charity on such a miraculous cow."[62]

Gandhi's anguish and despair at the Kumbh Mela are quite plain. He was disgusted with the sanctimonious hypocrisy that, on the one hand, revered a holy place like Hardwar and particularly the Ganga there, yet had no hesitation in dirtying the roads, the river banks and the river itself. Concluding his narrative, he writes, "The Hardwar experiences proved for me to be of inestimable value. They helped me in no small way to decide where I was to live and what I was to do."[63]

The gap between social precept and practice was again noticed by Gandhi on a visit to some other Hindu centres of pilgrimage. In November 1929, while touring the United Provinces, he went to Mathura, Govardhan and Vrindavan. This region is the home of the legendary Hindu God, Krishna, the cowherd, and as Gandhi was a devout Vaishnava, he had perhaps expected something from the visit. But he was sorely disappointed. Instead of boasting the finest cattle (Krishna's playmates) in the land and an ample supply of pure unadulterated milk, all he saw was "cattle with their bones protruding, cows who give so little milk as to be an economic burden".[64] The Hindus sold them for slaughter to the butchers. Things were worse in Govardhan for the Brahmins there were no longer "custodians of true religion", but lived as "beggars". In Vrindavan, he noticed a very large number of widows, principally from Bengal. He was grieved to hear that the poor among them were paid a small pittance daily for repeating the divine name of 'Radhey-Shyam' in the congregation.

On the occasion of the Buddha's birth anniversary celebrations in Kolkata in May 1925, Gandhi bemoaned the state of all Indian religions. "Buddhism, like every religion at the present moment," he said, "is really decadent. I am optimistic enough to feel that a day is dawning when all these great religions will be purged of all frauds, hypocrisy, humbug, untruthfulness, incredulity and all that may be described under the term, 'degradation'."[65] Only truth and love would be recognized as the true badge of religion, he hoped.

Gandhi also noted that immorality and dishonesty characterized the conduct of many of the so-called leaders of society. He had in mind the custom of very young girls being forced to marry old or middle aged widowers, who thus pretended to do social service, but in reality satisfied their "baser instincts".[66] He also published letters from trusted workers about "violence, untruth and corruption in the Congress". The most serious charge was that bogus membership existed on a very large scale, which resulted in large scale embezzlement of funds.[67] That the foremost political party of the nation indulged in such practices told its own tale about the state of the country.

Capital and Labour

According to Gandhi, the general erosion of human values in Indian society was also reflected in the relations between capital and labour. He believed that capital and labour were mutually complementary forces. But he noted that a work ethic had not evolved and wrote, "The masters care only for the service they get. What becomes of the labourers does not concern them. All their endeavours are generally confined to obtaining maximum service with minimum payment. The labourer, on the other hand, tries to hit upon all the tricks whereby he can get maximum pay with minimum work. The result is that although the labourers get an increment, there is no improvement in the work turned out. The relations between the two parties are not purified and the labourers do not make proper use of the increment they get."[68]

The living conditions of the labourers, he felt, were a great shame to the industrialists. He knew of labourers in Mumbai who lived in boxes, literally, though they were called houses. There was terrible overcrowding and no ventilation. They worked long hours in miserable conditions. Their food was almost inedible and they had no friends to give them advice.[69] Rootless, rudderless, they drank to forget their miseries, but only ended up creating worse problems for themselves.[70] His sympathy for the workers enabled him to see their problems in their proper perspective. As early as 1921, he wrote in the context of the outbreaks of violence during the Non-Cooperation

Movement: "We must not tamper with the masses. It is dangerous to make political use of factory labourers or the peasantry, not that we are not entitled to do so, but we are not ready for it. We have neglected their political (as distinguished from literary) education all these long years. We have not got enough honest, intelligent, reliable and brave workers to enable us to act upon these countrymen of ours."[71]

He blamed the educated classes for not caring to find out the wants and aspirations of the labouring classes. They had not taken the trouble to spread political consciousness among them. They kept aloof and yet expected them to help in a national cause about which they knew nothing.[72]

The labour component of society had to struggle for a harmonious relationship with its employers and also for common grounds of interest among themselves. From his own experience, Gandhi knew that there was no social contact and no mutual ties between the different labour forces in the country. Moreover, they were often under the influence of leaders who were provincial or communal in their outlook and sometimes even unscrupulous.[73] But in situations where there was no conflict of interest between the class of employers and the employed and the advisers to both sides had a genuine desire that both sides cooperate for mutual benefit, it was seen that the adversarial relationship between the employer and the worker could be replaced by harmonious interaction. This fact was illustrated, says Gandhi, by the successful working of the labour union of Ahmedabad Textile Mills, which was reorganized under him.[74] Gandhi was apparently looking for not only harmony, but also efficiency and a work ethic.

He noted the existence of bonded labour in various parts of the country. He saw in the system an example of the general prevalence of oppression and injustice in society and another instance of the shameful inequity and exploitation.[75]

Position of Women

The position of women in contemporary India was, in Gandhi's opinion, a reflection of the generally depressed state of the country, which had been enslaved for some two centuries under

British rulers. Added to this was the effect of Hindu culture, which encouraged excessive subordination of women and idolized wives who merged their identity into that of their husbands'.[76] On the one hand, the culture taught reverence of women as mothers, wives and goddesses, and, on the other, there were many double standards in the customs and rules relating to institutions such as marriage, purdah, widowhood and everyday life, which affected women adversely.[77] Most notable in the context of culture was the effect of authoritative Hindu texts, such as the *Smritis*,[78] and stray passages in some other great works, such as Goswami Tulsidas' *Ramcharitmanas*,[79] in which women were put on the same level as the Shudra, the fool, the drum and the animal, all of whom required to be beaten. As these works set the norms to be observed in society, their impact can well be imagined.

Another root cause of women's inferior status, Gandhi said, was the institution of private property and the rules governing it.[80] In order that property not be devalued by being shared among numerous offspring, it descended on the eldest male child or only on sons, leaving the daughters dependent on the charity of their brothers or marital families. Closely linked to this issue was the lack of an elite class that was forward looking and desirous of leading society in a positive direction. Both men and women of the rich and educated classes were busy advancing their selfish interests, rather than social ones.[81]

A further significant reason for the degradation of Indian woman was the absence of education on even a moderate scale in India. What little there was of it was in the urban areas, where barely 15 per cent of the population lived. This had led to a lack of self-consciousness in women about their own status and class problems. Sunk in ignorance, they quietly accepted what was imposed on them in the name of custom and tradition.[82]

Writing about their imperfect socialization, Gandhi noted that girls were brought up for the sole purpose of being married off and, hence, taught the ways of adorning themselves so much so that they thought it to be their true nature.[83] They hugged their fetters, says Gandhi. The limit of outside activities for women, generally, was going to the temple, and religion for them was mainly in terms of superstition, as very few could read. They had no conception of the freedom that true knowledge of religion gives – the freedom to think.[84]

It was Gandhi's contention that India was in a state of social paralysis due to the condition of her women.[85] Social and political movements for national advancement could have no effect because women did not participate in them. He was convinced that till women began to influence the political deliberations of the nation, there could be no real progress. Women had to become the equal partners of men before they could come into their own.[86] He said, "Our lot is like that of the penny wise and pound foolish trader, who does not employ enough capital in his business."[87]

Gandhi believed that the sexual exploitation of women was almost entirely due to their lack of economic independence, which, in turn, was caused by the absence of any productive occupation among them. He was convinced that this was not the situation before the British overran the country; cottage industries had flourished then and India was an exporter of cloth and other articles. Spinning and weaving provided the much needed supplement to agriculture. But with this support system gone, women, very often with the knowledge of their men, turned to questionable means to make ends meet.[88]

There was a very small section of Indian women, Gandhi said, in some towns, which was conscious of the incompleteness of their lives. Due to their education and background, they were aware of the issues which hurt women the most and on which social action was necessary. Gandhi appealed to them to lead the women's movement in an intrepid manner.[89] The status and role of women was most significant for any social structure to be strong and mutual relationships in it to be equal. In Indian society, the weakness of the social structure and its degeneration was perhaps most noticeable in the position of its women.

Before concluding this chapter, it would not be out of place to note Gandhi's impressions of what he thought were positive signs of change in contemporaneous Indian society – although these were not dramatic or sharply in focus, nevertheless, he perceived them as auguring well for the future of India. In January 1925, he wrote: "Beneath the present disorganization, demoralization and lack of initiative, I can discover organization, moral strength and initiative forming themselves .... I know that I have nothing to offer in proof of my hope. It is based on immutable faith."[90]

One fact he highlighted was the positive role of the educated class in providing leadership to the national movement. He had criticized this class on numerous occasions for its false sense of superiority and alienation from the Indian masses. But he noticed that some of them had begun to identify themselves with the people and tried to raise their consciousness on national issues. He writes, "Without the closest cooperation of some of our educated young men and women, I should not have been able to establish contact with the masses and to serve them on a nationwide scale; and I am sustained by the hope that they will act as the leaven, and in time transform the entire mass."[91]

Even on the question of untouchability, which was a countrywide phenomenon, Gandhi was able to perceive significant signs of decline in its virulence and an awakening of conscience and humane values. In this context, the most illustrious example Gandhi could cite was that of Pandit Madan Mohan Malviya. From being a highly orthodox Hindu Brahmin, observing all the rules of untouchability, Malviya had been transformed into an ardent campaigner for the removal of untouchability and, in the process, had sometimes incurred the wrath of diehard Hindus.[92]

Another notable example was set by Jamnalal Bajaj, a wealthy Marwari merchant, who declared his magnificent temple in Wardha open to all untouchables. Gandhi observed, "The most remarkable thing about it is that from the record kept in the temple of the daily visitors, it was found that attendance had gone up, instead of declining since the admission of the untouchables to it."[93]

Thus, in Gandhi's perception of contemporaneous Indian society, one can see a society that was principally enmeshed in the shackles of poverty, tradition and superstition, with some signs of change becoming visible.

Notes

1. *CWMG*, Volume 11, p. 126.
2. *CWMG*, Volume 59, pp. 62–3.
3. Ibid., p. 64.
4. The Jat Pat Todak Mandal.
5. *CWMG*, Volume 61, p. 64.
6. *CWMG*, Volume 50, p. 225.
7. *CWMG*, Volume 39, p. 181.
8. Ibid., p. 331.
9. Ibid.
10. *CWMG*, Volume 10, p. 229.
11. *CWMG*, Volume 24, p. 123.
12. *CWMG*, Volume 14, p. 75.
13. *CWMG*, Volume 31, p. 214.
14. *CWMG*, Volume 53, p. 66.
15. *CWMG*, Volume 14, p. 175.
16. *CWMG*, Volume 57, p. 279.
17. *CWMG*, Volume 54, p. 399.
18. Ibid., p. 107.
19. Ibid.
20. Ibid., p. 108.
21. *CWMG*, Volume 41, p. 171.
22. Ibid.
23. *CWMG*, Volume 35, p. 116.
24. *CWMG*, Volume 51, p. 117.
25. *CWMG*, Volume 39, p. 315.
26. *CWMG*, Volume 51, p. 347.
27. *CWMG*, Volume 60, p. 440.
28. *CWMG*, Volume 14, p. 387.
29. *CWMG*, Volume 23, p. 274.
30. *CWMG*, Volume 40, p. 382.
31. *CWMG*, Volume 57, p. 200.
32. Ibid., p. 201.
33. *CWMG*, Volume 60, p. 189.

34. *CWMG*, Volume 38, p. 88.
35. *CWMG*, Volume 25, p. 479.
36. *CWMG*, Volume 18, p. 263.
37. *CWMG*, Volume 24, p. 448.
38. *CWMG*, Volume 19, p. 137.
39. Ibid.
40. *CWMG*, Volume 67, pp. 159–61.
41. *CWMG*, Volume 36, p. 260.
42. *CWMG*, Volume 24, p. 212.
43. *CWMG*, Volume 10, p. 29.
44. Ibid.
45. Ibid., p. 30.
46. Ibid.
47. *CWMG*, Volume 65, p. 320.
48. *CWMG*, Volume 10, p. 31.
49. *CWMG*, Volume 27, p. 154.
50. *CWMG*, Volume 26, p. 126.
51. *CWMG*, Volume 24, p. 150.
52. *CWMG*, Volume 26, p. 445.
53. *CWMG*, Volume 73, p. 50.
54. *CWMG*, Volume 18, p. 263.
55. N.B. Sen, ed., *Wit and Wisdom of Mahatma Gandhi* (New Delhi: New Book Society of India, 1960), p. 129.
56. *CWMG*, Volume 34, p. 125.
57. CWMG, Volume 17, p. 401.
58. *CWMG*, Volume 30, p. 62.
59. *CWMG*, Volume 18, p. 191.
60. *CWMG*, Volume 37, p. 263.
61. *CWMG*, Volume 21, p. 234.
62. *CWMG*, Volume 39, p. 309.
63. Ibid.
64. Ibid., p. 310.
65. *CWMG*, Volume 42, p. 155.
66. *CWMG*, Volume 27, p. 64.

67. *CWMG*, Volume 31, p. 243.
68. *CWMG*, Volume 62, pp. 371–2.
69. *CWMG*, Volume 17, p. 20.
70. *CWMG*, Volume 26, p. 394.
71. Ibid.
72. *CWMG*, Volume 19, p. 340.
73. *CWMG*, Volume 21, p. 163.
74. *CWMG*, Volume 33, p. 303.
75. Gopinath Dhawan, *The Political Philosophy of Mahatma Gandhi* (Ahmedabad: Navajivan Publishing House, 1951), pp. 288–9.
76. *CWMG*, Volume 46, p. 53.
77. Pushpa Joshi, ed., *Gandhi on Women* (Ahmedabad: Navajivan Publishing House, 1988), p. 206.
78. Ibid., p. 39.
79. M.K. Gandhi, *Conquest of Self*, eds., R.K. Prabhu and U.R. Rao (Mumbai: Thacker & Co, 1943), p. 168.
80. Joshi, *Gandhi on Women*, p. 15.
81. *Conquest of Self*, op. cit., pp. 153–54.
82. Joshi, *Gandhi on Women*, p. 37.
83. *Conquest of Self*, pp. 169–70.
84. Joshi, *Gandhi on Women*, p. 78.
85. Ibid., p. 49.
86. Ibid., p. 17.
87. Ibid., p. 24.
88. *Conquest of Self*, p. 169.
89. Joshi, *Gandhi on Women*, p. 33.
90. *Conquest of Self*, p. 182.
91. *CWMG*, Volume 26, p. 52.
92. *CWMG*, Volume 40, p. 58.
93. *CWMG*, Volume 52, p. 199.

CHAPTER 4

Issues in Social Change

Although seemingly a contradiction in terms, it may be said that Gandhi was both a conservative and a radical reformer. Through his experiences in South Africa, he realized the nature and scale of India's problems and his long and successful association with the Indians there gave him confidence in dealing with the Indians back home. He did not believe in change for the sake of it and would not mistake movement for progress. He clarified his views through his weekly journal, *Indian Opinion,* saying: "'Hasten slowly' should be the motto of the real reformer. We must be most careful before we uproot systems and customs that have been handed down for generations unless we know them to be immoral."[1]

In this chapter, an attempt has been made to highlight the various issues on which Gandhi focussed his attention and the solution to which he considered necessary for the nation's development. Some of these are education, civic rights, economic self-sufficiency, a national language and common script, Hindu–Muslim relations, untouchability, the position of women, equality of all productive labour, and the attributes of a public worker. Gandhi's analyses are peculiarly his own in that they illustrate his consciousness of the Indian reality and his attempts to mould it into a viable and humane social entity.

Education

In the sphere of social reform, and especially in the field of education, Gandhi was deeply influenced by the views of Gopal

Krishna Gokhale, the well-known nationalist and social thinker. Gandhi liked to quote Gokhale on the issue: "The prime necessity of the country today is education. By education I do not mean the mere rudiments of primary education, but a knowledge of our rights, and along with them of our responsibilities and duties."[2] Gandhi had a very high opinion of the role of a teacher and considered no calling as sacred as that of imparting knowledge. He often quoted the Sanskrit verse:

Kingship and learning are never equal
A king is worshipped in his own kingdom
But a learned man throughout the world.[3]

In the field of education, the issue of change was not the British system alone, but also some indigenous institutions. Gandhi was of the opinion that communal institutions of learning were the bane of India's educational system. He identified three such institutions: the Banaras Hindu University, the Aligarh Muslim University and the Khalsa College in Amritsar. It was his belief that they taught religious fanaticism and depended unduly on government aid and favour, as a result of which they hampered independent development of the scholars and teachers. "I do desire passionately," he wrote, "to destroy all these three institutions as they are, and would strive to raise purer and truer ones instead. I deny that these institutions are in any way true representatives of their respective cultures."[4] He wanted such institutions to be reconstructed so as to breathe in an air of freedom and tolerance.

The greatest drawback of the British system of education in India, Gandhi argued, was its medium of instruction, which was English, a foreign language. As a result, Indian students suffered a great handicap in attaining education. Elaborating on this, Gandhi wrote: "Suppose that we had been receiving during the past 50 years education through our vernaculars, what would we have had today? We should have had today a free India, we should have our educated men, not as if they were foreigners in their own land, but speaking to the heart of the nation, they would be working amongst the poorest of the poor, and whatever they would have gained during the past 50 years would be a heritage for the nation."[5] He made particular reference to the research of men such as Sir J.C. Bose and Dr P.C. Ray, whose findings, had they been in the vernaculars, would have been the common property of the people.[6]

Gandhi expounded his views on education in his article, 'National Education', which was published in *Young India* in September 1921, at the time of the Non-Cooperation Movement. To be relevant, he wrote, education should be related to one's environment. It ought to point out the defects and positive points in it and provide the means to make the most of one's life. India was an agricultural country and its system of education should highlight the dignity of manual labour. In a poor country like India, if education was to reach everyone, it had to be free. To achieve this goal, he recommended that "our children must be made to pay in 'labour' partly or wholly for all the education they receive. Such universal labour, to be profitable, can only be (to my thinking) hand spinning and hand weaving."[7] He qualified this by saying that labour could be in any form as long as it was productive.

This introduction of manual training, Gandhi believed, would serve a double purpose: It could pay for the education of the children and also teach them an occupation on which they could fall back later, if they chose, for earning a living. Such a system was bound to make them self-reliant, he felt. "Nothing will demoralize the nation so much as that we should learn to despise labour,"[8] he wrote. Gandhi was obviously concerned not only about the system and content of formal education, but also about its relevance to the life of the people. The people or masses were always at the centre of his reflections.

Gandhi was not opposed to foreign culture or the learning of the English language. He regarded English as the language of international commerce and diplomacy and, therefore, considered its knowledge essential at least among some Indians. He was aware that it contained some of the richest treasures of thought and literature and, as such, he would certainly encourage its careful study among those who had linguistic talents and expect them to translate those treasures for the nation into the vernaculars. "But, I do respectfully contend," he writes, "that an appreciation of other cultures can fitly follow, never precede an appreciation and assimilation of our own. It is my firm opinion that no culture has treasures so rich as ours has. We have not known it, we have been made even to deprecate its study and depreciate its value."[9]

Gandhi had very definite views about the aim and content of primary education. He was dismayed by the current emphasis on the alphabet and learning by rote from textbooks as he believed that they crushed the growth of the child. There was also the financial burden of buying expensive textbooks that came from Britain. Gandhi was of the opinion that during the primary stage, textbooks should be given only to teachers and their syllabi should be different. "Instead of teaching the child the letters of the alphabet in the beginning," he wrote, "I would teach him drawing so that the child, from the very beginning, learns to draw beautiful designs .... We can impart to him orally a lot of practical and religious instruction .... We can develop his memory by making him repeat verses from the *Gita* and other sacred books. Thereby his ears get tuned up, his tongue practices clear pronunciation, and his eyes learn to observe. Thus, all the powers of the child can be developed simultaneously. Meanwhile, the alphabet can be introduced to him as a distinct art." This last would also improve the handwriting of young people, he felt.[10]

Gandhi's reflections on educational issues led him to some experiments on the lines of his own thinking – primarily the setting up of the Gujarat Vidyapith in Ahmedabad with the help of some devoted followers. The Gujarat Vidyapith had many newly set up schools and colleges under its jurisdiction. Through this project, Gandhi made a qualitative change in the concept of primary education. "The task of this Vidyapith is not to turn out schoolteachers or clerks, but to train village workers ... its task is to contribute towards changing the attitude of the city if possible."[11] Included in the activities of the new schools were imparting knowledge of all the processes leading to the production of cloth, of carpentry to suit the needs of villagers, of sewing and, of course, the three Rs. The pupils were also to be made familiar with ancient literature such as the *Mahabharata* and the *Ramayana* and their modern spiritual meaning. They were to be taught village games and rules of hygiene. They were to be trained to be good home doctors and have a sound knowledge of village sanitation. "In other words," he writes, "education in these schools would be such that it enables the pupils to serve the villages in every way and the expenses incurred should be regarded as having been incurred on primary education."[12]

Gandhi was aware that getting teachers for the kind of schools he had in mind would be a difficult task. His conception of a teacher was that first and foremost, he would have to be a passionate nationalist and lover of his poor countrymen. His role would be multidimensional in keeping with the goal of swaraj. Among his fundamental duties would be the exclusive use and propagation of khadi, and thus the pursuit of the swadeshi ideal; campaigning for temperance and prohibition; and campaigning also for Hindu–Muslim friendship and the eradication of untouchability. Gandhi was fully conscious of the fact that the quality and training of the teacher was central to any scheme of education. His analysis of the educational issue took into account the content, the medium and the teacher.

Gandhi's scheme of vocational or manual training right from the primary stage attracted some criticism – he was accused of neglecting intellectual training. To this, he replied that the two fields were not exclusive, but necessary complements of each other. He would even say that "true development of the intellect is not possible without vocational training".[13] To explain his position, he gave an example: "The knowledge a mason requires to earn his livelihood is not education at all in my opinion. His education should comprise knowledge of the place of his vocation in society, of bricks and their importance, of the need for houses and what they should be like, and how closely they are connected with civilization."[14] Even university education should train "truly intellectual social workers" and include masons, carpenters and weavers, who would not merely be tradesmen, but active social workers.[15]

Gandhi felt, for instance, that the learning of economics should keep the focus on agriculture. A sound method of teaching economic principles would be to give the students practical lessons in the agricultural economy of India in a systematic manner. Through such practical training alone should the student learn the economics of India.[16] It is obvious that the notion of education had a very special meaning for Gandhi. He judged its value in terms of the benefits it held for the social and economic development of the masses and the nation as a whole and his desire was to devise a method by which this objective would be fulfilled. The aim of education, in Gandhi's view, was to mould an individual into a social human being, not by suppressing his individuality, but by adding new dimensions to it.

Development of Self-esteem

Gandhi's sojourn in South Africa had taught him to view with the highest regard the capacity for self-sacrifice and the degree of patriotism inherent even in poor illiterate Indians. As a result, on his return to India, he was deeply irked and ashamed to see the "state of perpetual fear" in which the masses and classes of Indians lived. He found that they not only feared the government, who were a small minority, but even the pundits and the priests. Gandhi diagnosed the cause of this fear to two sources, one a spiritual one and the other a material one. Indians, he wrote, had lost their spiritual strength because they had lost their healthy respect for religion. They had forgotten that there was divinity in each of them, which would guide them along the true path and the consciousness of which drove away all illusory fears, save the fear of God. To quote him, "Loyalty to the governor of governors supersedes all other loyalty and gives an intelligent basis to the latter."[17]

The other reason for the pusillanimity of Indians was the state of abject subjection in which they lived. The draconian policies of the British regime, Gandhi believed, had engendered in them a sense of impotence and fear, a sense which could only be dissipated by a proper exercise of their civic and fundamental rights. He wrote that from the very beginning, the British government had curbed the three most important vehicles for expressing and cultivating public opinion – freedom of the press, freedom of speech and freedom of association. These were the foundations of any democratic society. "Liberty of speech," he wrote, "means that it is unassailed even when the speech hurts; liberty of the press can be said to be truly respected only when the press can comment in the severest terms upon and even misrepresent matters; protection against misrepresentation or violence being secured not by an administrative gagging order, not by closing down the press, but by punishing the real offender, leaving the press itself unrestricted. Freedom of association is truly respected when assemblies of people can discuss even revolutionary projects, the state relying upon the force of public opinion and the civil police, not the savage military at its disposal, to crush any actual outbreak or revolution that is designed to confound public opinion and the state representing it."[18] The latitude that Gandhi recommends in the exercise of the civic rights is indeed wide. Only such freedom could in reality enable the people of a land to become true citizens, conscious of their social and political identity.

Gandhi deeply admired Lokmanya Bal Gangadhar Tilak, whose influence, he believed, was "multiplied a thousand-fold by his incarceration and his speech and his pen had acquired much greater power after he was discharged than before his imprisonment".[19] In a way, Tilak was the symbol of the struggle for freedom of expression, which, for Gandhi, was a fundamental right necessary for a people's self-confidence and self-respect. In Gandhi's opinion, only through the restoration of the three fundamental rights of speech, press and association could a sound basis be laid for swaraj or total independence.[20] Although the question of national self-esteem was related to the exercise of civic rights, Gandhi did not overlook the dangers of the abuse of freedom of the press, especially in the context of a multicultural milieu like India. He attributed a substantial portion of the blame for the assassination of Swami Shraddhanand, a well-known Arya Samaj leader, to the communal role played by newspapers owned by both Hindus and Muslims. In unequivocal terms, he wrote: "The newspaperman has become a walking plague. He spreads the contagion of lies and calumnies. He exhausts the foul vocabulary of his dialect and injects his views into the unsuspecting and often receptive minds of his readers .... Secret and insidious propaganda has done its dark and horrible work, unchecked and unabashed."[21]

Another consequence of the abuse of the freedom of the press was the capitalizing by some newspapers and journals on obscene and titillating information for the public. This practice brought the owners enormous financial gain. To check this, Gandhi suggested that the journalists' association cultivate a uniform code of morals and create public opinion that would make it impossible for a respectable journal to violate the prescribed code.[22] Abuses of freedom could be checked in various ways, but the restoration of rights to freedom was of prime importance. It was only the exercise of these rights that could destroy the perpetual fear from which Indians suffered.

Self-sufficiency

Gandhi's belief in the attainment of self-sufficiency was a pillar of his social philosophy. Only by being self-sufficient in vital matters could an individual or nation defend his independence and maintain an honourable existence. Dependence on another for one's sustenance ensured one's physical and mental servitude. Thus, Gandhi believed, the only guarantee against exploitation and domination of any kind was being self-sufficient. In this context, he wrote: "Our first duty is that we should not be a burden on society, that is, we should be self-dependent. From this point of view, self-sufficiency itself is a kind of service."[23]

His creed of swadeshi or belonging to one's own country was in reality an extension of this principle of self-sufficiency. Although India had the raw materials and resources, its manufacture was almost negligible as a result of deliberate imperial policy. The country had become dependent on Britain for all its needs. Gandhi realized that there was only one field in which, with herculean efforts on the part of his fellow countrymen, a degree of self-reliance could be achieved in a relatively short period of time. "We can take the full swadeshi vow only in respect of our clothing, whether made of cotton, silk or wool,"[24] he wrote. "When swadeshi pervades the country ... millions of men will have in their hands the key to the economic salvation of India."[25] By this, he obviously meant that only when India became self-reliant for almost all its requirements would it become genuinely independent.

Gandhi was aware of the difficulties that would arise initially in the changeover to swadeshi cloth on a massive scale as the infrastructure necessary for it was either forgotten or fallen into disuse. To boost the morale of his countrymen and urge them along the difficult path, Gandhi, himself a deeply religious person, formulated the swadeshi vow to be taken by them. "By taking a vow," he writes, "we draw a cordon round ourselves from which we may never be free and thus we avoid failures."[26]

Gandhi's pledge ran as follows: "With god as my witness, I solemnly declare that from today I shall confine myself, for my personal requirements, to the use of cloth manufactured in India from Indian cotton, silk or wool and I shall destroy all foreign cloth in my possession."[27] The full meaning of the pledge implied that the cotton had to be spun on indigenous spinning wheels and woven on indigenous handlooms. This was not immediately possible, he knew, so he declared that the requirements of the pledge were met so long as all the spinning and weaving was done in India. Gandhi made an emotional appeal to his countrymen through the English dailies of Chennai and Mumbai: "I beseech every Hindu, Mussalman, Sikh, Parsi, Christian, Jew who believes that he belongs to this country to take the swadeshi vow and to ask others also to do likewise .... Those who think deep will see that such swadeshi contains pure economics."[28]

Though in the opinion of the cloth mill owners of the time, some 50 years would be required to set up enough mills to produce cloth for the whole of India, Gandhi was not deterred in his mission. He was convinced that if women took to spinning again in their leisure hours, and weavers who had given up their profession resumed it with some help, and the unemployed among the educated and semi-educated classes also took up weaving as an occupation, India would be in a position to produce its own cloth within two or three years. He records his own experience for the benefit of the educated unemployed (or ill employed) that as a weaver, working for eight hours a day, he found he could earn more than a rupee a day. With regret, he wrote, "I have seen graduates slaving for a salary of Rs 30 a month, and they rot thus even after their exhausting work for examinations. Surely, the weaver's lot is better than the graduate's."[29]

Gandhi felt that there was tremendous potential for the spinning programme among the countless women of India if they could be persuaded to spin in their homes in their leisure time as they used to earlier. His frequent reference to the role of women misled many to think that spinning was specifically a women's occupation. To dispel this notion, he stated in unambiguous terms: "Looked at from every point of view, hand spinning is as essential for men as for women in India, so long as it has not become universal enough to be reinstated in our villages and to bring about total boycott of foreign cloth."[30]

Gandhi was pragmatic enough to perceive that there were certain obstacles in the path of his mission to popularize swadeshi cloth. The chief of these were the mode and implements of production, which had to be improved urgently. He was certain that, provided all the initial processes of picking, ginning and carding of raw cotton were done carefully, there would automatically follow an increase in output and an improvement in the strength and evenness of yarn. Another important factor, he realized, was the number of revolutions that a spindle made for every turn of the wheel. "Local workers," he said, "should examine every wheel in their place and make the necessary changes in the spindle and other parts, wherever necessary."[31]

Gandhi's views on the restoration of indigenous tools of production are of importance in the modern context of appropriate and indigenous technology. One of his principal followers, Dr P.C. Ray, who was a well-known chemical scientist of Bengal, became a convert to the cause of khadi. He designed a spinning wheel called the Khulna spinning wheel and supplied them to destitute people.[32] The spread and progress of the swadeshi movement as an instrument of social change will be discussed in the next chapter; here it will suffice to assert that self-sufficiency held a high place in Gandhi's analysis of social issues.

Reorganization of Village Life

Gandhi regarded the revitalization of villages as a central issue in the social sphere because of the overwhelming number of Indians who lived there. He wished to be thoroughly identified with these masses. He believed India's soul was to be found there. He clearly understood that the principle of self-sufficiency was the key to the welfare of the rural areas. The dependence of villages on cities for most of their needs had to be reversed in his opinion and local self-government at the village level was a necessity. He bemoaned the abysmal lack of civic arrangements and the collapse of the education system in the villages.

In his effort to study and ameliorate rural conditions, Gandhi wrote and spoke through countless forums. He even set up different organizations with the aim of raising the living standards of the masses. The message that Gandhi constantly gave his countrymen in the villages was that they were the government in their respective areas and were, therefore, responsible for the state of their villages.[33] They had to overcome their fear of outside officials and interact with them as true representatives of their village. Since they worked on the land, they were its real owners and they should not fear eviction or oppression of any kind. They should rather be prepared for the highest sacrifice to protect their rights.[34] There were two issues on which Gandhi laid a great deal of emphasis – self-reliance and healthy cooperation. The village as a whole, he said, should be self-reliant for its basic needs to avoid being dependent on outside help and subject to unjust pressures. The residents of a village should look after all its civic arrangements, such as the maintenance of lanes, wells, pastures and temples, and take care of the old, the infirm and the cattle. All these activities would require a great deal of mutual help and cooperation.[35]

The factors of religious tolerance and education in the context of village life did not escape Gandhi's attention. He asserted that India had a tradition of religious liberalism and this must continue in precept and practice. Education in the village, he said, must be available to everyone. The teacher must be born in the village and he must not teach for money. His livelihood should be provided for by the village. The school curriculum should meet the needs of the villagers – teach them to do their duty, as, for example, how to use their savings and how to best manage the occupations of agriculture and weaving. Such schools, he believed, could be run by four or five wise men in a village.[36]

Gandhi with Mahadevbhai on the way to a khadi exhibition in Lucknow in 1936

At an exhibition ground in Haripura with Amrit Kaur and Sushila Nayyar on 10, February 1938

Another major task that he suggested to those living in the villages was to take up the responsibility for carrying forward the swadeshi programme, or the work of spinning and weaving one's own cloth requirements. He described this as "their purest and holiest dharma (duty)", which would benefit them and their country immeasurably. The work of spinning could be begun immediately in their own homes by poor village women, who, till then, had worked outside their homes to supplement their income and faced many humiliations in the process.[37] The schemes that Gandhi set in motion to achieve the ends of village uplift have been discussed in the next chapter under instruments of social change.

Establishment of Hindi as the National Language

Gandhi realized that one of the most important factors for forging a nation was its capacity to communicate in a common language. Without this element, the different parts of the country would remain alienated from the national mainstream, thus laying the foundation for fissiparous tendencies. No language other than Hindi appeared to Gandhi to fulfil this role. He also felt the need for a common script that would facilitate communication.

One of the biggest obstacles that Gandhi perceived in evoking a sense of nationhood among his countrymen was the isolation of the different provinces caused by the great number of provincial languages and their respective scripts. Only a small number of educated people in different parts of India spoke English, but with a few exceptions, they were themselves cut off from their cultural roots. So their capacity for national leadership was almost nil, he realized.

Gandhi came to the considered conclusion as early as in May 1917 that Hindi alone could become the common language of the people of India. He based this on several premises. Firstly, as compared to learning English, learning Hindi was easy for most Indians. Secondly, the number of those speaking Hindi at the time was almost 65 million. The Bengali, Bihari, Oriya, Marathi, Gujarati, Rajasthani, Punjabi and Sindhi languages were "sisters of Hindi", he argued. People speaking these languages could understand and speak a little Hindi. If they were included, the number rose to 220 million. "How then can English," he asked, "which even a hundred thousand Indians cannot speak correctly, compete successfully with a language which is so widely used?" He believed it was due to "our cowardice, lack of faith and ignorance of the greatness of the Hindi language" that this realization had not happened before.[38]

The issue of language concerned communication between the classes and the masses, between regions, between urban areas and rural areas as well as the forging of nationhood. The changeover to Hindi from English necessitated its use for official work and this should begin, he asserted, in the national and provincial councils and government organizations. Gandhi proposed special efforts for the propagation of the national language in the southern states, where the languages were not related to Hindi.[39] The propagators he had in mind had to be endowed with special qualities, chief of which would be a high level of patriotism and capacity for hard work. His scheme specified that Hindi instructors "who are zealous, brave, full of self-respect and energetic should be sent to Madras and other provinces to teach Hindi without receiving payment". Self-instruction books should be prepared and distributed free. Famous speakers should be sent all over the country to bring home to the people the importance of learning Hindi.[40]

Gandhi posited some key concerns in delineating the "mission" for the spread of the national language. As there was no ready stock of funds for "this gigantic enterprise", he appealed to the wealthy to shoulder the financial responsibility. The organization of the effort should, he advised, be entrusted to a small committee of active workers alone. He also affirmed that the national language made no distinction between Hindi and Urdu. Why, indeed, he asked, should there be contention on this issue with the Muslims? "They may use the Persian script. A few among us know the Persian script and more will learn it. So long as our Muslim brethren have not learnt the Devanagari, both the scripts will continue to be used for national work. However, this is a matter we can decide in a fraternal spirit with our Muslim brethren. Right now, the chief task is to spread the national language throughout India in the Devanagari script.[41]

In 1917, Gandhi was invited by the Hindi Sahitya Sammelan,[42] a body that had established itself by that time as a premier organization in the field of promotion and propagation of Hindi, to preside over its eighth session at Indore. His presidential address[43] at the session may be regarded as a classic statement of his thinking on the issue of the national language; it encapsulated the ideas he had been expressing on the subject and displayed remarkable consistency with his prescriptions as elaborated in the 1920s and 1930s.

The issue of the national language became part of the Congress programme in 1917 at Gandhi's instance.[44] He included it in his national programme for satyagraha in 1919, saying that since satyagraha was "essentially a fight for truth, and if we have regard for truth, we shall have to admit that Hindi is the only language we can use as a national language. There is no other regional language with equal claims." In order to avoid being misunderstood, Gandhi specified the nature of the national language he had in mind. It was not to be a Sanskritized or Persianized Hindi, but a mixture of Hindi and Urdu as spoken by and large in the United Provinces, Bihar, Delhi and the Punjab.[45]

By 1927, teaching of Hindi had been established on a small scale in Tamil Nadu by instructors from the north of the country, who held free classes.[46] A beginning was made in Kolkata in 1928. Subhas Chandra Bose, chairman of the reception committee of the Hindi Prachar (Propagation) Conference, was the first to enlist as a learner. A committee was appointed for a term of one year to do propaganda work with a view to making it a permanent body. Eight eminent people, including Sir J.C. Bose, were appointed on the committee, while G.D. Birla consented to act as treasurer. Ten members offered their services as part time honorary Hindi teachers at the conference. There was also a handsome response to the appeal for collections as more than Rs 3,000 was collected on the spot.[47]

At the conference, Gandhi emphasized the importance of teaching Hindi without prejudice to any religion or community. Knowledge of the best works in the language, like that of Kabir and Tulsidas, which did not offer a distorted view of religion, should be disseminated, he said. For the promotion of Hindi at the school level, he suggested that every school should have an association armed with the duty to make progressive use of Hindi in all fields; to evolve new technical words; to make a sound study of abstruse books; to provide Hindi teachers wherever necessary; and to organize volunteer Hindi teachers for honorary work.

Gandhi suggested an important innovation to promote Hindi. As many Bengali and Assamese words resembled Hindi, he said, "Books to make this fact known should be written; pocket size Hindi-Bengali and Bengali-Hindi dictionaries should be prepared, Bengali books in Devanagari script and Hindi books in Bengali script should be published."[48] He believed that such books could pay their way as had been demonstrated in Madras (now Chennai). Moreover, when the books proved really useful, they would gain in value and become popular, he wrote.

An important landmark in the progress of Hindi as the national language was in the shape of two resolutions passed by the Hindi Sahitya Sammelan at Indore in 1935 under Gandhi's influence. One gave a comprehensive definition of Hindi and the other expressed the opinion that all the languages that had descended from or were largely influenced by Sanskrit should be written in the Devanagari script. The first resolution was designed, Gandhi wrote, to emphasize the fact that Hindi did not supplant the provincial languages, but supplemented them, and that it extended the knowledge and usefulness of the speaker as an all India worker. It also recognized the fact that the language written in the Urdu script, but understood by both Muslims and Hindus, was also Hindi. The Sammelan, he wrote, took particular care to disarm suspicion that it desired to undermine the Urdu script. The authorized script of the Sammelan would remain Devanagari, though it recognized the right of Muslims to write the language in the Urdu script as they had done till then. Thus, Gandhi kept all the dimensions of the language issue in view.

To implement the second resolution, a committee was appointed, with Kaka Saheb Kalelkar as chairman and convener, to explore the possibility of extensive use of the Devanagari script and make such changes and additions in it as were necessary to keep it simple and phonetically exact so as to represent the sounds not expressed by the existing letters. This would pave the way for increased interprovincial contacts and for a medium of communication between provinces, he believed. Qualifying these resolutions, Gandhi wrote, "Let no one run away with the idea that the reform will diminish the importance of the provincial languages. Indeed, it can only enrich them even as the adoption of a common script has enriched the languages of Europe by making intercourse between its provinces easy."[49]

A notable advance in the movement to spread awareness of the national language and to promote interaction between the provinces was marked by meeting of the Bharatiya Sahitya Parishad at Chennai in March 1937. One of its objectives was to collect gems from all provincial literature and make them available in Hindi. The other was, in Gandhi's words, "to stimulate in our people the desire to know languages of other provinces .... But to this end, a common script is quite essential."[50] In his opinion, the teaching of a common script on a national scale was not such a difficult undertaking as more than 90 per cent of the people were illiterate and so they could start on a clean slate. "Why should we not," he asked, "start making them literate by means of a common script?"[51]

Gandhi appealed to men of letters of all provinces to sink their differences and, while serving their own regional literatures, popularize the concept of a national language and devote themselves to writing only in the common script of the country.[52]

Hindu–Muslim Relations

More than any other national leader, Gandhi believed that India's social and economic development would remain stunted until Hindus and Muslims, the two major communities, agreed to resolve their differences in a spirit of understanding and to work together for their common betterment. Gandhi believed that the Hindus and Muslims had not so far really endeavoured to come together to adjust their differences and to live as friends and compatriots. Minor differences were blown out of proportion, often with the active connivance of the British rulers. He perceived a good opportunity to bring about communal accord when the issue of dismemberment of the Turkish empire arose at the conclusion of the First World War. This had agitated Muslims all over the world. Gandhi was of the opinion that as Muslims were an integral part of India, it was the duty of Hindus and other brother communities to come to their aid and share their grief. "If the Hindus wish to cultivate eternal friendship with the Muslims," he wrote, "they must perish with them in the attempt to vindicate the honour of Islam."[53] His vigorous efforts in this direction led to the historic cooperation between the two communities during the Non-Cooperation Movement between 1920 and 1922, though the concord did not last long.

Another dimension of Hindu–Muslim relations was the sharing of political power, for which Gandhi offered a courageous and unique solution. He asserted that the majority must take the initiative and leave the decision in the hands of the minority community. He voiced his opinion in *Young India*, saying, "I hold that it is up to the Hindus as the major party not to bargain, but leave the pen in the hands of, say, Hakim Saheb Ajmal Khan and abide by his decision. I would similarly deal with the Sikhs, the Christians and the Parsis and be satisfied with the residue. It is, in my opinion, the only just, equitable, honourable and dignified solution."[54]

This statement shows the latitude Gandhi was prepared to allow in order to gain the objective of Hindu–Muslim friendship. He was convinced that the Hindus, with their overwhelming numbers, could easily trust the minority communities and should agree to share political power with them in the proportion they desired. He also probably understood that once the power of decision making was given to anyone, reasonableness had a strong chance of holding sway. A minority community, when given the power to determine its rights, would hesitate to indulge in excesses. Any other adjustment, he felt, must leave a nasty taste in the mouth, for adjustment was possible only when the more powerful took the initiative without waiting for a response from the weaker community. Gandhi did not fear abuse or misuse of power by an unjust administrator, whether he was a Hindu, Muslim or any other, as the powerful remedy of satyagraha was always available to those who would use it.

The issue of Hindu–Muslim amity was considered by Gandhi at all levels – the religious, the political and the economic. Gandhi stated categorically that communal reservation of jobs in government departments and institutions would be fatal to good government. He believed that for administration to be efficient, it must always be in the hands of the fittest. The lowest posts could, if necessary, be filled by an examination by an impartial board consisting of men from different communities. But that is as far he would go.[55] Though Gandhi was not willing to compromise on the question of efficiency in administration, he asserted that the policy of the national government with regard to providing educational opportunities must be to favour the educationally backward communities.[56]

Gandhi observed that the Muslims of his time were generally more intolerant and fanatic than the Hindus. He traced the cause to a reaction, which, he felt, had taken place against the liberalism of Islamic teachers in the time of Harun-al Rashid and Maman. The reactionaries had gained an upper hand as there were many learned, able and influential men amongst them and they had very nearly overwhelmed the liberal teachers and philosophers of Islam. He wrote, "We in India are still suffering from the effect of that reaction. But I have not a shadow of doubt that Islam has sufficient in itself to become purged of illiberalism and intolerance."[57]

In a multi-religious and plural society like India, Gandhi realized, it would be preposterous to expect any particular culture or religion to dominate. The need of the hour was not one religion, but mutual respect and tolerance between the devotees of different religions. The attempt should be for a dynamic unity in diversity, rather than for a static homogeneity. Gandhi believed that any attempt to root out traditions, effects of heredity, climate and other surroundings was not only bound to fail, but would be sacrilege. "The soul of religion is one," he wrote, "but it is encased in a multitude of forms. The latter will persist to the end of time. Wise men will ignore the outward crust and see the same soul living under a variety of crusts .... Truth is the exclusive property of no single scripture."[58]

Disputes were bound to arise between followers of different faiths regarding certain issues, but they could be solved non-violently, Gandhi believed. For this purpose, it was necessary that the belligerents in the contending parties should be first convinced of the efficacy of non-violence. They should resolve, he wrote, "that neither party shall take the law into its own hands, but that all points in dispute, wherever and whenever they arise, shall be decided by reference either to private arbitration, or to the law courts if they wish. This is the whole meaning of non-violence so far as communal matters are concerned."[59]

Notwithstanding his intensive efforts, Hindu–Muslim tensions reached a peak in December 1926, with the assassination of Swami Shraddhanand, the prominent Arya Samaj leader, by a Muslim called Abdul Rashid. Though Gandhi was critical of his religious views, he had great personal regard for the swami as he was a fearless and active reformer. On his death, Gandhi was apprehensive about a Hindu backlash and the resulting communal inferno. He sought to calm passions by speaking to both communities through *Young India*. He counselled the Hindus to exercise self-restraint and evoke in themselves the innate quality of forgiveness associated with their religion. "Let us not ascribe the crime of an individual to a whole community ...," he said. "Let us not think of the wrong as done by a Mussalman against a Hindu, but of an erring brother against a hero."[60]

Gandhi called upon the Muslims to condemn the murder in unequivocal terms if they desired to prove their bona fides regarding a peaceful solution to the communal problem. He criticized them for being too free with the knife and the pistol, even though the sword was no emblem of Islam. It was unfortunate that Islam was born in an environment where the sword was and still remained the supreme law, he wrote. As a result of this, the message of the Prophet had not been received in the right spirit, even though, the word, 'Islam', meant peace. He asserted that the sword had to be sheathed if Islam was to live up to its name. Otherwise, it would be calamity for them and the world as the communal problem was a world problem. Reliance upon the sword, he said, was wholly inconsistent with reliance upon God.[61]

He hoped that the "martyrdom" of Swami Shraddhanand would bring both communities to their senses and help them make extraordinary efforts to reach a peaceful solution to their problems. The issue of communal harmony and understanding was by no means a simple one, but, as Gandhi saw, it was essential for the growth of a healthy, integrated society and the basis of harmony could only be mutual respect and mutual concessions.

Eradication of Untouchability

It was Gandhi who first raised the issue of untouchability to national heights when he found in it a complete antithesis of human dignity and universal values. In sharply critical language, he wrote, "Nowhere, either in Vaishnavism or in Hinduism, have I seen it laid down that Bhangis, Dom, et cetera, are untouchables. Hinduism is hemmed in by many old customs. Some of them are praiseworthy, but the rest are to be condemned .... The Sanatana Dharma will not be saved by defending every verse printed in the scriptures. It will be saved only by putting into action the principles enunciated in them – principles that are eternal."[62]

Gandhi knew that he had to tread cautiously in the matter of social and religious reform or his efforts would prove counterproductive. The movement against untouchability, he said, did not urge the untouchables to give up their vocations. The desire was to demonstrate that the function of removing garbage and filth was a necessary and sacred function and its performance could impart grace even to a Vaishnava. He wrote, "Those who pursue this vocation are not, therefore, degraded, but entitled to an equal measure of social privileges with those pursuing other callings; their work protects the country from a number of diseases. They, therefore, deserve the same respect as doctors."[63]

Gandhi's commitment to the cause of eradication of this social evil was complete. He made the following declaration: "It is my firm conviction that if, in the attempt to free Hinduism of this blot, I have to lay down my life, it will be no great matter."[64]

He sought to arouse a sense of shame in his co-religionists, the Vaishnavas, by asking them, "How can a dharma which holds that the entire universe is permeated by Vishnu believe that he is not present in the *antyaja*?"[65] He advised them that if they found it difficult to give up their traditional beliefs, they could at least render practical help to the untouchables in terms of digging wells, founding schools, arranging for medical help and contribute in other ways towards improving their life.[66] He drew the attention of the Jains of Gujarat to the contradiction in the theory and practice of their faith. He told them, "The dharma that you practice is neither Hindu dharma nor Jain dharma. He who is prepared to protect the bedbug, should he not protect the *antyajas* who are as weak as cows?"[67]

A section of opinion in the country was critical of Gandhi for including the issue of untouchability in the national programme, for they felt that it would prove to be socially divisive. Gandhi was not moved by this argument. He replied that some social questions were of such importance that they could not but be made political issues.[68] He included among these the question of Hindu–Muslim unity, the Brahmin–non-Brahmin quarrel and untouchability. No political or national party could afford to ignore these issues, he asserted. There could be no national progress or development without unity being achieved between the different segments of Indian society, as otherwise remove, the weak spots would pull down the whole structure. "We put the noose round our own necks by covering up our weaknesses, giving them the appearance of strength and postponing their reform,"[69] he said.

In order to change the attitudes of people and uproot their prejudices, Gandhi initiated the policy of holding common meetings in which members of both the touchable and untouchable castes would be present. He would not tolerate any kind of segregation at these meetings. He would also discourse on all important issues of the national struggle at the meetings, including that of untouchability. He put the blame squarely on the caste Hindus for the degraded condition of the untouchables. He asked them to study the question deeply and aim at being ideal scavengers. He said, "So long as you do not take the broom and the bucket in your hands, you cannot make your towns and cities clean."[70]

In his advice to the untouchable classes, he asked them to eschew those habits which fed the prejudices of the caste Hindus and thereby raise themselves in public estimation. Among them was the eating of beef, which was taboo for Hindus. If they could give up eating beef, they would, he believed, earn the goodwill of the Hindu masses. He buttressed this argument by highlighting the importance of dairy and cattle farming in the agricultural economy of India and, therefore, the need for the protection and care of cows.[71]

Gandhi was aware that there were sections of Harijans in different parts of the country who removed and disposed off dead cattle and ate their flesh. Eating such flesh was a heinous sin from the Hindu point of view. In response to his appeal to give up carrion eating, the Harijans pointed out that they were compelled by the upper castes to remove dead cattle and they did not dare refuse; secondly, the cost of the flesh was deducted from their remuneration; and thirdly, they had through long habit come to regard the cooked flesh as a delicacy.[72]

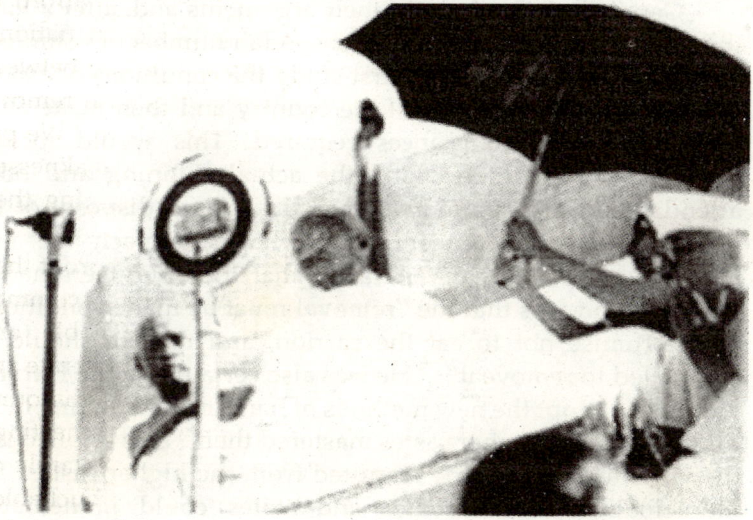

Gandhi declaring the All India Village Industries Association exhibition at Haripura open on 10 February 1938

Gandhi at a public meeting in Mardan in the North West Frontier Province (now in Pakistan) on 15 October 1938

Gandhi saw the force of their arguments and, after a lot of thought, put forth some suggestions. A fair number of volunteers were required, he wrote, to first study the conditions of carcass removal in different parts of the country and then make alterations as the circumstances required. This would include supervising and undertaking the actual skinning and other attendant processes and seeing to the proper disposal of the remains. These volunteers would have to teach the new methods to the Harijans. A factor that the volunteers had to keep in mind was that the "removal must be made conditional on a promise not to eat the carrion, and no one should be compelled to remove it".[73] He was also certain that the Harijans would not adopt the new methods of handling and curing hides till the so-called higher castes mastered them. This implied that the volunteers should be recruited from the higher castes. The municipalities, local bodies and states could immediately undertake the work of training volunteers in scientific skinning and hide curing, he said.[74]

Apart from their occupational problems, the Harijans suffered from several other economic disabilities. In the rural areas, the landlords had reduced them to the status of serfs and they were idle for a major portion of the year. In the urban areas, apart from the myriad social restrictions, there were bylaws to prevent them from holding even minor administrative posts. Their income, too, was much below their expenditure. Nevertheless, Gandhi noticed the glimmerings of a political and social consciousness among some of the untouchables. In Tamil Nadu, some untouchables told Gandhi that they were, in reality, the first holders of the land in India because they were the actual tillers of the soil. Gandhi agreed and told them that they must rely on their own strength to solve their problems. He wrote, "They have but to become conscious of their own strength which their numbers and their occupation give them, and they will become an irresistible force. Immediately they realize that they are slaves of nobody, and that after all, without their labour, the lands they are cultivating will become a horrible wilderness, then the day is theirs."[75] In effect, his message was to non-cooperate and offer satyagraha.

His advice to the landlords was that they should remember how heavily obliged they were to the Harijans for their own comforts. By crushing them, they would bring about their own downfall. They should look upon the labourers as members of their family and allow them to share in the happiness to which the labourers contributed so much.[76]

Municipalities could, according to Gandhi, play a useful role in alleviating the distress of the untouchables. They could examine the causes of their chronic indebtedness, help them repay outstanding loans, see that such loans were not improperly taken and form a cooperative society for their benefit. They could also help in standardizing their wages. A municipality could construct civic amenities such as wells, lavatories and schools for the untouchables as they were not allowed access to the existing ones, but in order to prevent segregation from being institutionalized, children of socially conscious higher caste people also ought to attend these schools. This would help maintain standards in them as well.[77]

Gandhi studied and analysed the problem of untouchability in all its dimensions and his suggestions and appeals were based on humanitarian, religious, economic and social grounds. He did not depend merely on exhortations and sermons, he put forward ideas and programmes that would work slowly but surely. Gandhi obviously realized that the issue was to bring about reform in the social structure without tearing apart the social fabric.

Empowering the Untouchables

Gandhi's biggest challenge on the issue of untouchability arose when the British government announced the Communal Award, which sanctioned separate electorates for the untouchables. Earlier, Gandhi had made it emphatically clear that any such attempt to sanction separate electorates to the untouchables would be resisted by him with his life. Therefore, he decided to undertake a fast unto death as soon as the award came into effect. He explained the reason for his opposition in a letter to the prime minister, Ramsay Macdonald, in the following words, "I sense the injection of a poison that is calculated to destroy Hinduism and do no good whatsoever to the 'depressed classes' .... What I am against is their statutory separation, even in a limited form, from the Hindu fold, so long as they choose to belong to it. Do you not realize that if your decision stands and a constitution comes into being, you arrest the marvellous growth of work of Hindu reformers who have dedicated themselves to the uplift of their suppressed brethren in every walk of life?"[78] Gandhi started his fast on 20 September 1932 and this led to momentous consequences.

In a letter, he wrote, "I have not a shadow of doubt that it (the award) will prevent the natural growth of the suppressed classes and will remove the incentive to honourable amends from the suppressors. What I am aiming at is a heart understanding between the two, the greatest opportunity of repentance and reparation on the part of the suppressors. I am certain that the moment is ripe for the change of heart among them."[79] He said he would rather have the widest possible franchise for the Harijans and hoped that a convention would be established between the two sections of Hindus for securing the proper election of representatives of the depressed classes.

Gandhi's fast is generally known as the Epic Fast and it evoked hectic negotiations and consultations between leaders of different sections of the Hindu community to arrive at an amicable settlement as soon as possible in order to save Gandhi's life. The Yeravda Pact was reached on 24 September between the leaders of the depressed classes on the one hand and the rest of the Hindu community on the other.[80] It gave sizeable representation to the depressed classes in the provincial legislatures of the country; in the central legislature, they were given 18 per cent of the seats allotted to the general electorate for British India. Numerically, the Harijans gained more seats in the legislatures than granted to them in the Communal Award. Another clause in the Yeravda Pact stated that no disability would attach to anyone on the grounds of his being a member of the depressed classes with regard to any elections to local bodies or appointment to public service.

Another fallout of Gandhi's fast was the extensive and vocal assertion of most Hindu leaders and organizations in the country that all efforts would be made to fully integrate the Harijans with the rest of the Hindu community. Under the chairmanship of Pandit Madan Mohan Malviya, many Hindu leaders of the country held a conference in Mumbai on 25 September 1932, in which they resolved that henceforth all those so far regarded untouchable would have civic rights equal to the rest of society and statutory recognition of these would be sought as soon as possible. Further, they would try by every legitimate and peaceful means to secure to them equal social rights, including the right to enter Hindu temples at par with other Hindus.[81]

Gandhi's conviction that religion played an important part in the life of the common man made him campaign vigorously for the right of temple entry for Harijans. He believed that it was the one thing that could give new life and new hope to the Harijans, as no mere economic uplift could do. The message of the temples, he said, would penetrate every Harijan hut; the message of economic and educational uplift would touch only those to whom it was personally brought. "This proposition of mine," he says, "can easily be understood by those, who, like me, believe in temples as an integral part of Hinduism, as churches and mosques are of Christianity and Islam. It is not necessary that every Harijan should at once enter the temples. It is enough and necessary if he knows that he has acquired the right."[82]

The temple entry movement launched by Gandhi came up against tremendous legal hurdles at the time. The British code of laws did not allow the entry of Harijans into temples on the grounds of custom and usage. This anomaly had to be removed, Gandhi realized, if temple entry were to become a reality. Under his inspiration, two bills, one in the Madras legislature (Dr Subbarayana's) and the other in the Central Legislative Assembly (Ranga Iyer's) were sought to be introduced to permit the entry of Harijans into temples where the opinion of the majority favoured it. The British government refused permission to the former on the grounds of its national ramifications, but allowed the latter on the condition that opportunity would be given to all sections of Hindus to express their opinions on it.[83]

During the campaign for the temple entry rights of the Harijans, Gandhi wrote to the private secretary to the Viceroy that the English Law of Trusts barred the progress of reform in India as, in many places, the trustees of the temples and the Hindu congregations there wished to admit the Harijans, but were helpless on account of the law. Apart from this, he reminded the government that it had, by accepting the Yeravda Pact, bound itself morally to facilitate as far as it lay in its power the observance by caste Hindus of all the other conditions of the pact, which had reference to social and religious matters.[84] He urged the government to pass both the bills as soon as possible and thereby end state interference in cultural matters and allow society to evolve naturally.

For Gandhi, the field and scope for social service in India was as wide as India itself, but the centre of it was Harijan service because, in serving the Harijans, the worker would meet with every conceivable social problem in a concentrated form and he would have to possess the best qualities to face them and solve them.[85]

Women as Partners and Motivators

Gandhi's views on the position of women in society were quite radical. At the Gujarat Political Conference in Godhra in November 1917, he said, "We have kept our women away from these activities of ours and have thus become victims of a kind of paralysis. The nation walks with one leg only. All its work appears to be only half or incompletely done."[86] This was his usual refrain at all public meetings, with the result that women, initially of the upper classes, began to attend these conferences and also started organizing themselves for participation in public activities. When Gandhi began the Rowlatt Satyagraha in April 1919, it is reported that women of all classes and communities held a meeting at China Bagh in Mumbai to record their emphatic protests against the Rowlatt Legislation.[87] Gandhi addressed this meeting and appealed to the women of India to cooperate with the men and join the satyagraha movement in large numbers.[88]

When Gandhi launched the swadeshi movement in the country, he brought to light the powerful role Indian women could play in it by accepting and acting upon the message of swadeshi. They had ancient traditions of spinning and weaving, but, except in a few isolated parts of the country, these occupations had been forgotten. India had become totally dependent for its textiles on Britain, although only 150 years ago, it had not only been self-sufficient, but even a major exporter of cloth. Appealing to their ethical and common sense, Gandhi asserted boldly at women's meetings: "Using foreign cloth for the last 150 years, we have violated dharma and morals and lost our industries .... We serve both our economic interest and dharma through swadeshi, the former because our wealth remains in the country and the latter because we take work from our neighbour, so that his talents may have scope."[89] Gandhi was trying to bring the women into the national mainstream, which, in turn, would make them and their men aware of their changing roles, their capacity and their rights.

Gandhi spoke to the women about the famine conditions in many parts of the country caused by lack of occupation and, consequently, of purchasing power. Spinning and weaving, he said, would be the best occupations, provided there was a demand for khadi. They should, he emphasized, teach their children the value of wearing swadeshi cloth and persuade their men to gift them only khadi saris. If the saris were found to be heavy, they should, he pleaded, find out the defects and help make the necessary improvements, rather than discard them.

Knowing the importance of religious vows in India, he formulated a pledge that the women could take on Bhima Ekadashi,[90] the day when the traditional Chaturmas[91] vow was taken. The pledge was that they would wear out what they had, but would not buy any more foreign material. He added a rider saying that he would not be satisfied if they alone used locally produced cloth, they must also persuade all women of their area to use such cloth. If women all over the country would make similar resolutions in relation to their respective areas, he said, "I cannot estimate the resulting increase in prosperity .... [W]e should have this result in no more than a year or two."[92] By producing hand spun yarn, women could boost the inadequate national output of yarn. Gandhi suggested that rich women could donate such yarn to the authorized stores, while poor women could earn enough for their needs through spinning. The latter would be supplied spinning wheels, the cost of which would be deducted from their remuneration in easy instalments. He estimated that they could earn three annas per pound of yarn. If spinning and weaving became universal occupations as before, he believed foreign cloth would disappear in 11 days and economic conditions would improve immensely.[93]

Gandhi was familiar with the fact that exploitation of women began in the family. He was aware of the inequalities, the repression and deprivation women suffered and he, more than any other leader, advocated equality for them in every sphere – the family, the economy and the polity. In a letter to his pupil, Premabehn Kantak, he wrote, "A wife is not a servant, she is a friend with equal rights, a partner in dharma. Each is the guru of the other. A daughter's share should be equal to a son's. A husband and a wife have equal rights in what either earns. The husband earns with the wife's help, even if she does no more than cook for the family .... A wife has the right to live separately from her husband if he ill treats her. The two have equal rights over the children. After the children have grown up, neither has any. If the wife is unfit to exercise her right, she loses it. And so does the husband. In sum, I do not admit any differences between men and women, except those created by nature, which all of us can see."[94] This was the crux of the issue concerning women – the removal of the differences between men and women.

Gandhi was firmly of the opinion that ownership of property bred pride and arrogance and led to the exploitation of those who had no property, including women. In his opinion, the concept of material property had to be abandoned before a radical change in the social position of women could be effected. He would have women acquire equal legal status with men and frame appropriate laws for the abolition of property. The only property that could be bequeathed properly to one's children was a good education and exemplary character, he felt.[95]

Denouncing the patriarchal norms of society, he wrote, "Lustful men have degraded women .... They have taught her to adorn herself. Woman did not see in all this her slavery and her degradation."[96] Women, too, consented to get their noses and ears pierced, put fetters on their feet and became slaves. Women had to rise above this social and psychological trap and realize themselves. He asserted that women must cease to consider themselves objects of men's lust. The remedy was more in their hands, than in men's. They should refuse to adorn themselves for men, including their husbands, if they wished to be their equal partners. He felt compelled to say, "I cannot imagine Sita ever wasting a single moment on pleasing Ram by physical charms."[97] Gandhi was decrying women's love of gold and jewellery, which, he pointed out, led to their willing enslavement by men. The conditioning of women's minds was an important dimension of the whole issue of their status in society.

Gandhi was quite clear that he expected women of all classes to share the financial burden of running the household to the extent they reasonably could.[98] For this purpose, he suggested ways in which the drudgery of cooking could be reduced. One was that the diet should be simple and that food should be cooked only once. Cooking was a necessity, so it should be shared by both husband and wife. If both worked in a spirit of service, he believed, many ways of saving time could be discovered.[99] His ideas on the kind of occupation that women could undertake underwent considerable evolution. In *Hind Swaraj*, written in 1909, he had said disdainfully that women in the west were slaving away in factories when they ought to be queens of their households. But in January 1935, he advised Congressmen in Nagpur, "I insist on the industrial education of girls. That will make them independent. They will not have to depend on others if they are not married. If married, they can lend a helping hand at home. If widows, they can earn their own living."[100]

Child Wives and Child Widows

An issue that moved Gandhi passionately was the plight of child wives and child widows in Hindu society. There was no restriction, ironically, on Hindu widowers marrying any number of times and neither was there any social sanction against polygamy. On the other hand, young widows, often 10 or 12 year old girls, were subjected to the worst kind of oppression and exploitation. Apart from the fact that they could not remarry, they were expected to conform to the ideals of self-sacrifice and renunciation. Gandhi rebelled against these double standards for widows and widowers, which he rightly felt were related to the bigger and more basic issue of equality.

He defined what a true marriage meant to him: "If marriage is, as it ought to be, a sacrament, an entrance into a new life, the girls to be married should be fully developed, should have some hand in the choice of companions for life and should know the consequences of their acts. It is a crime against God and man to call the union of children a married state and then to decree widowhood for a girl whose so-called husband is dead."[101]

In 1925, Gandhi was moved to formulate rules that he considered necessary for preserving the dignity of a widow's life and for preserving order in Hindu society. These rules were:

1. No father should get a daughter under the age of 15 married.
2. If a girl below this age has already been married and has become a widow, it is the father's duty to get her married again.
3. If a 15 year old girl becomes a widow within a year of marriage, her parents should encourage her to marry again.
4. Every member of the family should look upon the widow with the utmost respect. Her parents or parents in law must provide her with the means of improving her knowledge.[102]

These, he said, were not hard and fast rules, but should serve as a guide for parents.

Knowing the difficulty of implementing these rules, Gandhi was of the opinion that parents should try to persuade the leaders of the community and, if they failed in this, they should break the shackles of caste and look outside their caste for a suitable groom for the widowed girl. They should not be afraid of being socially ostracized, but they should not provoke the leaders unnecessarily either. The remedy, he suggested, was moral persuasion through self-suffering, or satyagraha. Using this method, he was certain, widow remarriage would be accepted by all. The work of promoting widow remarriage was one that could not be done by any institution, he said. It had to be done by individual reformers, whose relatives had become widows, and they should carry on a vigorous, dignified and restrained propaganda in their own circles, and whenever they succeeded, they should give the widest possible publicity to the event.[103]

When the Child Marriage Restraint Bill, which sought to raise the age of consummation of marriage for girls to 14, came up before the Central Legislative Assembly, Gandhi asked that it should be raised to at least 16. But Gandhi knew that even if the bill was passed, the actual conditions would not change unless there was a strong body of public opinion to back it. There was need for constant and continuous agitation, he said, if any impression was to be made on the Hindu public.[104]

Male chauvinists, alarmed by Gandhi's espousal of the cause of widow remarriage, expressed misgivings that were the practice to become common, there would be a breakdown of the social order. Gandhi's distaste for the double standard is apparent in his reply to this: "The rights or latitude allowed to widowers should also be allowed to widows. Otherwise, widows become victims of coercion and coercion is violence, out of which only harm can come. The question raised about widows is not raised about widowers. It can only be because the laws applying to women have been framed by men. If law making had been the business of women, they would not have given themselves fewer rights than men enjoy."[105]

Gandhi said the fears of the chauvinists that all widows would want to remarry were baseless as he knew from personal experience that many widows did not wish to remarry, though there were no restrictions imposed on them.

The cause of widow remarriage was spread with missionary zeal by Gandhi, especially among the younger generation, through his speeches and writings. On 7 September 1927, he asked the students of Panchaiyappa's College, Chennai, to make the sacred resolve that they were not going to marry a girl who was not a widow, they would seek out a widow to marry, and if they could not do so, they were not going to marry at all. They should announce their decision, he said, to the world, including their parents and sisters. Another novel suggestion he made at the time was that the minimum marriageable age of girls should be 20 and men should not marry girls aged less than 20. Some Brahmin boys raised the objection that Brahmin girls did not remain unmarried till 20, to which Gandhi replied that they should then forget caste considerations and marry a girl from outside their caste. Criticizing their religious orthodoxy, he said, "Brahminism I adore .... But Brahminism that can tolerate untouchability, virgin widowhood, spoliation of virgins, stinks in my nostrils. It is a parody of Brahminism .... It is undiluted animalism."[106]

Gandhi expressed similar views on the issue of sati. It was a Hindu custom, mainly of the middle and upper classes, in which a widow immolated herself on the funeral pyre of her husband to prove her fidelity. He declared that the custom had its origin in superstitious ignorance and the blind egotism of man. He was of the opinion that the laws and vows of marriage should apply equally to both sexes. If the wife had to prove her fidelity and undivided devotion to her husband, the husband, too, had to prove his allegiance and devotion to his wife. "Yet," he wrote, "we have never heard of a husband mounting the funeral pyre of his deceased wife .... Satihood is the acme of purity. This purity cannot be attained or realized by dying. It can be attained only through constant striving, constant immolation of the spirit from day to day."[107]

Gandhi was also an uncompromising critic of the purdah system, which literally meant that women were to be kept behind the veil in seclusion. He wrote that the observance of the custom pained and humiliated him deeply as he thought of the wrong being done by men to the women of India by clinging to a barbarous custom that did incalculable harm to the country.[108] He was of the opinion that the custom created moral weakness in women as they considered themselves incapable of withstanding the attention of men.[109] By being kept caged and confined in their houses and little courtyards, women remained ignorant of affairs outside their homes and their growth was stunted. He questioned the right of men to deprive women of the same freedom that they allowed themselves. He remonstrated, "Men, to be men, must be able to trust their womenfolk even as the latter are compelled to trust them. Let us not live with one limb completely or partially paralyzed .... By seeking today to interfere with the free growth of the womanhood of India, we are interfering with the growth of free and independent spirited men .... Let us then tear down the purdah with one mighty effort."[110] Gandhi constantly stressed the equal role of women in the family and society and campaigned for the removal of hindrances in the fulfilment of that role.

Gandhi's analysis of the issue of women's status took into account the double standards practised by society: the restrictions imposed on women, the suppression and repression they had to suffer, and the evils of which they became victims. For instance, he took note of the dowry system, which, he believed, affected the middle class alone. Gandhi felt that dowry could be abolished only if people had the courage to marry outside their own caste as the two systems were connected intimately. Girls, he said, must refuse to marry boys whose parents demanded a dowry and they must be prepared to remain spinsters, if need be. Only proper education, he thought, could revolutionize the mentality of the youth of the nation and inspire them to refuse to take or give dowry. Armed with such education, they could fight this and other social evils.[111]

The fact that fundamental social reforms could not be rushed through in society, but had to be nurtured with painstaking work was made clear by Gandhi in the suggestions he made for ameliorating the lot of the devadasis. The devadasis were a community of women in south India who lived by prostitution. They were originally dancing girls, who were initiated into the service of the temples. Their children were social outcastes. Gandhi was approached by one of them to help them regain social respectability and root out the devadasi system itself. Gandhi knew the enormity of the task. He thought the reform could be planned along two lines. Firstly, the devadasis would have to be provided a source of livelihood in place of prostitution. Secondly, the reformers would have to appeal to the reason and heart of those who engaged them for their base ends and explain to them the cause for which they were fighting. The reformers should not expect instant results, he said, because all reform was a kind of education, which yielded results only when pursued systematically.[112]

Gandhi's perception of women's issues was discerning and sympathetic. He was keenly aware of the huge handicaps under which women lived as well as their tremendous potential for nation building activities. It was this potential that had to be given an opportunity to find expression, he said. Gandhi fully recognized and appreciated the services rendered by some Indian women to the national cause. Foremost among them, he said, was Sarojini Naidu. Naidu was his choice for the presidentship of the Congress in 1924,[113] and she became the first Indian woman president of the Congress. By supporting Naidu's candidature, Gandhi did a big service to the cause of Indian women and actively contributed to their being recognized as a major political force. Indeed, Gandhi did not merely perceive the potential of

Indian women, he actively took up the cause of bettering their lot and making them conscious of their own power.

A Sound Work Ethic

An important factor of national life that Gandhi highlighted for the first time was the necessity for a sound work ethic to achieve national goals. When Gandhi arrived on the scene, political and social work was being done in India, but in a haphazard and uncoordinated manner. Through personal example, Gandhi tried to inculcate the habits and attitudes of a disciplined nation. He said at a civic reception in Bangalore in 1915, "A charge has been brought against us that we as a nation are too demonstrative and lack businesslike methods. We plead guilty to the charge .... You and I have to act on the political platform from a spiritual side and, if this is done, we should then conquer the conquerors."[114]

Gandhi missed no opportunity to bring this message home to his countrymen. On many occasions, the crowds proved unmanageable at his meetings. Invariably, he would publicly upbraid them and their leaders for their conduct. He would say that there was no room for such methods in the country's non-violent struggle. A non-violent army demands, and should insist upon, he said, greater discipline, self-restraint and orderliness than necessary in an army equipped with arms.[115] With a novel kind of militancy, he pursued this cause and advocated the practice of drills by volunteers for the purpose of managing meetings, processions and crowds.[116]

Related to these ideas was Gandhi's belief that the human psyche was an integral whole and there could be no lack of correspondence between the private and public activities of a person. His conviction is contrary to the modern western belief that private morals are less relevant for public action and realms of conduct can be differentiated.[117] A public worker, in Gandhi's opinion, had to have integrity to be able to truly fulfil his role. He wrote, "A man whose desires are not under his control, who is incapable of the least self-discipline, is such a man fit to be in public life?"[118]

In Gandhi's view, a work ethic and discipline were important, and equally important were organization and efficiency. He believed that all activities associated with political and social life should reflect care and consideration for human life. He, therefore, disliked slovenliness in both private and public life. For instance, he was deeply concerned about the arrangements made for the annual sessions of the Congress, which left much to be desired. So, when the Congress session of 1921 was to be held in Ahmedabad, Gandhi gave detailed suggestions regarding the arrangements. Two factors were uppermost in his mind – simplicity and cleanliness. The two were not contradictory, as many modern people believed, he said. To prove this, he outlined the sanitary facilities that were to be arranged at the Congress session at minimum cost and with full consideration for hygiene. To implement the suggestions, one factor was essential – that all the delegates from Gujarat become volunteers and demand no service for themselves; given this, there would be no mismanagement, he said.[119]

Gandhi believed in commitment and sincere desire and had no patience with local leaders who expressed their inability to do social work because of lack of resources. He found this inexcusable because he was of the opinion that if there were selfless "leader–workers", men and money would never be in short supply. Expressing disapprobation in *Young India,* he said, "... many Congressmen do not care so much for constructive work as for excitement and work that will bring them into prominence without costing them much labour, if any at all. This mentality has to be changed before we can have a steady supply of workers." He reminded Congress subcommittees in the villages and talukas that they were absolutely autonomous, and urged these to collect money immediately and initiate reforms. The stress was on quiet and sincere work.[120] Any issue of social reform had to be taken up with tireless conviction and norms of selfless service had to be maintained for achieving progress and reform; Gandhi preached this not only at the level of principles, but also cited day to day examples that drove the point home more effectively.

His idolizing of ethical norms in private and public work had an important effect on those who participated in the national movement and became part of the tradition of national work.

Equality of Labour and Standard Wage

The principle of equality of all labour was firmly held by Gandhi and he thought of it in terms of an issue to change social norms and mentality. He set up his ashram with this ideal and attempted to implement it through the various organizations he formed for public work. Closely related to the principle of equality of labour was his belief in a minimum standard wage. In a letter, he defined his views: "All types of social service, whether spinning or weaving or cleaning lavatories, should be valued at the rate of one anna per hour of work."[121]

But to enforce this principle on a general scale was, he knew, difficult, and even the All India Spinners Association (AISA), founded by him to promote khadi on a commercial scale, paid spinners one-sixth of the wage given to weavers and carders, as this was the traditional rate governed by prevailing prices. To remedy this state of affairs, he wrote in, *Harijan*, "The time has come for the association to equalize, if not also to stabilize, the prices of all labour regulated by it .... [I]f the doctrine of equality of wages for all productive labour is sound, the association must strive to approach the ideal as near as may be."[122] Gandhi's ideas may have been questioned on the grounds of wages for skilled and unskilled labour, but the issue which he obviously wished to emphasize was the value of labour, which often got lost in a hierarchical society.

Gandhi encountered the problem of implementing the doctrine of equality of wages for all productive labour in the All India Village Industries Association (AIVIA) and he made strenuous efforts to promote this concept. He founded AIVIA with the aim of bringing about the economic and social uplift of villages. It gave villagers incentives to produce the best handicrafts, markets for which were to be found by AIVIA. Even though a good deal of labour and skill was required, and in spite of his best efforts, Gandhi was dismayed to find that the wages of artisans were perforce very low because it was argued that the goods would otherwise be too dear for the buying public, who preferred cheap machine made goods.[123]

Gandhi focused a good deal of attention on the issue of a standard wage for artisans. On behalf of AIVIA, Gandhi prepared a questionnaire to be sent to its agents and others on the need for such a standard wage. This standard, he said, should be the same for both sexes for equal quantity of work. It could be based on an eight hour day with a prescribed minimum output. This wage would enter into the cost of the product and the price should be fixed in relation to this. Prices should be fixed for articles that did not enter into competition, but were chosen for their special virtues, which were appreciated by customers. The questions framed by him were, firstly, whether it was feasible to fix a minimum daily wage and ensure it to workers by fixing prices; secondly, whether an ultimate standard should be fixed and whether they should work towards it or whether they should start with a low minimum wage and then raise it as they proceeded; thirdly, on what basis the minimum wage should be arrived at and could they suggest a subsistence wage taking into consideration only food for the time being as clothing should be made by personal effort; and finally, would half an anna per hour be too low?[124]

Unfortunately for Gandhi, he did not get a very encouraging response from those to whom he sent the questionnaire. There was no general awareness about the need for a standard wage for artisans. One response from the agents was that consumers were mostly interested in buying goods cheap and were not concerned about whether the artisans got adequate return for their labour.

Gandhi was not cowed down by this attitude. He replied through *Harijan*: "The buying public has to be instructed to know the abject condition of the people. If we are to do justice to the toiling millions, we must render to them their due; we must pay them a wage that will sustain them; we must not take advantage of their helplessness and pay a wage that would hardly give them one full meal."[125] Gandhi's concern for adequate wages for labour, for the respectability and value of labour, for the discipline and ethics of work were pertinent issues, not altogether familiar or easily accepted in an inegalitarian social setup.

Economy of Resources

A social value that Gandhi epitomized, and the establishment of which he continually propagated, was the economizing of resources. He attached the greatest importance to the collection, conservation and proper utilization of public resources.

Gandhi became accustomed to handling large sums of public money from the time he began to organize the Natal Indian Congress in 1894. He took meticulous care to account for the smallest sums and insisted on giving receipts. But instead of having receipt books and reports printed, he ran them off on a cyclostyling machine in his office because he knew that in public work, at times, minor expenses absorbed large amounts of money. "Such economy," he wrote, "is essential for every organization, and yet I know that it is not always exercised."[126]

He also disapproved of the practice of sending greeting cards and messages and suggested that the time and money spent on them could be better devoted to constructive activities.[127] He also advocated the use of old envelopes by pasting slips of paper on the writing and thus saving the money on additional stationery.[128] His philosophy of wasting nothing that could be used finds expression in an interesting rule of the ashram, which reads: "The split twigs used for tooth brushing should be washed well and collected in a pot. When they dry up, they should be used for starting a fire, the idea being that nothing which can be used should be thrown away."[129]

Gandhi also endeavoured to regulate public expenditure. He would urge every local unit of the Congress and the various reception committees to scrutinize every item of expenditure.[130] Once, while he was touring Malabar, Gandhi came to know that 50 per cent of the purse collected for Harijans was spent on feeding his entourage. He expressed his sense of outrage and shame in a public speech and said, "I assure you that I do not want a single convenience which cannot be cheaply supplied."[131] He reproached all those responsible for the lapse. He asserted that neglect or carelessness on the part of trustees – and everyone connected with the movement was a trustee – amounted to a crime,[132] as they contravened the ideals of simplicity, economy and responsibility towards society and the country.

One of the important items of the Fundamental Rights Resolution passed by the Congress in February 1931 was the resolution limiting the salary of government servants to not more than Rs 500 per month or Rs 6,000 per year. This was in stark contrast to the enormous salaries paid by the British government to its civil servants. Gandhi hoped to establish some correspondence between the modes of life of the government servants and the masses. He even appealed to the business classes and professionals to remodel their lives in keeping with the public interest.[133]

That Gandhi also understood the importance of preserving a natural environment is apparent in his answer to a request that an orchard of the ashram be uprooted because it was a useless investment. He wrote, "An orchard always increases the value of the land, helps the soil to retain moisture and cools the air. This is a universal experience."[134]

For Gandhi, conservation of natural resources was part of his unified outlook on life in which the balanced functioning of the various parts helped in maintaining the integrity of the whole. This fact is recognized in a statement of Dr Indu Tikekar, renowned ecologist and second in command of the Chipko[135] movement: "We Chipkoites are warriors of Gandhiji. We are not fighting for any 'ism', but for the establishment of an egalitarian society based on fundamental unity and oneness of life."[136] Gandhi's attempt was to infuse new values and new attitudes into a society suffering from the degradation of imperial enslavement and he paid meticulous attention to almost all aspects of social activity.

Trusteeship in Action

Gandhi was the first national leader to demand publicly that the rich classes should do their duty towards those less fortunate than themselves. He used every forum to convey this message and he got a good response to it. His doctrine of trusteeship spelt out the duty of the rich – that they should voluntarily surrender their superfluous wealth in trust for the poor. It was during Gandhi's time that the Tatas, the Bajajs, the Birlas and others contributed substantially to many national causes.

On a tour of south India, Gandhi appealed to the rich Chetti community to form a union for the common welfare and for the welfare of the peasantry that lived in their midst. He asked them to alter their lavish lifestyle and adopt a simple, clean life and, thus, save on wasteful expenditure. He warned them against spending foolishly on dubious charities and innumerable temple trusts and feasts for the poor as a salve to their conscience. In his opinion, the greatest charity that they could do at the time was to promote khadi, which would provide work and sustenance to the starving villagers of India. They could, if they wished, finance and organize the whole of the khadi movement in Tamil Nadu, if not in all of India.[137]

Rich people with a sense of social responsibility could, he wrote, shoulder several other tasks of national importance. There was urgent need for good dairies and tanneries in the country for, even though the raw materials for both were in abundant supply, they fell to waste through sheer ignorance and superstition. There was also vast scope for social service in trying to ameliorate the lot of the untouchables. By taking up such work, the privileged classes could come closer to the masses and pave the way for a more just society. "I am most anxious," he wrote, "to bridge the gulf between the rich people of India and its paupers. I see no way of finding abiding happiness for this land unless there is a living bond created between these two."[138]

One of the issues of social change that disturbed Gandhi greatly was the lack of a sense of hygiene among the people. Indians could learn a great deal in this matter from Europeans who had, he wrote, deduced an elaborate code of sanitation from the principles laid down in their great religious works. The Indians did not implement such measures even though they knew of them. Gandhi suggested the formation of useful sanitary associations, whose members would deem it a privilege to take up the broom, the shovel and the bucket.[139] Boys and girls who desired to join the national movement could begin with the work of sanitation, he asserted. The modern public toilet facility, Sulabh Shauchalaya, appears to be the answer to this problem.

Another issue that stirred Gandhi deeply was the need for a radical change in the diet of the masses so that their health and, consequently, the quality of their lives would improve. This was one of the main themes emphasized by him in *Harijan*. He wrote, "Since the economic reorganization of villages has been commenced with food reform, it is necessary to find out the simplest and cheapest foods that would enable villagers to regain lost health."[140] With this in mind, he highlighted the individual properties and values of fresh green leaves and salad vegetables in the diet, especially those that grew wild or at least very easily. He also described the way in which they should be washed carefully and prepared for consumption.[141] He explained the importance of eating unpolished rice, whole wheat and gur, rather than their milled forms, which had gained popularity.

So great was Gandhi's concern for a healthy diet that he would make personal experiments in diet reform and then record their results and publicize them. He also obtained the conclusions reached by organizations concerned with the science of nutrition and published these in his journals. One of these was that "a well balanced diet need not cost more than Rs 4 per month".[142] This information was given to him by Dr Akroyd, director of nutrition research at Coonoor, who also gave him the details of such a diet. Other bodies that sent him the results of their research were the Bombay Health Association and the Baroda State Food Survey Office. One important leaflet dealt with soybeans, detailing where they were to be had, how they should be sown and the ways in which they could be cooked.[143] One can easily imagine the potential value of such literature.

One of the biggest drawbacks in the field of dietary reform in India was, Gandhi knew well, the acute shortage of wholesome milk in the country. In order to deal with this problem and also to prevent cruelty to cattle, he advocated that dairy farming should become the monopoly of the municipality in every city.[144] The merits of such a scheme can be debated, but one cannot deny the crying need for some sort of systematization of milk supply in most parts of India, as has been accomplished in the four decades since 1970.

Gandhi provided a strong fillip to the movement for the uplift of tribal and semi-tribal people. These people form a significant percentage of the population of the country and their problems were an important social issue. A.V. Thakkar, better known as Thakkar Bapa, was a close friend and associate of Gandhi and it was due to Gandhi's constant encouragement that he spent his whole life doing social service among the tribals of central India. In fact, Thakkar Bapa once expressed his keenness to undertake other responsibilities in addition to tribal uplift work, but Gandhi rebuked him by saying that ambitious plans were of no use and his own cause was big enough for a lifetime.

Gandhi sponsored the first conference of backward communities, such as the Kaliparaj and Bhils. Common issues were discussed freely at the conference. In his Gujarati weekly, *Navajivan*, Gandhi wrote, "Excellent work is being done among both these communities .... We should pray that there should be an awakening among both the communities and that they should join in serving the country. It is not a small service to humanity in becoming human ourselves."[145] Gandhi was the inspiration for the successful mobilization of the Kaliparaj people during the Bardoli Satyagraha of 1928.[146]

Mention must also be made of Gandhi's association with the cause of the physically handicapped. In 1915, he inaugurated a small school for the deaf and the dumb in Ahmedabad and undertook to run it for their benefit. He requested the wealthy people of the city to set up many such schools and demonstrate their thankfulness to God for the gifts of speech and hearing. He was aware that not even a fraction of the afflicted were cared for in India and the most the public did was to give them alms, which only aggravated the problem because it turned many of them into idlers. Some were made to work like slaves. Their main need, he felt, was suitable education and skills, which would enable them to become self-reliant. He said, "Let the educated class make money, but instead of amassing wealth for themselves, they should give its benefits generously to others – this is my humble prayer."[147]

Some of the issues that Gandhi raised, such as eradication of untouchability and establishment of self-esteem of various levels in the social order, vocational education, economic self-sufficiency, communal harmony, according women equal position in society, equality of all productive labour, and the maintenance of high moral standards in public and private life, are burning questions even today and demand positive action.

Notes

1. *CWMG*, Volume 11, p. 196.
2. *CWMG*, Volume 4, p. 161.
3. Ibid., p. 165.
4. *CWMG*, Volume 18, p. 378.
5. Ibid., Volume 18, p. 216.
6. *CWMG*, Volume 21, pp. 39, 40.
7. Ibid.
8. Ibid.
9. Ibid., p. 40.
10. *CWMG*, Volume 25, p. 244.
11. *CWMG*, Volume 36, p. 316.
12. Ibid., p. 344.
13. *CWMG*, Volume 36, p. 422.
14. Ibid.
15. Ibid.
16. *CWMG*, Volume 42, pp. 7–8.
17. *CWMG*, Volume 13, p. 261.
18. *CWMG*, Volume 22, p. 177.
19. Ibid.
20. Ibid., p. 178.
21. *CWMG*, Volume 32, p. 475.
22. *CWMG*, Volume 34, p. 51.
23. *SWMG*, Volume 4, p. 348.
24. *CWMG*, Volume 4, 196.
25. Ibid., p. 200.
26. Ibid., p. 195.

27. Ibid., p. 198.
28. Ibid., p. 201.
29. *CWMG*, Volume 16, p. 226.
30. *CWMG*, Volume 25, p. 153.
31. *CWMG*, Volume 61, p. 33.
32. *CWMG*, Volume 22, p. 325.
33. *CWMG*, Volume 16, p. 187.
34. Ibid., p. 189.
35. Ibid., p. 187.
36. Ibid., p. 188.
37. *CWMG*, Volume 16, p. 190.
38. *CWMG*, Volume 13, p. 419.
39. Ibid., p. 420.
40. Ibid.
41. *CWMG*, Volume 14, pp. 120, 121.
42. The Hindi Sahitya Sammelan, mooted by a conference called at Varanasi in 1910 by the Kashi Nagari Prachirini Sabha, at the initiative of Madan Mohan Malviya and other leading members of the Sabha, began functioning as a permanent body in Allahabad from 1911. For an excellent account of the founding and work of the Sammelan, see Francesca Orsini, *The Hindi Public Sphere 1920–40: Language and Literature in the Age of Nationalism* (New Delhi: Oxford University Press, 2002).
43. For an English rendering of Gandhi's seminal address to the Eighth Session of the Sammelan, see *CWMG*, Volume 14, pp. 292–7.
44. *CWMG*, Volume 15, p. 242.
45. *CWMG*, Volume 35, p. 58.
46. *CWMG*, Volume 38, pp. 329–30.
47. Ibid., p. 65.
48. *CWMG*, Volume 61, pp. 31–2.
49. Ibid., pp. 32–3.
50. Ibid., p. 27.
51. Ibid., p. 29.
52. Ibid.
53. *CWMG*, Volume 20, p. 90.

54. *CWMG*, Volume 24, p. 152.
55. Ibid., pp. 152–3.
56. Ibid.
57. *CWMG*, Volume 25, p. 179.
58. Ibid.
59. *CWMG*, Volume 24, p. 141.
60. *CWMG*, Volume 32, p. 474.
61. Ibid., pp. 474–5.
62. *CWMG*, Volume 14, pp. 75–6.
63. Ibid., pp. 76–7.
64. *CWMG*, Volume 20, p. 320.
65. Ibid.
66. Ibid.
67. *CWMG*, Volume 28, p. 412.
68. *CWMG*, Volume 20, p. 507.
69. Ibid., pp. 509–10.
70. Ibid., p. 177.
71. Ibid.
72. *CWMG*, Volume 54, p. 65.
73. Ibid.
74. Ibid., p. 66.
75. *CWMG*, Volume 34, pp. 529–30.
76. Ibid.
77. *CWMG*, Volume 41, p. 32.
78. *CWMG*, Volume 61, pp. 31–2.
79. *CWMG*, Volume 51, p. 111.
80. *CWMG*, Volume 61, Appendix II, pp. 463–5.
81. *CWMG*, Volume 51, p. 139.
82. *CWMG*, Volume 53, p. 132.
83. Ibid., p. 14.
84. *CWMG*, Volume 53, p. 203.
85. Ibid., p. 471.
86. *CWMG*, Volume 14, p. 61.
87. *CWMG*, Volume 15, p. 189, note 1.

88. Ibid.
89. Ibid., p. 441.
90. The 11th day of the bright half of the Hindi month of Ashadh, roughly corresponding to July.
91. Literally, a period of four months – the term signifies a vow of fasting and semi-fasting during the four monsoon months.
92. *CWMG*, Volume 15, p. 443.
93. Ibid., pp. 444–5.
94. *CWMG*, Volume 50, pp. 90–1.
95. *CWMG*, Volume 42, p. 5.
96. Ibid., p. 255.
97. *CWMG*, Volume 20, p. 441.
98. *CWMG*, Volume 56, p. 10.
99. *CWMG*, Volume 34, p. 32.
100. *CWMG*, Volume 60, p. 125.
101. *CWMG*, Volume 31, p. 314.
102. *CWMG*, Volume 23, p. 524.
103. Ibid., pp. 188–9.
104. *CWMG*, Volume 28, p. 116.
105. *CWMG*, Volume 41, pp. 179–80.
106. *CWMG*, Volume 34, p. 481.
107. *CWMG*, Volume 46, p. 75.
108. *CWMG*, Volume 33, p. 44.
109. *CWMG*, Volume 24, p. 278.
110. *CWMG*, Volume 33, p. 45.
111. *CWMG*, Volume 62, p. 436.
112. *CWMG*, Volume 58, p. 449.
113. *CWMG*, Volume 24, p. 399.
114. *CWMG*, Volume 13, p. 82.
115. *CWMG*, Volume 21, p. 140.
116. *CWMG*, Volume 14, p. 77.
117. Rudolph and Rudolph, *Modernity of Tradition*, pp. 193–4.
118. *CWMG*, Volume 21, p. 51.
119. Ibid., p. 52.

120. *CWMG*, Volume 40, p. 390-1.
121. *CWMG*, Volume 50, p. 25.
122. *CWMG*, Volume 61, p. 233.
123. Ibid., p. 247-9.
124. Ibid.
125. Ibid., p. 250.
126. *CWMG*, Volume 39, p. 125.
127. *CWMG*, Volume 16, p. 174, 247.
128. *CWMG*, Volume 44, p. 105.
129. Rudolph and Rudolph, *Modernity of Tradition*, p. 225.
130. *CWMG*, Volume 33, p. 121; Volume 46, pp. 160–2.
131. *CWMG*, Volume 57, p. 27.
132. Ibid.
133. *CWMG*, Volume 47, pp. 227–8.
134. *CWMG*, Volume 49, p. 56.
135. A public satyagraha kind of movement to protect trees from commercial logging and preserve forest ecology begun in the Garhwal region of Uttarakhand.
136. *The Times of India*, New Delhi, 25 April 1988, p. 1.
137. *CWMG*, Volume 35, pp. 19–21.
138. Ibid., p. 22.
139. *CWMG*, Volume 28, pp. 461, 462.
140. *CWMG*, Volume 60, p. 229.
141. Ibid.
142. *CWMG*, Volume 62, p. 26.
143. Ibid., pp. 26–7.
144. *CWMG*, Volume 65, p. 320.
145. *CWMG*, Volume 29, p. 337; Volume 26, pp. 15, 17, 18, 22.
146. *CWMG*, Volume 36, pp. 412, 443
147. *CWMG*, Volume 37, pp. 242–3.

CHAPTER 5

Instruments of Social Change

Gandhi's analysis of the instruments of social change is quite unique to him. He did not accept the Marxist view that forces and relations of production – or the economic structure of a state or society – determine its social and ideological structure and any change in the former will automatically lead to change in the latter. Gandhi considered the human being superior to his environment and believed that he had the capacity to influence it on his own. For him, any individual who would use his will and moral strength could rise above his circumstances. Therefore, in Gandhi's analysis, besides specific methods and movements, it is quite often the individual in his personal capacity who is the instrument of social change.

Satyagraha

Basic to his philosophy of social and moral change was the technique of satyagraha or resistance through absolutely truthful means. Apart from this, there were special movements to spread the message of swadeshi, to remove untouchability, to promote village reconstruction and special efforts to enable women to take their due place in society, to establish communal harmony, to implement a revolutionary scheme of education and to reform the Indian National Congress to serve as an instrument of social and political change. Satyagraha was chosen as the starting point in the analysis because that was the quintessence of Gandhi's ideology. To quote him, "It is a force, which, if it became universal, would revolutionize social ideals."[1] Here, it will be considered as the means Gandhi employed all his life to solve various problems and conflicts in society.

Specifically, satyagraha is a method of resolving disputes through moral pressure. It is a force that, according to Gandhi, could be used at all levels of human interaction – political, social and domestic. He believed that genuine social and economic equality could only be attained through the extensive use of this method and ordinary people could easily adopt it provided they had dedicated leaders. In this context, he wrote, "True democracy or the swaraj of the masses can never come through untruthful and violent means for the simple reason that the natural corollary to their use would be to remove all opposition through the suppression or extermination of the antagonists. That does not make for individual freedom. Individual freedom can have the fullest play only under a regime of unadulterated ahimsa."[2]

It would be worthwhile to briefly discuss the three localized satyagraha campaigns that Gandhi led between 1917 and 1918. The first of these, in Champaran district of Bihar in April 1917, was in response to an urgent demand from the peasants there for mediation in a case of extreme agrarian exploitation. As the details are well known, they need only a brief summing up here. The European indigo planters forced the petty farmers of Champaran to grow indigo on the best portion of their land for a paltry consideration through a system called *tin-kathiya*. Where indigo cultivation had stopped because it ceased to be a commercial proposition for the planters, the peasants were made to pay heavy damages or compensation in the form of *tawan* or *sharabheshi*.[3] Though there was great resentment among the farmers, they were helpless against the planters who had the support of the local government.

Soon after Gandhi arrived in Champaran, the district magistrate ordered him to leave the district immediately, but Gandhi disobeyed the order saying he was compelled by the higher law of his conscience.[4] He suffered a brief period of incarceration as a result. After his release, he carried out a vigorous and thorough investigation of the charges against the planters with the help of local pleaders and volunteers. The peasants were solidly behind him as was proved by the thousands who came to give their statements in spite of threats from the planters.[5] They were carefully instructed by Gandhi in the principles of satyagraha, especially regarding the value of non-violence and firm adherence to their demands. As Gandhi desired his enquiry to appear genuine, the planters and officials were allowed free access to the proceedings. He also kept the district authorities constantly informed of his activities. The upshot of his campaign was that the government was impelled to appoint a committee of enquiry in which Gandhi served as the peasants' representative. All his charges were accepted and the *tin-kathiya* system was abolished.[6]

There are several points to be noted in this whole exercise. The emphasis on fair means was obvious and firm, but it was the non-violent resistance to oppression that achieved the objective. Despite the mass mobilization in the area, there was no incidence of violence by the peasants, which naturally added to the credibility of the technique of satyagraha. The self-confidence of the peasants was greatly enhanced for they realized that there was a plausible solution to their problems through a method that involved no violent confrontation with authority.[7] For Gandhi, this was only the beginning as he saw in Champaran a reflection of the true condition of the peasantry in India.[8] Their extreme poverty and backwardness motivated him to take steps towards improving their social conditions.

The greatest need, he perceived, was for all-round education, both for children and adults. He could now rely on an enthusiastic response and, with the help of local people, in November 1917, he set up several schools, where the teachers were all volunteers with independent means, many of them from Mumbai and Gujarat.[9] Gandhi also invited the help of the local authorities in the task, which he felt would benefit everyone. With regard to the main purpose of these schools, he wrote, "The chief thing aimed at is contact of the children with men and women of culture and unimpeachable moral character. That to me is education."[10]

There was also a programme of adult education aimed at women who lived in purdah and the chief content of this education was to teach the elementary rules of hygiene and the advantages of joint action for the promotion of community welfare, such as the making of proper village roads, the sinking of wells, and the construction and maintenance of village latrines. Free medical aid was also given as far as was possible by some of the volunteers who were trained in the work. The secretary of the Servants of India Society, Dr M.S. Dev, an eminent surgeon and physician, came from Pune with three volunteers to help in the work. Gandhi left the work among the women to his wife, Kasturba.[11]

Through his social activities in Champaran district, Gandhi was able to highlight two factors important for those seeking social change through satyagraha. He showed that the trust of the local masses had to be gained by identifying with their problems and issues, and that material resources for voluntary work would not be lacking once the credibility of a cause was established.

However, the Gujarat (Kheda) Satyagraha was more important from the point of view of raising peasant consciousness and realization of the latent strength of the Indian peasantry. Gandhi stated the significance of the campaign in the following manner: "The movement is intended to assert the right of the people to be effectively heard in matters concerning themselves."[12] The Kheda campaign began in March 1918 and bore all the classic characteristics of Gandhi's satyagraha technique. The cause was the government's refusal to grant a remission in revenue even though the peasants claimed their crops had failed. After carrying out a thorough examination, Gandhi found the peasants' demand to be just and wrote to the local authorities requesting suspension of revenue.[13] When this request was not granted, he advised the peasants to simply refuse to pay the revenue and prepare stoically for the consequences.[14]

There were several important features of this campaign. As satyagraha demanded total commitment to truthful means for pursuing a cause, Gandhi believed that the taking of a public pledge would greatly enhance the resolve of a people undertaking satyagraha. He, therefore, instituted the system of taking a pledge publicly and formulated the pledge on behalf of the peasants. It was a solemn declaration that they would not pay the government dues and would undergo all the suffering this might entail.[15]

The pledge was taken by most peasants in all the villages of the district. Gandhi personally toured the villages, propagating his message of firm non-violent resistance and tried to keep up the morale of the peasants, who suffered silently as they saw their goods auctioned and cattle sold off. He posted circulars about the situation to the villages concerned and wrote extensively to the newspapers, explaining the issues involved.[16]

A very important plank of the campaign was Gandhi's direct appeal to the women in the villages. He urged them to fully support their men in the fight for justice and self-respect and bear with patience whatever loss was incurred.[17] As in Champaran, in Kheda too, Gandhi was assisted by a band of committed volunteers who helped him sustain the tempo of the campaign. His written instructions to them illustrate the importance he attached to the values of non-violence, honesty and courtesy.[18]

Finally on 3 June 1918, the government reluctantly granted relief to the peasants. The campaign ended, but Gandhi was led to remark, "The above orders have not been passed either with generosity or with the heart in them."[19] This fact apart, there is no doubt about the psychological impact of this struggle. The national press carried frequent reports of it and Gandhi and satyagraha became familiar topics of discussion throughout the country. It was recognized that even the poor and backward could, if they wanted, get justice from the rulers without force of any kind, provided they were prepared to suffer.

The satyagraha campaign that Gandhi undertook in February 1918 in Ahmedabad was also significant because it defined a new and harmonious relationship between capital and labour. The crux of the dispute between the textile industrialists and their workers was that while the workers demanded a 50 per cent wage increase, the mill owners were prepared to grant only

20 per cent. Gandhi was asked to intervene by Ambalal Sarabhai,[20] a mill owner and a friend of Gandhi. Arbitration proceedings had started, but the workers in some factories struck work. In retaliation, the mill owners cancelled arbitration and gave the workers the option of accepting a 20 per cent increase or being discharged after being paid their due wages. The workers chose the latter and the mill owners declared a lockout on 22 February 1918.[21]

On his own initiative, Gandhi undertook to lead the workers and get them their just demands. After a survey of the wage scales in Mumbai and Ahmedabad, Gandhi persuaded the workers to accept a 35 per cent increase in wages as a fair demand,[22] but the mill owners refused to grant this.

Gandhi believed that if the workers could demonstrate that they were prepared to suffer all hardships and stick to their demand and not use violence or threats of any kind, they would win their case. He asked all of them to take a public pledge to this effect.[23] Among others, Gandhi received wholehearted support from Ambalal's sister, Anasuyaben, who was also a confidante of the workers.[24] Through public meetings, visits to workers' homes and instructive leaflets, Gandhi and his co-workers tried to drive home to the striking workers the significance of their struggle – the fundamental role of workers in society, the question of their rights and self-respect, and the need to remain non-violent and maintain themselves through other means, such as manual labour.[25]

In spite of Gandhi's efforts, the workers began to lose hope and some of them returned to work when the lockout was lifted on 13 March 1918. Gandhi realized that only through a drastic personal example would he be able to restrain the remaining workers from betraying their pledge. Therefore, he declared his resolve to fast from 15 March till either the workers got a 35 per cent increase in wages or they simply repudiated their pledge.[26] Apart from its immediate positive effect on the workers, the fast put great moral pressure on the mill owners, some of whom got ready to concede the workers' demand. But Gandhi regarded this concession as unfortunate and asked them to be guided in their decision by their sense of justice, rather than concern for him.[27] Gandhi's suggestion of appointing an arbitrator was accepted by the mill owners and a settlement was arrived at on 18 March, whereby the workers were granted a 35 per cent increase in wages.[28]

Three important principles were illustrated by the Ahmedabad satyagraha campaign. First, serious industrial disputes could be settled by peaceful arbitration, rather than militant protests. Second, the two classes of capitalists and workers were interdependent and could work in harmony. Third, wealthy industrialists could behave as their workers' 'trustees'. Gandhi's intervention in the Ahmedabad textile mill workers' strike had a significant impact on labour relations in the Ahmedabad region. In 1920, Gandhi organized the Ahmedabad Textile Labour Association, which became one of the most powerful labour unions in the country. It was based on the system of joint arbitration and conciliation. Its constitution provided for recourse to strikes only in case of failure of arbitration. The association contributed to a genuine improvement in the social conditions of the workers through comprehensive welfare measures. From 1937, the association also trained its members in a supplementary occupation to provide sustenance for rainy days, as, for example, during a lockout.[29]

Gandhi's experience of the three localized satyagraha campaigns discussed above was the prelude to similar campaigns led by him at the all India level. The efficacy and credibility of this instrument of change was established in both the agrarian and industrial spheres. Later, it was to prove itself also in the political arena. Just as the three local campaigns left deep impressions in their areas of operation, the all India satyagraha campaigns between 1919 and 1942 led to extensive changes in India's overall character. From being a thoroughly backward and deeply divided society, there emerged in India widespread social and political consciousness, which penetrated the countryside on a major scale.[30]

Basic Education

Apart from satyagraha, which aimed at the peaceful resolution of conflicts, the foremost among the other instruments of change, in

Gandhi's view, was education. It will be relevant to examine some of the concrete schemes of education that Gandhi conceptualized and implemented with the help of his associates and also those schemes that he visualized for the future.

To exemplify his concept of "real education", Gandhi set up a school through voluntary effort and he hoped that its success would help in obtaining public support, including that of the government. His first experimental school, the National Gujarati School, was established in Ahmedabad in 1917. The basic principle, in his own words, was that the education would be "physical, intellectual and religious".[31] By physical education, he meant that there would be training in agriculture, hand weaving, carpentry, smithy, drill and civil defence. It would also include some basic instruction on how to maintain bodily health. Intellectual training would include a study of Gujarati, Marathi, Hindi and Sanskrit as compulsory subjects and Urdu, Tamil and Bengali as optional. English would not be taught in the first three years. Mathematics would be taught and would include instruction in book keeping and weights and measures. History, geography and the elements of astronomy and chemistry would also be taught. Regarding instruction in religion, he wrote that the pupils would be made familiar with general ethical principles, especially truth and non-violence, and learn from the conduct of the teachers.

Gandhi's earliest scheme of education had much to commend itself as it had special value for the state of the country, but it was too idealistic to be implemented fully. Teachers were hard to get, enough funds were not available and there were not sufficient numbers inspired to organize such schools. So, progress was slow.

In 1921, at the height of the Non-Cooperation Movement, Gandhi established the first national university in Ahmedabad, the Gujarat Vidyapith. He said the principal objective of the Gujarat Vidyapith was to prepare educated workers of character and conscientiousness, who would help in the conduct of the swaraj and connected movements. As the institution was set up to further the objective of non-cooperation with the government, including its educational system, Gandhi decided that the

Gujarat Vidyapith would not seek any aid from the government and, in keeping with the creed of the Non-Cooperation Movement, it would always uphold the principles of truth and non-violence. From this, it naturally followed that the Gujarat Vidyapith would not recognize the custom of untouchability in any form. The students would spin regularly, even if for a short while, and wear khadi habitually so that, on the one hand, they would boost the production of swadeshi cloth and thereby promote the country's self-reliance and, on the other, they would identify with the lives of the overwhelming majority in the villages of India. To pre-empt an artificial division between the classes and the masses, the medium of instruction would be the language of the province. To promote national integration, the learning of the national language – Hindi-Hindustani in both Devanagari and Persian scripts – would be a compulsory part of the curriculum. Manual training was to receive equal importance with intellectual training and only such occupations would be taught as were necessary for the good life of the nation. The change in attitude and perspectives that Gandhi hoped to achieve was the identification of the interests of the classes and the masses, compatibility in home and school, and a new perception of educational aims, including value for dignity of labour and lack of ambition for making money.

Gandhi said religious instruction should be a part of the curriculum so long as it was in consonance with truth and non-violence. There should be complete tolerance of all established religions. Physical exercise and training should be a compulsory part of the curriculum for the physical well-being of the nation. Gandhi's wish was to make this kind of national education a living force, so as to cover every village in Gujarat, and finally to produce social workers who would serve the country in all its villages.[32] It is obvious that national service was an indispensable part of education as far as Gandhi was concerned.

The Gujarat Vidyapith received a good response from the people initially, but then, the enrolment numbers began declining. To remedy this, in February 1928, Gandhi reorganized it by shifting the management from the senate to a board of trustees. This had a positive effect on its functioning. Other national institutions such as the Kashi Vidyapith and the Jamia Millia Islamia (initially in Aligarh, but later shifted to Delhi) were set up along the lines of the Gujarat Vidyapith in many provinces in the 1920s and they maintained a viable existence even without government help. After independence, they received support from the government.

Gandhi wanted to make education self-supporting because he saw that the problem of obtaining adequate funds was never going to go away. His scheme of self-supporting education gained greater importance when the Congress, under his influence, accepted prohibition as one of its goals – this cut off a major financial source for education as the excise on liquor had customarily financed state education. The concept of self-supporting education was translated into action after 1937, when the Congress came into power in seven provinces.

Gandhi's scheme is described as Basic Education or the Wardha Scheme of Education. Explaining its underlying principle, Gandhi said: "Taken as a whole, a vocation or vocations are the best medium for the all-round development of a boy or a girl and, therefore, the syllabus should be woven round vocational training, primary education thus conceived as a whole is bound to be self-supporting, even though for the first or even the second year's course, it may not be wholly so."[33]

He explained that every handicraft had to be taught not merely mechanically, but scientifically so that the child would know the why and wherefore of every process.[34] By this means, subjects such as history, geography and arithmetic would be partially or wholly covered, he believed. Language and grammar would also be associated with the crafts. He described the course as primary education and it would extend over a period of seven years. The vocations would include all the processes of hand manufacture of cotton, wool and silk products, embroidery, tailoring, papermaking, cutting, book binding, cabinet making, toy making and gur making. These, he felt, could be learnt easily without much capital outlay.[35] Dignity of labour also received emphasis during this process of learning.

The products manufactured in the schools were to be bought by the state at prices fixed by it. In this way, education would be self-financing. The boys and girls trained at these schools would be guaranteed employment by the state in the vocations they had learnt.[36] When he was asked whether Basic Education would be different in rural and urban areas, Gandhi replied that he did not visualize any fundamental difference. In fact, he said, it was time cities made good their debt to the villages from which they had drawn sustenance thus far. To establish what he called a "healthy moral relationship" between cities and villages, the vocations through which the city children would receive their education ought to be directly related to the requirements of villages, just as village production had always been geared to the requirements of cities.[37]

An obvious criticism that one could make of the Basic Education scheme was the high degree of state control visualized in it. But Gandhi foresaw far reaching social consequences if the scheme was implemented in the right spirit. It would, he said, check the progressive decay of our villages and lay the foundation of a more just social order in which there was no unnatural division between the haves and the have-nots and everybody would be assured of a living wage and the right to freedom. All this, he believed, would be accomplished without a bloody class war or colossal capital expenditure on extensive mechanization.[38] Gandhi was of the opinion that women could play an important role as teachers in this scheme. The women he had in mind were not needy women looking for jobs, but patriotic women with the leisure and zeal to serve the people and their country.[39]

The first school under the Basic Education scheme was set up in April 1938 at Wardha under the aegis of the Hindustani Talimi Sangh. It was called the Vidyamandir Training School. On 21 April, the students took a solemn pledge that bound them to serve without a break for 25 years on a monthly salary of Rs 15. Out of the 5,000 applications received, 166 were granted admission.[40] During 1938 and 1939, several Basic Education schools were set up and Gandhi writes that the economic results of the spread went far beyond their expectations.[41]

In October 1939, the first Conference of Basic National Education was held at Pune to review the progress of the scheme in its first year of working., The secretary of the Hindustani Talimi Sangh, E.W. Aryanayakam, said that the conference and the exhibition (on Basic Education) had finally lifted the scheme above the realm of controversy and proved to the educational world that the claims of the new education system about the fundamental principles, content and methods were justified by a year's experience of work with the teachers and children.[42]

After independence, however, the economic development of India took a turn different from that visualized by Gandhi, so the necessary political will and faith required for Basic Education was no longer available. As a result, the scheme languished after the first five or six years and the few schools that continued under the rubric of Basic schools remained so in name alone. Public opinion could not be mobilized adequately nor did the state structure remain supportive.

Gandhi at the convocation ceremony of the Thackersey University for Women (SNDT) in Mumbai on 1 July 1939

Gandhi studying leprosy germs at Segaon in December 1939

On the subject of higher education, Gandhi's considered opinion in later years was that it should be left to private enterprise and that it should meet national requirements, whether in the various industries, technical arts or fine arts. The state universities should, he said, be purely examining bodies, self-supported through the fees charged for examinations.[43]

In conclusion, it may be said that Gandhi considered education not an end in itself, but a means to an end. It was seen as an instrument to serve the purpose of the all round development of individual personalities and the needs of the nation.

Anti-Untouchability Movement

The issue of untouchability assumed a truly national dimension after Gandhi offered unqualified support to the Vykom Satyagraha launched by some local leaders of Travancore in modern day Kerala, who were trying to remove the ban on the entry of untouchables on the roads surrounding the Vykom temples. Through *Young India*, Gandhi informed the country about the sufferings of the *satyagrahis* and, soon after that, the cause was taken up by the national press.[44] In March 1925, he went personally to Vykom, addressed public meetings and held discussions with the leaders of the orthodox section who were opposing the campaign. The satyagraha bore fruit and, in January 1926, the Travancore government announced the opening of the public roads around the temples to the untouchables. Through the press, Gandhi appealed to the Travancore government to go the full logical extent and insist on throwing open all public institutions, including temples, to the untouchables on the same terms as the rest of the population.[45]

At its Karachi session in March 1931, the Congress adopted the Resolution on Fundamental Rights drafted by Gandhi.[46] Relevant sections of it constituted a legal attack on the institution of untouchability. Section 4 declared that all "citizens are equal before law, irrespective of caste, creed or sex". Section 6 endowed all citizens with equal rights and duties with regard to wells, tanks, roads, schools and places of public interest maintained out of state or local funds or dedicated by private persons for the use of the general public. Section 10 decreed universal adult suffrage. These principled statements were later included in the Constitution of India.

The strongest impetus that the anti-untouchability movement received was from the heroic fast unto death Gandhi undertook against the implementation of the Communal Award on 20 September 1932 and its aftermath – the Poona or Yeravda Pact, as it came to be known. To quote him: "My politics are derived from my religion, If God has ordained death by starvation, I know that it will set the last seal on my political leadership. Nationalism will be the stronger for sacrificial death. The vast majority of the Indian community has instinctively recognized the correctness and implications of this fast."[47]

Gandhi described the Yeravda Pact, which was reached on 24 September after hectic negotiations, as "a generous gesture on all sides". As stated earlier, the pact gave larger representation to the Harijans on the legislative councils of the country than the Communal Award. Gandhi was well aware that it was merely a political settlement achieved partly as a result of his fast and only the beginning of the end of the untouchables' travails.

In order to better organize the campaign for the amelioration of the untouchables' condition, Gandhi set up a new body in October 1932. It was first named the All India Anti-Untouchability League and later renamed the Harijan Sevak Sangh.[48] Local branches of the body were set up in the provinces, while the central body was in Mumbai. Gandhi began to call the untouchables Harijans – a term not associated with the many derogatory and derisive words used for identifying them. Harijan meant "creation of God". Today, it is regarded as a patronizing term for the untouchables, who themselves prefer to be known as Dalits. However, although perhaps less politically correct in the current context, Gandhi never intended this word to have any kind of negative connotation.

The pattern of management of the Harijan Sevak Sangh highlights Gandhi's zeal to set up an organization that would help the Harijans in the most efficient manner. On the subject of a democratic structure, he said: "In an institution like ours, there is no room for election, democracy or anything of that sort .... To run an elective institution means expense and delay. Our aim is to distribute the funds among the Harijans with as little expenditure and delay as possible .... We are mere trustees and the trust descends to those whom we appoint .... And if we are to have the highest amount of efficiency, we have to select the best and the most honest workers.[49]

It is perhaps due to this attitude that Gandhi was sometimes misunderstood and accused of dictatorial ways, but his obvious anxiety was to achieve results with the least possible fuss.

Gandhi initiated the movement to open public temples to the untouchables and played a central role in the opening of the famous temple at Guruvayur in Kerala to the untouchables. In early 1932, he had declared his intention and that of another well-known *satyagrahi* leader of Kerala, K. Kelappan, to undertake a fast unto death from 1 January 1933 if the temple was not opened to everyone by then. This campaign bore the special marks of Gandhi's style of functioning. He suggested the carrying out of an open referendum of temple goers to elicit their opinion on the issue, and in this, he visualized a prominent role for women. In order that the referendum be absolutely above board, signatures should be taken, he wrote, "at public meetings in the presence of witnesses known to the signatories, with their full names, addresses and occupations, together with age and sex".[50] The women, he said, should undertake the work of conducting the referendum as they had good powers of persuasion. To quote him, the women should "convince the bona fide temple goers that true religion will open the hearts of the people and the gates of the temple to every human being and will brand no one as an outcaste".[51] Their cause, he said, would be obviously strengthened if they were able to recruit the local upper caste Namboodiri and Nair women of Malabar to lead the work.

The result of the referendum was momentous. A decisive majority of eligible voters expressed themselves in favour of the entry of Harijans to the Guruvayur temple.[52] The same procedure with the same result was followed for the opening of the Madurai temple.[53] In this way, a trend was established and, over the next few years, many famous temples opened their doors to the general public.[54] Gandhi was thus getting people actively involved and committed to the issue of eradication of untouchability. Exhortations and pleas would not have had the same effect as his strategy of involvement in action. A continuing commitment was ensured by Gandhi's wise understanding.

In early February 1933, Gandhi, with the help of G.D. Birla, R.V. Shastri and Mahadev Desai, brought out a weekly journal called *Harijan* in English and, by March, vernacular editions were also out. The chief purpose of the magazine was to carry out propaganda work for the removal of untouchability. The journal continued for many years even after Gandhi's death. It did not carry any advertisements because he wanted it to be self-supporting. Since it supplied a felt want, he claimed that its circulation should depend solely on subscriptions.[55] Again, one can see Gandhi's desire to get people actively interested and committed. It is not difficult to imagine that subscribers would begin to look upon the task of continuing the campaign as their own responsibility. This plan of getting more and more people actively involved was extended to other areas also. Gandhi gave his wholehearted support to a private donation scheme begun by a philanthropist of Mumbai to finance the higher education of selected Harijan boys. Thousands of rupees were collected under this scheme and a selection board was set up to screen the students' eligibility.[56]

On 1 August 1933, with the concurrence of his co-trustees, Gandhi dedicated the Sabarmati Ashram for the exclusive use of Harijans. The management and property were transferred to the central board of the Harijan Sevak Sangh. He laid down the following objectives for the new trust:

1. To settle on the ashram ground approved Harijan families;
2. To open a hostel for Harijan boys and girls with the liberty to take non-Harijans as well;
3. To conduct a technological department to teach all the processes of leather manufacture and shoe making; and
4. To use the premises as offices for the central board or the Gujarat provincial organizations and allied uses.[57]

As a result of Gandhi's work, important changes were effected in different parts of the country by various institutions and authorities for the uplift of the depressed classes. One of these was the resolution passed by the Nagpur University and the High School Board of the Central Provinces in October 1933, stating that no examination fees would be charged from students belonging to the depressed classes and the aboriginal tribes, until 1940 in the first case and five years in the others.[58]

The provincial and local branches of the Harijan Sevak Sangh tried to bring about significant reforms both in villages and cities, sometimes against great odds. Gandhi advised that a house to house collection of signatures to an anti-untouchability pledge be made and money contributions solicited. He undertook this task personally in Ahmedabad, where a Harijan girls' hostel was opened and every effort made to induce them to join.[59] The Mumbai branch spent a great deal of money on scholarships and ran three *chawls*, which provided accommodation for nearly 200 families. Gandhi offered suggestions for further relief work, like providing clean eating houses for Harijans, giving them employment in domestic service and in offices, and above all, providing them with greater facilities for education by voluntary workers of recognized status.[60]

During his tour of the country in 1934, Gandhi stressed the important role that local boards and municipalities could play in relieving the economic distress of Harijans and the lack of sanitation in their quarters.[61] This countrywide tour was wholly devoted to the cause of the Harijans.

An important opportunity for alleviating the distress of the depressed classes arose when the Congress party took office in seven out of 11 provinces in 1937. The party members were prevailed upon by the executive committee of the Harijan Sevak Sangh to vigorously undertake measures and programmes for the social and economic uplift of Harijans in their respective provinces.[62] In 1938, the Removal of Civil Disabilities Act was passed by the Madras legislature, which provided that no Harijan would be disabled from any social or public amenity. In the same year, the Madras legislature also passed the Malabar Temple Entry Act, which threw open the temples in Malabar to the untouchables. Gandhi expressed his hope that even the non-Congress provincial governments would undertake this work.

Though Gandhi was always conscious of the fact that exclusive institutions for Harijans would in a way perpetuate untouchability by maintaining segregation, he was also aware that waiting for such public opinion to emerge as would allow free entry of Harijans into public institutions was a long drawn out process. Therefore, for the sake of the untouchables' immediate benefit, he was prepared to recommend exclusive institutions for their proper education and training. Gandhi's dream of establishing an ideal industrial training school exclusively for Harijans was fulfilled to some extent in 1939, when he presided over the first convocation of such a school in Delhi, set up by the Harijan Sevak Sangh in 1936. It followed the system of education cum manual training, which included training in vocational subjects such as carpentry, tailoring, leatherwork and paper making. Twenty-one students passed out of the school that year. Gandhi's view was that in such an institution, the teacher–taught relationship ought to be that of the parent–child and, even after the students left, the superintendent should keep in contact with them to see that they faced no undue difficulty in pursuing their chosen tasks. Of all the activities of the Harijan Sevak Sangh, Gandhi lauded its educational activity in a home like this the most, for, to use his words, "if this institution throws up even a few boys of sterling worth who would give themselves to the service of the Harijans, they will solve the problem of untouchability in a most substantial manner".[63]

Gandhi received considerable financial aid from some business houses to carry on his reform work. One instance was the scheme of model schools for Harijans proposed by G.D. Birla, who was also president of the Harijan Sevak Sangh. Birla was of the opinion that the education provided so far to the Harijans in a few places was of an inferior kind and this only added to their inferiority complex. The need, he said, was to establish a few residential schools mainly, though not exclusively, for educating Harijan boys of a standard that would compare favourably in every respect with a well conducted public school. Personal attention to students should be a speciality, he said. Education should be imparted through the medium of the mother tongue and English should be taught as a second language. Another important element should be the teaching of useful handicrafts. The underlying idea, according to Birla, was that the boys should not feel the want of a college education. There would, of course, be no bar to such an education if they desired it. It was also hoped that equipped with this education, the boys would not find it difficult to earn an honest livelihood. It would be the duty of the board of the Harijan Sevak Sangh to place boys who so wished in particular places of employment. Finally, the education for the Harijans would be free.[64] Gandhi approved of this scheme wholeheartedly for he regarded such schools as "patent instruments for exorcising the demon of untouchability".[65]

Gandhi's contribution in ensuring justice and equity for Harijans in the Constitution of India cannot be undervalued. "The constitution which I could influence," he said, "would contain a provision making the observance of untouchability in any shape or form an offence. The so-called untouchables would have seats reserved for them in all elected bodies according to their population within the electoral area concerned."[66] Indeed, reservation of seats was established under the Yeravda Pact and Gandhi's relentless efforts created a climate for the state to accept the responsibility for improving the lot of this deprived section of society.

The Indian Constitution proclaimed in Article 17 the principle of equality to all citizens, irrespective of caste differences, and made discrimination on the basis of caste punishable in a court of law. The Untouchability Offences Act, 1955, enacted in pursuance of this principle of the Constitution, abolished the practice of untouchability and made it a punishable offence. Finally, the Hindu Marriage Act, 1956, removed the legal obstacles in inter-caste marriage. Article 46 of the Constitution makes it the responsibility of the state to promote with special care the educational and economic institutions of the weaker sections of people, in particular scheduled castes and scheduled tribes, and to protect them from social injustice and all forms of exploitation. Articles 330 and 332 provide for the reservation of seats for the scheduled castes and tribes in the Lower House of Parliament and the legislative assemblies of the states, respectively. Gandhi's ideas were, as can be seen, respected by the makers of the Constitution.

In concluding this section, it can be said that Gandhi made the removal of untouchability one of the chief planks of his programme for the resurgence of India. He attacked the injustice being done to a section of human beings at all levels – religious, social and political. He tried to give them dignity, education and political rights, and contributed effectively in the creation of a mass consciousness about this major problem.

Swadeshi Movement

A very significant instrument of social change, in Gandhi's view, was the precept and practice of swadeshi, which implied self-reliance and self-sufficiency at the level of the individual, the village and the nation. By following the swadeshi principle, the nation's confidence and prosperity could be assured. It would be appropriate to quote him on the rule of swadeshi: "Swadeshi is that spirit in us which restricts us to the use and service of our immediate surroundings to the exclusion of the more remote.

Thus, as for religion .... I must restrict myself to my ancestral religion ..., if I find it defective, I should serve it by purging it of its defects. In the domain of politics, I should make use of the indigenous institutions and serve them by curing them of their proved defects. In that of economics, I should use only those things that are produced by my immediate neighbours and serve those industries by making them efficient and complete where they might be found wanting. It is suggested that such swadeshi, if reduced to practice, will lead to the millennium.[67]

Thus, all Gandhi's wide ranging activities, whether in the sphere of Hindu–Muslim relations or the removal of untouchability or khadi and rural uplift, could be subsumed under his ideal of realizing swadeshi.

However, the importance of swadeshi in the economic field was the greatest, he said, because departure from the principle resulted in loss of independence and poverty for the nation. India was a case in point. To undo the evil was not difficult, provided the thinking portion of the community took the vow of swadeshi, even though observing it could cause considerable inconvenience for a time. It should be accepted as a religious discipline, he said. As a temporary measure, he was willing to confine swadeshi to a given set of articles.[68]

Gandhi did not just conceptualize the instruments of change, he also showed their efficacy by use. He began the manufacture of swadeshi cloth on a small experimental basis at the Sabarmati Ashram in 1917. He found five families who had been weavers till a few years ago and were willing to resume their occupation if they were given some help. The ashram supplied them with yarn and its volunteers took delivery of the cloth woven and paid them cash at the market rate.[69]

Gandhi's work and commitment attracted to him the resources of many wealthy and patriotic Indians. This enabled him to go ahead with many of his cherished programmes.[70] The khadi work at the ashram grew gradually, but steadily, and hundreds of men and women, many of them untouchables, found an independent vocation. Some segments of the business community in Mumbai helped Gandhi to extend the production and sale of swadeshi cloth. In June 1919, some philanthropic merchants set up the Pure Swadeshi Cloth Store in Mumbai, which offered for sale all types of cloth woven out of yarn spun from indigenous cotton, wool and silk. The proprietors, Narandas and Jerajani, vowed not to charge more than 5 per cent on the cost price as profit and no profit at all on cloth that was completely hand spun and hand woven.[71] Gandhi appealed to other merchants also to set up stores on such "purely patriotic lines". He asked for volunteers who would take up the work at the individual and group level and help produce swadeshi cloth. The most notable among those who helped him was Gangabehn Majumdar of Vijapur – she was instrumental in organizing the spinning wheel movement in Gujarat.[72]

Khadi activity received a great impetus during the Non-Cooperation Movement of 1920–22 because it was part of the constructive programme together with the boycott of foreign cloth. The charkha had been introduced in national schools and vigorous attempts were made to produce finer yarn that would attract a bigger market.[73] A unique feature of the programme during the non-cooperation days was Gandhi's appeal to established mill owners and cloth merchants to help make the swadeshi movement a success. They should see that middlemen did not exploit the people, he said.[74] His message to the big cloth merchants who sold mainly imported cloth was: "Swaraj means that you and I put our country's trade before ours. The appeal to you to refrain from importing foreign cloth is in other words an appeal to subordinate your individual gain to the country's." They should instead aim at making the country self-sufficient in cloth by organizing hand spinning and hand weaving on an extended scale. His appeal did not fall on deaf ears. In June 1921, three principal merchants of Mumbai agreed to stop importing foreign cloth.[75]

The far reaching impact of the charkha movement began to manifest itself soon after its launch. The value of imports of foreign cloth fell from Rs 102 crore in 1920–21 to Rs 57 crore in 1921–22. Import of British cotton piece goods was 1,292 million yards and 955 million yards, respectively, in the same years.[76]

The local impact of the charkha movement was also noteworthy. T.K. Mahadevan, editor of the *Deshabhimani* in Kollam (then known as Quilon) and a leader of the Ezhavas (untouchables) of Travancore, said to Gandhi, "My community has been much benefited – morally much more than materially – by your charkha movement .... The enthusiasm you have created for Indian made clothes is partly responsible for the removal of the social stigma attached to weaving – we are trying to push up weaving."[77]

Similarly, in many places, indigent women – many of them Muslim – were provided with employment at home. This led Mian Mohammad Chotani, a wealthy Muslim of Mumbai, to donate one lakh spinning wheels to Gandhi, saying that they should preferably be used for members of the Maiman community.[78] Gandhi's instruments for change were beginning to gain popular appeal and commitment, which was in itself proof of his understanding and the rationality of his vision.

The viability of carding and spinning as supplementary occupations was demonstrated in flood and famine affected areas as well. In June 1922, a severe flood hit Hooghly district in Bengal. The local Congress committee introduced spinning wheels in the area and work started with a few women plying them. By June 1924, 200 people were employed. There were many Muslim women among them. A correspondent who was helping in the relief work wrote to Gandhi that "women who used to beg for their sustenance were now well off. They no longer quarrelled among themselves because they had no idle time left after carding and spinning. Their husbands could not now ill treat them as they were contributing considerably to the family fund; and lastly, but not the least, their *izzat*[79] was saved."[80]

In some places, khadi work was associated with other programmes such as national education, arbitration and social service. In Hooghly district, a separate propaganda department was set up, which published a litho weekly called *Congress Sambad*. The weekly contained expositions on topics such as non-violence, non-cooperation, khadi and untouchability. The organization was called the Satyagraha Sangh.[81]

An Adivasi greets Gandhi with a piece of khadi in Ramgarh on 14 March 1940

During a march through the fields of a Noakhali village in December 1946

By September 1925, the charkha movement had spread so widely that Gandhi found it necessary to set up a separate organization that would carry forward the economic programme of the nation more efficiently. This was the All India Spinners Association (AISA), which had its central office at the Satyagraha Ashram in Sabarmati. Gandhi described it as an expert and permanent organization for the development of hand spinning and khadi. Though it was an integral part of the Congress organization, it had an independent existence and powers. The association took over the funds and assets of the All India Khadi Board and all the provincial khadi boards and their existing financial obligations.[82]

To carry the message of the charkha, Gandhi toured extensively and addressed public meetings and women's gatherings. He collected donations for the khadi fund, which was meant for the *daridranarayan*,[83] to use his phrase. He hoped to make AISA the largest cooperative society in the world.[84] The thrust of his message everywhere was to help make the people and the country self-reliant and, thereby, truly independent.

In April 1930, with the launching of the civil disobedience movement, Gandhi desired to focus the attention of the nation on the importance of the swadeshi movement. With this in mind, he introduced a major change in his khadi programme, which would also meet the increasing demand for khadi and make the boycott of foreign cloth more effective. In his words, "No one who wishes to buy khadi will get it for money – it will be sold only against hand spun yarn. This is the only way to make it clear to people that khadi is not a mere commodity, like foreign cloth ... but that it is a symbol of the nation's strength and aspiration."[85] He made it clear that it was not necessary for the prospective buyer to spin himself; he could get it done by someone else. This would involve some trouble, he was aware, but the sacrifice was necessary for the nation, he declared.

As spinning wheels could not be produced fast enough to meet the demands of the whole country, he suggested the home manufacture of simple *taklis* (handheld spindles) to supplement them. Provided the *taklis* were well made and one had sufficient practice, the output of yarn on a *takli* could be quite high. He also disseminated instructions for making *taklis* at home at practically no cost.[86]

By August 1935, Gandhi discovered that though khadi sales had increased immensely and prices had been reduced on account of growing efficiency in every department of khadi production, the main purpose of the khadi movement had not been served – spinners were still not getting subsistence wages.

In the provincial centres of production, it was found that khadi was neither popular nor self-supporting. All the concentration was in the big cities. At Gandhi's instance, AISA adopted a new and radical policy. He ordered that private trade be almost stopped and the large staff of the big urban stores be substantially reduced.[87] He warned patrons of khadi that prices had to go up to give better wages to the spinners; greater technical skills needed to be developed among khadi workers; and a greater spirit of self-sacrifice had to be evoked amongst all classes connected with the production and distribution of khadi.[88] He demanded that the reports of AISA must henceforth state the increase in spinning wage. His personal opinion was that it should be equal to a weaver's hourly wage as the work required equal, if not more, skill.

This new directive sent the price of khadi up a considerable extent, yet sales increased noticeably in March 1937. The biggest Khadi Bhandar (store) in Mumbai recorded daily sales of Rs 1,000. With some satisfaction, Gandhi wrote, "For me, the sale of khadi is the best thermometer for measuring India's peaceful progress .... I presume that people have increasingly begun to understand the significance of khadi and those who wear khadi are satisfied by the higher rate paid to the women spinners and thus their enthusiasm for wearing it has increased."[89] He also found that since the rate of spinning had been increased and the work was being supervised, the "softness and durability" of khadi had increased.

For Gandhi, India's development at the grass-roots level and the khadi programme were so closely linked that when the question of another civil disobedience campaign came up in 1940, his chief instruction was that every Congress committee should become a satyagraha committee and enrol Congressmen who believed in the constructive programme. The registered *satyagrahis* would not only use khadi exclusively themselves, but also persuade the primary members to do likewise. Only such a disciplined, non-violent army could be led to battle. "I as your general must insist on your taking to the charkha, which will be your uniform," he stated.[90]

In short, it may be said that the goal of Gandhi's swadeshi programme was to make India self-sufficient as far as her needs of food and cloth were concerned and to provide an adequate means of livelihood for the needy. This, he believed, would pave the way for the real emancipation of the masses and provide the basis for building a dynamic nation.

Cordial Hindu–Muslim Relations

In Gandhi's view, in addition to swadeshi and the removal of untouchability, the necessity of cordial relations between Hindus and Muslims was a leading factor in the social progress of the country. He made this issue, too, an essential component of the constructive programme launched in 1920. Though he did not sponsor a specific movement for the purpose, he repeatedly suggested, in word and action, ways and means of promoting communal harmony. On several occasions, Gandhi was able, through individual action and sheer force of personality, to bring communal riots to an immediate halt. Social and political change could not be planned without taking this factor into consideration, according to him.

Gandhi's long and lively association with both Muslims and Hindus in South Africa had made him conscious of the fact that both had much in common and their traditional harmony, which had been somewhat fractured in the preceding decades, could be re-established in India. He perceived the Khilafat demand[91] as presenting an excellent opportunity for bringing the Muslim masses into the national struggle for freedom and for restoring amicable relations between Hindus and Muslims. Gandhi asked the leaders to submit a calm, dispassionate and reasoned statement of the Mahommedan claim to the British authorities. Till then, though pro-Khilafat sentiments had been running high among the Muslims, there had been no organized plan of action on the issue. Through discussions, Gandhi persuaded the Khilafat leaders to chalk out a national programme of non-violent action. He obviously estimated that if non-Muslims joined the Muslims on the Khilafat issue, it would be a big step towards the emotional integration of the country.

Gandhi was aware of Muslim reservations about the issue of non-violence as a technique of agitation, but after several consultations with Maulana Abdul Bari, who commanded wide influence, he managed to persuade him and others of its necessity.[92] He published letters in leading newspapers and his own journals[93] on the justice of the Khilafat issue. Important leaders such as Moti Lal Nehru, C.R. Das, Swami Shraddhanand and Bamanji of Saharanpur gave him full support.[94]

In November 1919, the Khilafat demand was made an issue of the all India satyagraha campaign that had been launched that April.[95] This was the first major step taken by Gandhi to bring about Hindu–Muslim harmony and identify common issues between the two communities. Gandhi's impact on the Muslims can be judged from the conduct of Maulana Abdul Bari, who began preaching about the need to stop cow slaughter out of regard for Hindu sensibilities. On 6 September 1919, when Bakri Eid was being celebrated, he wired Gandhi: "In celebration of Hindu–Muslim unity, no cow sacrifices in Firangi Mahal this Bakrid – Abdul Bari."[96]

Unfortunately, the phase of communal harmony that began in 1919 proved to be short-lived. Turkey itself made the Khilafat question redundant by abolishing the sultanate in 1924. Thus, the focal point of Hindu–Muslim political cooperation disintegrated. Communal riots broke out soon after the withdrawal of the non-cooperation movement in February 1922 and continued sporadically till 1924, when Gandhi morally compelled the communities to sign a truce in his own unique way – through a fast. Gandhi felt himself responsible for the unprecedented scale of communal violence because it followed a period of communal cooperation initiated by him.[97] He began his 21 day penitential fast on 17 September 1924 in the house of his close friend, Mohammad Ali, as a visible demonstration of his love for the Muslims. Gandhi perceived his own role in the following manner: "I am striving to become the best cement between the two communities. My longing is to be able to cement the two with my blood, if necessary."[98]

The upshot of his fast was that Hindus and Muslims got together and held a unity conference in Delhi on 26 and 27

September 1924 and passed a resolution drafted by Gandhi. This resolution was remarkable for its contents because it showed a genuine effort by both parties to re-establish a friendly atmosphere. It deplored the cruelties perpetrated during the riots and stated that it was "unlawful and irreligious for any person to take the law into his own hands". The conference was of the opinion that all differences should be referred to arbitration or a court of law. A board of arbitrators was appointed. On the controversial issues of cow slaughter and the playing of music before mosques, it was agreed that neither Hindus nor Muslims should use force, but rely on each other's good sense and the growth of better relations between them. Newspapers and pamphlets that inflamed communal passions came in for sharp criticism and the board of arbitrators was asked to scrutinize such writings from time to time and publish correct versions.

Another important achievement of this conference was that it authorized the board of arbitrators to frame a scheme for the protection of the rights of minorities and, for this purpose, invited representatives from all parties and all sections of society. The scheme, it was proposed, would be published and be binding on all parties for a period of five years ending in 1929, when it would be revised by a joint conference representing all interests. On the subject of religious conversions, the resolution stated that *tabligh* or *shuddhi* of minors or adults without education and clear understanding was contrary to moral sense and should be abandoned. Every conversion must be done openly and after notice to the relatives of the people concerned.[99]

As in other spheres, Gandhi had great expectations of women being able to play a positive role in the betterment of inter-communal relations. He had been deeply impressed by their powers of suffering and sacrifice during the civil disobedience movement.[100] He asked them to use the weapon of satyagraha now to secure Hindu-Muslim unity. They should, he advised, not cooperate with the men at home and starve themselves and their men till they gave up communal squabbles. "Assure me of your cooperation," he said, "and you will add tremendously to my strength and to my power of pleading."[101]

Another approach Gandhi tried was to draw the influential classes among the Muslims into the sphere of national and social development. In a speech at the Jamiat-ul-Ulema Conference in Karachi on 1 April 1931, he asked the delegate ulema[102] to use their influence with the masses to propagate non-violent methods in resolving disputes, just as he was doing among the general public. He also appealed to the ulema to set an example by adopting the nationwide programme of swadeshi and give up their love of imported cloth. Muslim zamindars could also do their bit, Gandhi believed, in improving relations with their Hindu neighbours. His message was especially for those in the province of Sindh, where they were feared and distrusted by the Hindus. A successful experiment in Sindh would be easily emulated in the other provinces, he thought.[103]

In searching for a more enduring solution to the problem of communal riots, Gandhi mooted the idea of forming Peace Brigades. But their members had to have certain qualifications, according to him. Among these were a living faith in non-violence and equal regard for all the principal religions of the world. They were required to be local men and women who would cultivate, through personal service, contacts with people in their locality so that they were trusted by them. They would thus be in a position to anticipate trouble and deal with it accordingly. They would also need to be in such occupations as to leave them leisure for this sort of voluntary service. He suggested that they should wear a distinctive dress so that they would be easily recognized.[104] It hardly needs to be said that such peace brigades could render valuable service in any part of the world.

Though Gandhi's efforts to establish Hindu–Muslim unity did not succeed in the long run due to many extraneous factors, it cannot be denied that his lack of bias, his zeal for establishing harmonious relations between different sections of India's population, and his personal integrity won him the love and trust of important segments of the Muslim community.

Women as Catalysts

Gandhi visualized a fundamental role for women as instruments of social change because they constituted the primary influence on the future citizens of the country and half the nation's strength in terms of population. Gandhi's unconscious guide in shaping his attitude to women was his mother, Putlibai, whom he deeply revered for her "saintliness". His intellectual guide was the image of the ideal wife of Hindu literature, whom he describes as *ardhangana*, the better half, and *sadadharmini*, the helpmate.[105] His perception of women as instruments of social change was influenced by two 'sexist' assumptions, which nevertheless did not have a negative impact on his thinking. These were the conservative and non-violent temperaments he assumed women to possess.[106] Women were slow to give up their traditions and customs because they were conservative, but for the same reason, they could discriminate better between the good and the bad in their heritage and cherish the good. Gandhi was of the opinion that women were superior to men in their moral and spiritual strength. They had greater powers of self-sacrifice and suffering. On this account, women were capable of infinite strength, which they only needed to realize and channel.

Women had a key role to play in the family, in Gandhi's opinion. The family was the crucible of society where future citizens, leaders and lawgivers were nurtured. Hence, it was here that the mother could mould the values and traits of her children in a direction that could lead to social progress. The ultimate aim was to teach children to be self-reliant and not keep them dependent on the family's resources.[107]

Gandhi had strong views on another key subject relating to women. This was the value of equality between the sexes. He was definitely against gender bias in the training of children. He asserted that girls ought not to be taught to adorn themselves as that identified them as objects of desire without any other distinct human qualities. The latter had to be highlighted if they wished to be accepted as equal partners of men. He was also of the opinion that housework must be divided equally between boys and girls as the home belonged to both.[108] Also, both boys and girls ought to have vocational training in some occupation so as to assure them a future livelihood when the need arose.

Gandhi envisaged an important political role for women vis-à-vis the power structure in society and the foundations of an equitable and non-violent social order. He wanted women to view their families in the larger perspective of the entire human family and to transfer some of their concern and devotion to the latter.[109] They must realize, he said, that as a class, women had been suppressed for centuries and it was now time for them to rise in rebellion and prove their worth. With the backing of education and the discriminating use of their political rights, they could affect the process of decision making in the nation and initiate appropriate changes at all levels to promote the values of social and economic equality. Though laws by themselves had not much meaning, they were very important for setting norms, so politically and socially conscious women should agitate for the framing of legislation, which accorded them equal status in society.[110] Simultaneously, strong and continuous agitation through the press and other platforms was necessary to rouse public opinion, which was the best sanction of law.

From the very beginning of his public career in India, Gandhi made strongly worded appeals to women to join the national struggle in large numbers. The response was overwhelming. In the non-cooperation campaign of 1920–22, women's contribution to the satyagraha fund in terms of personal jewellery was phenomenal;[111] they also played a notable part in the propagation of khadi in defiance of government orders,[112] and in picketing liquor shops as part of the temperance campaign.[113] In his plan for promoting communal harmony, eradicating untouchability and popularizing his revolutionary scheme of Basic Education, Gandhi held that women could play a central role as they had creative powers and a tremendous capacity for self-sacrifice.

To deal with issues specifically affecting women, such as child marriage, dowry, sati, purdah and prostitution, there was a need to change certain deep rooted values in society.[114] Gandhi felt that dedicated women would have to approach men and launch a widespread campaign to rouse public opinion against these social evils. Victims of prostitution should be sought out and given opportunities for rehabilitation. This was work of massive dimensions, but had to be undertaken if women were to take their rightful place in society. Gandhi not only exhorted women to undertake the tasks of their own 'uplift', but also squarely attacked the scriptures and the social customs and conventions that had devalued women's status and upheld women's social, political and legal equality. In short, as far as his perception of women as instruments of social change was concerned, Gandhi felt that they could play a most dynamic role in society – in fact, that they could provide the mainsprings of revolutionary thought and action.

Remodelling the Congress

Gandhi reconstituted the Congress in 1920 to function as an instrument of both social and political change. He was destined to play a leading role in the Congress in subsequent years, which greatly enhanced his social effectiveness. The objective of the Indian National Congress as specified by him in 1920 was "the attainment of swarajya by the people of India by all legitimate and peaceful means",[115] an objective that highlighted the point that only honourable and non-violent methods would be employed to attain the goal. A revolutionary feature introduced by Gandhi was the redistribution of British India into territories on a linguistic basis for the purpose of Congress organization, with Congress units constituted in each. Thus, 21 provincial Congress committees were created. This, together with the fact that each Congress delegate would represent 50,000 of the population of the province concerned, succeeded in transforming the Congress from an elite organization to a popular one, as the delegates became real representatives of those who wanted to participate in the political life of the country.

In order that the Congress could serve as a more efficient vehicle for creating popular awareness, Gandhi substituted its dilatory and casual manner of working with detailed rules for its efficient and democratic functioning at all levels – taluka, district, province and all India. A bold innovation introduced by him and which had significant consequences was that in the election of delegates, due regard was to be given to the representation of women, minorities, special interests or classes needing special protection and every variety of political opinion, through the system of proportional representation by a single transferable vote.

About these fundamental changes in the constitution, Gandhi wrote, "I have attempted to give the Congress a representative character such as would make its demands irresistible."[116] Through such changes, social issues at the village level could become political issues at a much broader level and appropriate programmes of action could be formulated and implemented. Regarding Gandhi's contribution to Indian politics, it has been observed that "Gandhi modernized Indian politics by moving it in a professional and democratic direction and by providing the organizational base, procedures and habits for national politics".[117] These new political forces affected the social life of the nation in a positive manner by creating a much wider distribution of the power structure and producing a great deal of social mobility.

Gandhi's resolution on non-violent non-cooperation,[118] passed by the Congress in September and December 1920, asked all Indians to non-cooperate with the government and all its institutions; at the same time, they were requested to remain absolutely peaceful and contribute to a national fund to set up national schools and other institutions to replace government ones. To promote national solidarity, the resolution appealed to the people to refrain from all communal quarrels and root out the "evil" practice of untouchability. In an effort to make India truly self-reliant, everyone was requested to give up wearing foreign cloth and take up hand spinning and weaving and wear only swadeshi cloth. Such a multifaceted programme had never been contemplated before and even less acted upon, that too on a national scale. The non-cooperation campaign produced a qualitative change in Indian society. It was proved to the "pusillanimous Indians" (as Gandhi felt about many of his compatriots) that the awesome might of the British empire could be challenged and its prestige given a severe jolt.

In subsequent years, the goal of Congress activities under Gandhi's guidance was the channelling of material and manpower resources towards the development of Indian society on an egalitarian basis. With this purpose in mind, Gandhi initiated the charkha or spinning wheel programme to provide work in villages, with the number of charkhas in each province to be in proportion to its population.[119] Meanwhile, he began the process of setting up panchayats for the purpose of social arbitration in local areas and launched a massive campaign against liquor addiction. People's participation was essential for the success of all these projects.

To bring the Congress more in line with the masses, Gandhi declared in September 1924 that the Congress would henceforth confine its activity to the propaganda of hand spinning and hand spun khaddar, the achievement of Hindu–Muslim unity and the removal of untouchability,[120] issues that most touched the life of the common people and were vital for the social and economic progress of the country. The Congress had also the responsibility of carrying on the existing national institutions set up for education and vocational training and it was asked to open more of them on an independent basis. Though it could not be said that these institutions supplied the need for education on a national or even provincial scale, their role was seminal in the freedom movement in India because of the direction they gave it.

"In an independent India," Gandhi had said in a speech at the "Subjects Commettee" meeting of A.I.C.C. III on January 1, 1930 that, "every problem is to be solved on a national basis and not on a communal basis,"[121] – presumably, he meant a democratic basis. At the same time, he assured Muslims, Sikhs and other minorities that no solution in any future constitution would be acceptable to the Congress that did not give full satisfaction to the parties concerned. The two parts of the resolution appear contradictory, but it seems that it was a compromise solution that Gandhi arrived at in keeping with the difficult times. The only real answer, he said, to the whole communal question was that the Congress should be joined in large numbers by the Muslims, Sikhs and others who would have India as one united nation. By joining it, they could participate in the direction of national affairs and help in solving the common problems of the country. This by itself would foster social cohesiveness.

Gandhi had a special piece of advice for Congressmen when Congress ministries were formed in seven of the 11 provinces of India after the elections of 1937. He said that as they were the representatives of one of the poorest nations in the world, they should observe rigorous simplicity in their personal life and administration. Such economy would save thousands of rupees, which could benefit the poor and also set an example for the rest of the nation, where the gulf between the rich and the poor was startling. The programmes of Congressmen, Gandhi said, should be oriented towards villages rather than cities and should have a secular and non-communal foundation. Without these administrative and policy changes, he felt that either there would be a bloody revolution or mass civil disobedience on a scale never attempted before.[122]

In pursuance of these guidelines, the scheme of Basic Education, the movements against liquor addiction and untouchability, the promotion of the charkha programme and indigenous industries received a great boost, particularly in the provinces where the Congress formed the government. The Congress government of Mumbai accepted prohibition as part of its policy, bringing it into force on 1 August 1939. Gandhi described the liquor prohibition act as "due fulfilment of the national will definitely expressed nearly twenty years ago".[123]

To ensure that the Indian National Congress did indeed constitute an instrument of social change, Gandhi emphasized the importance of all elected members to set examples in social and national service. In this context, he wrote, "The Congress is a revolutionary body in the widest and the wisest sense. It must be original. All its activities must be derived from its creed of non-violence."[124] But by 1940, Gandhi had come to realize that the existing Congress organization was incapable of functioning as an agent of social change on account of the corruption and lack of crusading zeal that had seeped into it.

Gandhi came to regard the Indian National Congress as a purely political body the goal of which was the attainment of complete independence. In 1947, he told his countrymen: "We must recognize the fact that the social order of our dreams cannot come through the Congress party of today .... There is so much corruption today that it frightens me .... [B]anish the idea of the capture of power and you will be able to guide power and keep it on the right path."[125] Gandhi wished to disband the Congress and raise in its place a purely social service organization. But by then, the party had tasted power and his wish remained unfulfilled. Gandhi's attempt to mould the Congress into a major instrument of social and political change met with only partial success. His dream floundered in the face of political power in all its dimensions and facets.

Rural Regeneration

For Gandhi, the state of the villages in India was the true index of the state of the country – if the state of the country was to be satisfactory, the state of its villages had to improve. Gandhi's solution was the regeneration of villages through a comprehensive programme of rural uplift covering all areas such as health, education and employment. Village based industries had to be revived and a taste for their goods had to be created in urban areas.[126]

In his programme of rural uplift, volunteers like himself had a key role to play. They should go to a selected village and live among the peasants there in the simplest way possible without any fuss and teach them through precept and practice to live a healthy life. Gandhi propagated his views through his journals, *Navajivan*, *Young India* and *Harijan*. These were copied or translated into other languages in various parts of India and became common knowledge.

Gandhi was of the opinion that the village worker should expect no more than a living wage from the All India Spinners Association or the new national provincial scheme that was being organized because India was a poor country and its service excluded a living beyond its means.[127] Gandhi also expressed his opinion about the "village–worker ratio" that would make his scheme of rural regeneration effective. Villages, he wrote, should be grouped into blocks, each with a radius of ten miles and covering around ten villages. In such a scheme, there would be one worker for every block and 70,000 men and women volunteers would be required to cover the more than seven lakh villages in the country.[128]

He outlined in meticulous detail the schedule of work for the village worker. Firstly, he should undertake a census of all the cattle to find out the average yield of milk; a census of the untouchables and a report of their conditions; a detailed survey of the village, including its area, crops, land revenue, crafts, industries, wells, fruits, and types of trees.[129] All this information needed to be recorded carefully because it would be of invaluable help not only to the worker, but also for chalking out uplift programmes. The local volunteers would prove most valuable in this task.

In response to Gandhi's call, dedicated volunteers opened centres for village service in different parts of the country and, fortunately, some records of their progress are available. In Tamil Nadu, a Gandhi ashram was set up by C. Rajagopalachari near Trinchengodu.[130] In Comilla, in Bengal, the Abhoy Ashram[131] was run by Drs S.C. Banerji and P.C. Ghosh. In Meerut, the Gandhi Ashram[132] managed by Acharya Kripalani was a big organization with branches in several places. Among the activities at these ashrams were spinning, medical relief, national education, dairy, agriculture, rural sanitation, removal of untouchability and fighting liquor addiction.

An important development in the programme for improving the state of villages was, as described in Chapter 4, the setting up of the All India Village Industries Association (AIVIA) in October 1934. AIVIA was constituted under the advice and guidance of Gandhi by J.C. Kumarrappa as an autonomous body, independent of the political activities of the Congress, but nevertheless a part of it. Gandhi outlined the work of AIVIA as follows:

1. To encourage and improve the known industries that are likely to perish for want of support;

2. To take charge and sell the products of these industries;
3. To carry on the survey of such village industries as need to be revived and supported; and
4. To attend to village sanitation and hygiene.[133]

He perceived the role of AIVIA thus: Village services as conceived by AIVIA had a unique mission. Town parties would go out to villages to clean, instruct and purchase. Parties of villagers would be organized to go to towns to sell articles made in their villages and demonstrate their usefulness. This village movement was to be one of decentralization and restoration of health and comfort and the skill of the artisan to villagers.[134]

Genuine service in the villages by those living in the towns epitomized for Gandhi his concept of bread labour, which denoted that each person should do adequate manual labour either for a living or to undo the unfair division of labour in society. By following it in society, Gandhi believed, there would be enough food and leisure for all and the common problems of overpopulation, disease and poverty could be alleviated.[135]

To create popular awareness about the village uplift programme, Gandhi conceived of the scheme of holding khadi exhibitions to synchronize with the annual sessions of the Congress. It was decided that AIVIA and AISA would jointly organize these exhibitions. The first such exhibition was held in March 1936 and it, as Gandhi says, "is not a spectacular show like its predecessors .... You will find here craftsmen and craftswomen from Kashmir and South India, from Sindh and Assam, and learn how they earn their scanty living. You will find that it is within your power to add a little to their income and to enable them to have a square meal, if only you will make up your mind to pay for their wares enough to ensure them a living wage."[136]

Gandhi was aware that the work of rural reconstruction on the scale that was needed in India was impossible without the active support of the government, which was the only body that could command the vast resources and manpower that was needed. Hence, when Congress governments were formed in seven provinces in 1937, he gave them guidelines on how they could further the work of AIVIA. He gave suggestions for the rapid promotion of select village based industries and for finding markets for their products outside the villages of production.[137]

Though, in the ultimate analysis, Gandhi's efforts for the revitalization of the villages of India did not achieve very much in concrete terms, they undoubtedly did bring into sharp focus the basic issues of social and economic change in India.

Decentralization of the Economy

Fundamental to Gandhi's economic approach was the idea that each individual should have the wherewithal to feed and clothe himself adequately. For the universal realization of this ideal, it was necessary, he wrote, that "the means of production of elementary necessaries of life remain in the control of the masses .... Their monopolization by any country, nation or groups of persons would be unjust."[138] Neglect of this principle was the cause of the destitution that was a worldwide phenomenon. So, it can be said that decentralization of the production of essential commodities was the pillar of Gandhi's economic philosophy. His own khadi movement, he said, was an example of this approach.[139] In it, poor peasants were given advances to buy cotton and spinning wheels from AISA units and the cotton they spun was bought at fixed prices by AISA and passed on to the weavers. The weavers were also given help where required and the cloth they produced was retailed at fixed prices in shops set up specifically for the purpose. Gandhi formulated rules that khadi should not be sold outside the locality or province where it was produced. In this manner, the whole enterprise was supervised and coordinated by AISA with the aim of assuring a living to those who needed it the most.

Gandhi was in favour of granting total protection to indigenous industries by banning import of articles that could be produced in the country itself, even if the cost of production was greater and the quality inferior in the initial stages. He would permit import facilities[140] for only those articles that were an absolute necessity and could in no circumstances be produced in the country.

A major advance in Gandhi's economic thinking was marked by the Resolution on Fundamental Rights and

Economic Changes,[141] which he drafted for the Karachi Congress in March 1931. It was his picture of swaraj in which the exploitation of the masses would end only when their political freedom included real economic freedom. The economic clauses in the resolution included special protection for women workers, prohibition against employment of children in factories, and the right of workers to form unions to protect their interests. In the agricultural sector, the resolution provided for a substantial reduction in the rents paid by the peasantry and, in the case of uneconomic holdings, exemption from rent for such period as might be necessary. Relief would be given to small zamindars wherever necessary by reason of such reduction. A progressive income tax was to be imposed on agricultural incomes above a fixed minimum.

Other measures to rationalize and improve the state economy included a graduated inheritance tax; reduction in military expenditure by at least one half of the prevailing scale; and considerable reduction in expenditure and salaries in civil departments. A truly radical clause was that no servant of the state, other than specially employed experts and the like, was to be paid above a certain fixed figure, which should not ordinarily exceed Rs 500 per month. The clauses relating to the industrial sector sought to provide protection to indigenous cloth by exclusion of foreign cloth and foreign yarn from the country; control over the exchange and currency policy to help Indian industries and bring relief to the masses; and control of key industries and ownership of mineral resources by the state. Thus, Gandhi envisaged a major economic role for the state. Provisions in the resolution that had a moral undertone, but also an economic impact, were the total prohibition of intoxicating drinks and drugs; abolition of duty on salt manufactured in India; and control of direct or indirect usury. Describing the intention of the resolution in unambiguous terms, Gandhi said: "By passing this resolution, we make it clear to the world and to our own people what we propose to do as soon as we come into power .... They (the clauses) are also meant to forewarn all concerned. Let them prepare themselves for the coming legislation by modelling their lives in the light of coming changes."[142]

In the next few years, Gandhi's thinking turned more and more towards economic equality, but he knew that it was an ideal that could only be approximated. Therefore, he wrote largely about equitable distribution of wealth. He would not, as far as possible, recommend compulsion to achieve this object because he believed in non-violence. His faith in the essential goodness of man made him adhere to his theory of trusteeship. The rich, he held, could not accumulate wealth without the cooperation and labour of the poor in society;[143] therefore, they should hold their superfluous wealth in trust for them and not squander it on luxuries. If they refused to do so, the poor should collectively refuse to cooperate with the proprietors of wealth and offer non-violent resistance, or satyagraha. This was, he was convinced, the only enduring remedy for the crushing inequalities in society.[144]

In 1942, Gandhi was ready to consider trusteeship as a legalized institution and not merely the whim of a lone philanthropist. "A trustee has no heir but the public," he wrote in *Harijan* in reply to a pointed question from a correspondent. "In a state built on the basis of non-violence, the commission of trustees will be regulated. Princes and zamindars will be on par with the other men of wealth."[145] Though Gandhi himself accepted and practised the ideal of non-possession and voluntary poverty, he did not, unlike the Marxists, forsake the notion of private property altogether. However, he favoured many limitations on it to secure the ends of social justice and community welfare.

In retrospect, one may say that all Gandhi's plans and policies were aimed at a comprehensive social and economic transformation of Indian society in which the emphasis was on the villages as they contained more than 80 per cent of the country's population. He desired the cities to function so that, instead of exploiting the villages, they would provide them sustenance through their leadership and expertise. This, he hoped, would usher in a mutually reinforcing, rather than antagonistic, relationship between urban and rural areas. Only in this way would their development be founded on social and economic justice.

The application of the technique of satyagraha for the resolution of social and political conflicts; the production of swadeshi goods for mass consumption and export; the all round uplift of villages; an integrated pattern of adult and primary education; uprooting of the social stigma of untouchability; fostering of communal harmony; mobilization of women as prime movers in society; an all India organization for popular mobilization; and a socialistic pattern of economic development were among the foremost instruments of social change as perceived by Gandhi.

Notes

1. *CWMG*, Volume 12, p. 462.
2. *Harijan*, 27 May 1939, p. 143.
3. *CWMG*, Volume 13, pp. 387–8.
4. Ibid., p. 375.
5. Ibid., 391; Appendix VI, pp. 573–4.
6. Ibid., p. 561.
7. Ibid., p. 426.
8. *CWMG*, Volume 14, p. 96.
9. Ibid., p. 88.
10. Ibid., p. 94.
11. Ibid., p. 96.
12. *CWMG*, Volume 14, p. 289.
13. Ibid., p. 281.
14. Ibid., p. 282.
15. Ibid., p. 279.
16. Ibid., pp. 288–92.
17. Ibid., pp. 313, 325.
18. Ibid., pp. 350–1.
19. Ibid., p. 417.
20. Ibid., p. 185, n. 3.

21. Ibid., p. 214.
22. Ibid., p. 212, n. 2.
23. Ibid., p. 215.
24. Ibid.
25. Ibid., pp. 185–256.
26. Ibid., p. 257.
27. Ibid., p. 264.
28. Ibid., p. 267.
29. Dhawan, *Political Philosophy of Mahatma Gandhi*, pp. 288–9.
30. Sumit Sarkar, *Modern India, 1885–1947* (Delhi: Macmillan India, 1984), pp. 210–24, 296–307, 394–404.
31. *CWMG*, Volume 13, p. 333.
32. *CWMG*, Volume 36, pp. 6–8.
33. *CWMG*, Volume 66, p. 143.
34. *CWMG*, Volume 65, p. 450.
35. *CWMG*, Volume 66, pp. 194–5.
36. Ibid.
37. Ibid., p. 169.
38. Ibid., pp. 169–70.
39. Ibid., p. 280.
40. *CWMG*, Volume 67, p. 35.
41. *CWMG*, Volume 70, p. 274.
42. *CWMG*, Volume 72, pp. 353–4.
43. *CWMG*, Volume 66, p. 195.
44. *CWMG*, Volume 23, p. 457; Volume 25, p. 164.
45. *CWMG*, Volume 29, p. 425.
46. *CWMG*, Volume 45, pp. 370–71.
47. *CWMG*, Volume 51, pp. 128–29.
48. Ibid., p. 263.
49. *CWMG*, Volume 58, pp. 259–60.
50. *CWMG*, Volume 52, p. 43.
51. Ibid., p. 48.
52. Ibid., p. 305.
53. *CWMG*, Volume 53, p. 71.

54. *CWMG*, Volume 64, p. 125; Volume 69, p. 421.
55. *CWMG*, Volume 53, p. 265.
56. *CWMG*, Volume 55, p. 435.
57. *CWMG*, Volume 56, p. 42.
58. Ibid., p. 88.
59. *CWMG*, Volume 55, p. 280.
60. *CWMG*, Volume 58, p. 77.
61. Ibid., p. 101.
62. *CWMG*, Volume 66, p. 302.
63. *CWMG*, Volume 70, pp. 32–33.
64. *CWMG*, Volume 75, pp. 320–1.
65. Ibid.
66. *CWMG*, Volume 76, p. 314.
67. *CWMG*, Volume 13, p. 219.
68. Ibid., p. 537.
69. Ibid.
70. *CWMG*, Volume 14, p. 467; Volume 15, p. 352.
71. *CWMG*, Volume 15, p. 372.
72. Ibid.
73. Ibid., p. 162.
74. Ibid., pp. 31–2.
75. Ibid., p. 321.
76. Sumit Sarkar, *Modern India*, p. 207.
77. *CWMG*, Volume 21, p. 185.
78. Ibid., p. 374.
79. Honour.
80. *CWMG*, Volume 24, p. 183.
81. Ibid.
82. *CWMG*, Volume 28, pp. 227–8.
83. Literally, God of the poor, but usually used for the poor.
84. *CWMG*, Volume 35, pp. 71, 74, 76, 78, 84.
85. *CWMG*, Volume 43, p. 305.
86. Ibid., p. 314–5.
87. Ibid., p. 315, 396.

88. *CWMG*, Volume 61, pp. 322–3.
89. *CWMG*, Volume 65, pp. 29–30.
90. *CWMG*, Volume 71, p. 366.
91. Sumit Sarkar, *Modern India*, p. 195.
92. *CWMG*, Volume 15, p. 298.
93. *CWMG*, Volume 16, pp. 269–94.
94. Ibid., p. 319.
95. Ibid., pp. 307–12.
96. Ibid., pp. 91, 305.
97. *CWMG*, Volume 25, p. 200.
98. Ibid., p. 202.
99. Ibid., pp. 214–5.
100. *CWMG*, Volume 45, p. 270.
101. Ibid.
102. Muslim theologians or scholars.
103. *CWMG*, Volume 45, p. 384.
104. *CWMG*, Volume 67, pp. 126–7.
105. *Conquest of Self*, p. 156.
106. Ibid., p. 165.
107. Ibid., p. 154. Also see Chapter V.
108. Joshi, *Gandhi on Women*, p. viii.
109. *Conquest of Self*, op. cit., p. 177.
110. Ibid., p. 154.
111. *CWMG*, Volume 19, p. 39.
112. *CWMG*, Volume 22, pp. 22–3.
113. Ibid., p. 206; Volume 37, p. 252; Volume 43, p. 191.
114. See Chapter IV.
115. *CWMG*, Volume 19, p. 199.
116. *CWMG*, Volume 18, p. 3.
117. Rudolph and Rudolph, *Modernity of Tradition*, p. 240.
118. *CWMG*, Volume 19, p. 208.
119. Ibid., pp. 496–7.
120. *CWMG*, Volume 22, p. 131.
121. *CWMG*, Volume 42, p. 359.

122. *CWMG*, Volume 65, p. 408.
123. *CWMG*, Volume 69, p. 83.
124. *CWMG*, Volume 68, p. 224.
125. Ibid., p. 223.
126. *CWMG*, Volume 59, pp. 409–10.
127. *CWMG*, Volume 60, pp. 118–9.
128. *CWMG*, Volume 46, p. 337.
129. Ibid.
130. *CWMG*, Volume 37, pp. 74–5.
131. Ibid., p. 309.
132. *CWMG*, Volume 46, pp. 305–6.
133. Ibid., p. 304.
134. Ibid., p. 329.
135. *CWMG*, Volume 61, p. 212.
136. *CWMG*, Volume 62, pp. 297–300.
137. *CWMG*, Volume 70, p. 39.
138. *CWMG*, Volume 37, p. 412.
139. Ibid.
140. Ibid., p. 413.
141. *CWMG*, Volume 45, pp. 370–71.
142. Ibid., p. 372.
143. *CWMG*, Volume 72, p. 401.
144. *CWMG*, Volume 64, p. 73.
145. *CWMG*, Volume 76, p. 10.

CHAPTER 6

Theory of Social Change and Contemporary Relevance

The preceding chapters have sought to discuss the different aspects of the issues and theory of social change in the writings of Mohandas Karamchand Gandhi. In the light of their contents, an effort has been made in this chapter to sum up Gandhi's views on the basic issues of social change and outline his theory of social change. This chapter also attempts to estimate his contemporary relevance.

Basic Issues of Social Change

In his voluminous writings, Gandhi touched or dwelt upon myriad issues of interpersonal, intergroup and individual–group relations that affected society and called for reform and even revolutionary change in the structure, institutions, processes and value orientations of society. Although his perspective was universalist in nature, his point of departure was the contemporary Indian situation. Social change in India constituted his immediate goal and priority. In the pursuit of this objective, he fashioned a programme of social reconstruction that evolved from his experiences and experiments in various areas of social life in a kind of trial and error process. He was deeply conscious of the inertial drag of tradition as well as the natural propensities of man to pursue narrow and immediate interests and dominate his fellow beings.

The central feature of Gandhi's thought is that it is man centred, not system centred. Its premise is the moral autonomy of man and the possibility of his lasting liberation from his own lower self and the impersonal and compelling dictates of the structure of society. The ideal social order is that which gives man the opportunity to realize his moral autonomy and encourages him always to exercise this autonomy in an enlightened manner that is conducive to individual and collective well-being. The movement from the existing imperfect state of man and society towards perfection requires the inculcation of certain fundamental values by man along with the establishment of social instrumentalities, which will promote and ensure the perennial primacy of these values. However, Gandhi postulates the inseparability of 'ends' (values) and 'means' (instrumentalities), that is, the dialectical unity of cause and effect. Therefore, a logical discrimination between values and instrumentalities is not possible – nor even desirable – in his thought.

It is in this context that the basic issues of social change in his writings have to be identified. In other words, these issues cannot be classified into neat categories labelled 'values' and 'instrumentalities'. Rather, they form a configuration that can only be analysed in terms of certain objectives, which need to be woven into the social fabric. From this point of view, we may identify the basic issues of social change prescribed by Gandhi as the institution of human dignity and equality; the elevation of labour to a high dignity; the quest for self-reliance; the propagation of the principle of trusteeship; the pursuit of truth and ahimsa; the establishment of a socially purposive system of education; the recognition of tolerance as a primary value; the realization of the inseparability of ends and means; and the urge towards a rational and scientific view of life.

Before proceeding to a brief elucidation of these issues, it is necessary to point out that, in contrast to other modern thinkers, Gandhi distilled most of his ideas from a-secular premises. This is clearly seen, for instance, in his justification of equality and his prognosis for sustaining the egalitarian imperative. Modern egalitarianism has been derived from a positivist theory of natural rights, or from the logic that it is not possible to determine relative primacy between the infinite hierarchies of classification, or from the irrationality of discrimination between incomparable individualities. Gandhi, on the other hand, eschews such abstract considerations and bases his concept of equality on the monistic premise of advaita philosophy that all sentient beings possess divinity as ultimately inalienable parts of the Supreme Being.

His belief in the Supreme Being, who manifested himself inter alia in an immanent moral law of the universe and was the ultimate reality, identical with the absolute truth, was the core of his thought. But his theism was rationally constructed and argued and it was devoid of mystical elements. Indeed, his calculus of good and evil was based upon secular and rational criteria and it is possible to argue that his references to the Supreme Being had a metaphorical quality inasmuch as they sought to enjoin socially constructive conduct. To him, religions were valuable not because they were built on the idea of communion with God, but because they gave strength to ethical principles and conduct. In other words, despite the a-secular foundations of some of them, his social ideas were rationalistic in their content and orientation.

To return to the issues of social change identifiable in Gandhi's vision, the institution of human dignity and equality as the guiding principles and objectives for social reconstruction derived from his belief that every human being, by virtue of the element of divinity in him, must be recognized as having intrinsic worth and as deserving of the highest respect, and he should feel and be free to achieve his full potential. Denial of dignity or equality to an individual was thus unacceptable, not so much for being offensive to formal human rights, as for its effect of crushing his spirit and denying the Supreme Being itself. The dismantling of the artificial barriers that categorized human beings according to descending scales of dignity and equality was a sine qua non for the ideal society and necessitated a conscious realization of the moral indefensibility of these categories on the part of those who were responsible for their sustenance and benefited from them. But it also required the assertion of the right to dignity and equality by the victims of their denial.

Gandhi extended the application of these concepts beyond individuals to group identities, such as religious communities, cultural and linguistic entities, regions, and other distinctive social collectives. His view that the oppressed and the underprivileged must struggle for their own liberation is evident in his social crusades against untouchability and for gender equality, for all through, he insisted that it was as much a duty for the untouchables and women to strive for their emancipation from social degradation and inequality as it was for the rest of society. Although he was categorical in upholding the principle of merit, he did not reject the principle of positive discrimination outright and, in fact, recognized the urgent need for providing the conditions and wherewithal for the backward and the underprivileged to bring them on par with the privileged sections of society. He also maintained that if an equitable social order reflecting the ideal of respect for human dignity and equality was founded on the inner realization that this ideal was an inalienable element of the moral law of the universe, instead of on formal laws and social sanctions, it would not have the tendency to regress towards older or new patterns of indignity and inequality.

However, Gandhi's conception of equality went beyond the right to equal dignity and opportunity, for it envisioned the right to equitable sustenance by society for individuals contributing to the social process to the best of their ability and potential. This was imperative to preclude the persistence and steady enlargement of inequality on account of the differing capacities and needs of individuals and the cooperative nature of social life. This, in turn, required the removal of artificial distinctions between different kinds of labour, and particularly between intellectual and manual labour, through the universal acceptance of bread labour and the pursuit of self-reliance by individuals as well as different levels of collective life from the family to the nation, which was represented by such ideals as the self-sufficiency of villages with respect to their essential needs and use of swadeshi. A significant component of this approach was the minimization of wants and the related idea of non-retention of what was surplus to the satisfaction of natural needs. In order to ensure against the resultant accumulation of unproductive wealth, Gandhi postulated the principle of trusteeship whereby the rich were to act as trustees for their superfluous wealth, which was to be used for society.

It is true that dignifying of labour, self-reliance and trusteeship are generally associated with the economic realm of Gandhi's thought. Yet, they are of central relevance to the process of social change for several reasons. Firstly, Gandhi himself insisted on the comprehensive and integral nature of his ideas and their categorization is, therefore, anathema to his scheme for social transformation. Secondly, these ideas, despite their apparent economic orientation, are basically concerned with and provide important instrumentalities for social change through the metamorphosis of man into a social being in the true sense. Thirdly, their operation represents and reinforces the innate higher traits of social commitment and sympathy in human nature. In the ultimate analysis, the elevation of labour to a high dignity, the quest for self-reliance and the propagation of the principle of trusteeship are important basic issues of social change because they have a direct bearing on extant social structures and human tendencies that militate against progress towards the ideal society.

Truth and ahimsa were regarded by Gandhi as forming an inseparable complex, logically distinguishable only in that the former is the end and the latter, the means. Although he defined truth variously in different contexts, there is no inconsistency in his formulations. To him, truth (the absolute truth) is identical with the ultimate reality which pervades the universe (the eternal principle or God). However, man cannot realize this absolutely and is prone to regarding a particular facet of it, relative in time, place or substance, as the end itself. This may generate conflict between specific relative truths.

However, in the contest between different relative truths, there can be no place for asserting the superiority of one over another and, therefore, for the imposition of one's own perception over an opponent. This necessitates the adoption of ahimsa as an operative creed, indeed as a supreme duty, not merely in the negative sense of not inflicting physical or emotional injury on any living being, but also – and more importantly – in the positive sense of active empathy with and love for the opponent, even to the extent of inviting and experiencing self-suffering. The struggle for social change, therefore, requires the inculcation of persistent concern for the disclosure of the absolute truth. This implies that each individual must recognize the relative character of his own variant of the truth and commit himself to non-violence. In other words, social change has to be predicated on a conscious and continuing pursuit of truth and ahimsa, the mode of its articulation being satyagraha.

To Gandhi, education could subserve social change only if it gave primacy to character building over the acquisition of knowledge and occupational skills, and was moreover related to the individual's environment and oriented towards its betterment. The character building aim of education ought, he felt, to be directed to the inculcation of selfless values and attitudes, and should contemplate the whole life by informing and pervading its learning and occupational functions. Education for its own sake or for acquiring specialized information in isolation from the process of development of society was, he believed, a contradiction in terms. His Basic Education scheme sought to universalize education by making the school complementary to the home and integrating value orientation with vocationalization, while ensuring the economic self-sufficiency of the school. His urgent stress on the establishment of a socially purposive system of education reflected the importance he attached to education as an efficacious agent for social change.

Gandhi's emphasis on the recognition of tolerance as a fundamental value arose only incidentally from his concern over the apparently endemic tensions and strife afflicting contemporary inter-communal relations in India. This was so because, to him, tolerance as a basic principle derived from his conceptions of equality among the constituents of plural societies, truth and ahimsa (as set out earlier in this section). Each collective identity had the same rights as the others, irrespective of size, and could claim to espouse no more than a relative truth. Moreover, it could only exercise the right to self-expression if it conceded the same right to others, which implied the practice of ahimsa. An injured party was enjoined to seek redressal only through the medium of satyagraha. Tolerance demanded that contentious issues be resolved through dialogue, arbitration and compromise without sacrifice of the fundamental principle. Tolerance alone could, he believed, provide lasting foundations of overall integration and harmony in plural social orders.

Gandhi was emphatic in turning down the assertions that an object could be detached from the means adopted to attain it and that the individual had the freedom to employ any from a range of optional means to achieve a desired end. To him, ends and means were inseparable and, in fact, convertible terms, and both ought to be equally pure. Moreover, since means were themselves ends in the process of realization, different means lead to substantially or qualitatively different outcomes, and fair results can only emerge from fair means. His stress on the fairness or purity of means was also derived from his belief that man can only strive and cannot command results, for he has control over means alone, never on ends. What an individual achieves through impure means only degrades him and makes him a lesser mortal instead of aiding him (as pure means do) to realize his full stature. Impure means (such as violence, hypocrisy and treachery) also involve the exploitation of other individuals and, therefore, even when they achieve immediate results, they sow the seeds of dissension and reaction among those who have been used and render the results unstable or ephemeral. Good means, or those consistent with truth, ahimsa and justice, may take longer to fructify, but their fruits are enduring. Gandhi, therefore, insisted that the realization of the inseparability of ends and means was essential for positive social change.

Although the premises of some of Gandhi's ideas were distinctly a-secular and he employed an idiom and a metaphor that were spiritual in appearance, he (as pointed out earlier in this section) developed his ideas in a rational manner and reached his conclusions through the scientific method of observation, hypothesis and experimentation. He readily admitted errors and varied the experiment to discover the proper way to the solution of a particular social problem. He always made the first test of a hypothesis on himself before he asked anyone else to try it.[1] In 1933, he stated that he had developed the "science of satyagraha" through "scientific research", to which he had applied "all the skill of a scientist". His approach to social problems, including religious and traditional issues, was always critical and he advocated the test of reason to prove the soundness of any doctrine or custom. His critique of the methods and activities of the cow protection societies, the concept of untouchability, and contemporary Hindu and Muslim fundamentalism was out and out rationalist in temper, as was his advocacy of the revisions of the (Hindu) *Smritis* in the light of contemporary goals and needs. He believed that his own concepts of equality, truth, ahimsa, swadeshi and bread labour would find universal recognition only when vindicated by popular rationality. It is true that he gave faith a higher pedestal than reason in some respects, but at the same time, he held that while faith transcended reason, it did not contradict it, and reason remained a valuable guide to man in his social life. Thus, to Gandhi, the urge towards a scientific and rational view of life was an important instrumentality for social transformation.

The foregoing account of the basic issues of social change has sought to identify the different prongs of the interventionist thrust of Gandhi's reconstructive social programme, the aims of which were twofold: to instil in man a deep and abiding concern for certain values and social goals, and to institute practical arrangements which would serve to reinforce them and prevent (and, in fact, obviate) regression towards unsocial and self-centred tendencies. The agent of this intervention would be man himself, with the vanguard comprising persons, who, "through a revolutionary transformation of self", would initiate "a process of social reordering" and help "create institutions that install and sustain a normal civilization".[2] This vanguard would mobilize the people by example more than precept into a collective drive towards the ideal society. The values and social goals prescribed by Gandhi were to be the essential elements of the personal ideology of the individuals constituting the vanguard, but their ultimate test was their acceptance by the people as their operative creed.

Theory of Social Change

Gandhi did not construct a theory of social change in the sense that most social analysts do. But scattered through the vast magnitude of his writings are many pointers and indications through which one can delineate his design for social reordering. This design is radically different from that of other social thinkers. It is pertinent to remember that his ideas were partly the result of his interaction with and disapprobatory assessment of modern civilization as typified by the rich industrial countries and partly the outcome of his political and social struggles in South Africa and India. His upbringing and readings also played a major part in his orientation towards man and society. His proposals for social change are different because they are not concerned with the progress of civilization or the historical process; his main concern is the destiny of man, which according to him is self-development, and he judges a civilization according to its capacity to fulfil this purpose. Material well-being is the prime consideration of modern civilization; opposed to this is Gandhi's view of progress as the movement towards self-discovery or self-realization of man.

Therefore, it is necessary in this context to begin with an examination of Gandhi's theory of human nature, or his conception of man. He begins with the recognition that in his basic inclinations, man is essentially a brute and easily led towards the gratification of his fundamental brutish nature or lower self. This phenomenal personality of man is subject to the law of nature (or, the egocentric urge to survive and dominate by whatever means) that governs all living beings. However, man is also endowed, unlike the brute, with reason, discrimination and free will, which invest him with the capacity to choose the kind of life he would lead and the kind of relationship he would have with his fellow beings, or the rest of humanity. As a result, "the law of nature as applied to ... [man] is different from the law of nature as applied to the ... [brute]",[3] for these endowments enable him to be aware of the self-destructive consequences of the unfettered expression of his brutish instincts. As Gandhi put it: "If all men were to act according to their lawless law, there would be perfect chaos within 24 hours. Man being by nature more passionate than the brute, the moment all restraint is withdrawn, the lava of unbridled passion would overspread the whole earth and destroy mankind."[4]

Moreover, man also possessed a moral and spiritual tendency because of the element of divinity present in him. Under his phenomenal exterior, there was an inner, higher core that distinguished him from the rest of creation. This was the real self of man (the 'self'), which lay unmanifest and unrevealed. The exterior personality of man and his inner self were both socially oriented, as man was a social being by nature as well as the compulsions of survival. But while the phenomenal exterior tended towards the lower instincts of dominating and exploiting fellow beings, the real self sought fulfilment through the actualization of the moral instinct of fraternity and sympathy. However, the real self remained suppressed as long as the exterior personality held sway over the individual. Gandhi held that each individual had in him the potential to rise above his natural inclinations, or lower self, and strive to become a total human being, provided he understood the moral and spiritual aspects of his nature and exercised his will for the purpose. The effort to move towards a higher plane of existence initiated the process of the uncovering of the real self – of self-realization.

Gandhi, however, rejected the notion that the endeavour of the individual for self-realization, or rising above the law of nature, could only be meaningful if he transcended the pulls of the phenomenal world by renouncing all existential concerns and withdrawing from the social realm. Instead, he postulated the doctrine that the duty of the individual "lies in remaining in the world and engaging in action not motivated by self-interest, but directed towards ameliorating the suffering of others".[5] To Gandhi, real freedom meant liberation from (or rising above) the law of nature and recognizing the fundamental unity of man and equality of individuals. In other words, laws designed to protect man's individuality and enshrine his rights were not the essence of liberty, for what was important was the freedom of the self to evolve and take man towards disinterested altruism, which represented his duty and destiny to toil tirelessly for perfection.

However, the path to genuine self-discovery is strewn with numerous pitfalls. The first of these is the seductive pull of material comfort and the gratification it brings to the senses. Gandhi maintained that "man must choose either of the two courses, the upward or the downward, but as he has the brute in him, he will more easily choose the downward course than the upward, especially when the downward course is presented to him in a beautiful garb".[6] A second pitfall is that out of ignorance, he is not able to discriminate between worldly concerns and the imperatives of self-realization. A third arises from the bind of *samskaras*, or the socially conditioned or acquired habits of thought and behaviour, which cloud his vision and make him veer towards actions reflecting his lower self. Finally, engagement in any kind of action (including philanthropic action), without constant awareness of the need to remain detached from the fruits (even the socially beneficial fruits) of such action, activate the ego and open the door for the assertion of the lower self and immersion in the phenomenal world.

But Gandhi had faith in the ultimate redemption of man. In his view, the individual was not only perfectible, but also had the spark to search for perfection, and this quest itself, however humble or limited, initiated the process of social transformation. However, his effort could have no content or meaning in isolation from his fellow beings – from society. Therefore, the question of the relationship between the individual and society was at the centre of his social theory. Gandhi believed that the individual and society were parts of an organic whole in which were included all living beings and material objects. There was an essential unity underlying all phenomena, which underscored the fact of mutual dependence between them. He gives a graphic description of this relationship in the following passage: "Individuality is and is not, even as each drop in the ocean is an individual and is not. It is not, because apart from the ocean it has no existence. It is, because the ocean has no existence if the drop has not, that is, has no individuality. They are beautifully interdependent. And if this is true of the physical law, how much more so of the spiritual world?"[7]

However, there is no doubt that for Gandhi, the individual was the prime factor and corporate growth was determined by individual growth. He would often say that "a chain is no stronger than the weakest link in it".[8] But this did not mean that the individual was supreme, for his very individuality would lack relevance if it developed without reference to the individualities of others, or if their needs were subordinated to his requirements. Indeed, man's effort for self-realization would defeat itself if it became a quest for personal salvation or a private enterprise in which society was merely a necessary facility. An individual moving on the path towards the uncovering of his real self had no superior claim to social resources than one who was steeped in the demands of his lower nature. On the contrary, the first condition of moral growth was the recognition of the priority of the needs of others, of the indivisibility of man and his fellow beings – of the essential oneness of the individual and society.

Gandhi thus posits the concept, not so much of the interdependence of man and society, as their integrity. To him, the dichotomy of the individual and society is false. Society is not something external to the individual, but a projection of his own identity or an extension of the self. Gandhi's doctrine, therefore, rejects both the Marxian view of man as an ensemble of social relations whose nature is governed by the objective conditions of his existence (the basic material structures of social life) and the liberal view of man as a free agent in a milieu, which arises "mechanically and independently of the individual will, from the actions of countless autonomous individuals on each other and in response to each other, behaving as rationally as possible for the protection of their private interests ... with no regard for any trans-individual authority or values".[9]

In his scheme, the individual is potentially a morally autonomous entity, entrapped by his lower nature into subservience to the false imperatives and values of the phenomenal world, but capable of being aroused to his moral freedom to pursue the call of the higher self. This quest begins independently of the social fabric, but the course of this movement towards self-realization reshapes his environment in accordance with the moral and spiritual concomitants of the higher self, which are built on disinterested altruism, or the imperative of submerging individual identity in the service of humanity.

In the light of the foregoing discussion, one may recapitulate, in outline, Gandhi's theory of social change. At first glance, it would appear that his ideas, with their emphasis on the divinity of man and union with God as the ultimate destiny of the individual, are derived from spiritualist premises and have spiritualist objectives. However, on deeper reflection, it becomes clear that these concepts are metaphorical (and not substantial) in his theory and their purpose is to stress the necessity for considering each individual as absolutely equal in social regard and to elevate selfless endeavour to the highest level of human conduct. He does not postulate any divine design for the universe, or the operation of a divine law which entails retribution for transgressions of the will of God, or any afterlife. His view of the primary brutish instincts of man and the possibility of their sublimation through the effort for self-realization, or the movement from false consciousness to real consciousness, is an essay in the psychology of man, which has a striking concordance with modern theories of human behaviour.

To Gandhi, truth was, in its essence, the state of freedom from self-regarding motives and the continuous urge to overcome the bewitchment of false consciousness. His belief in the perfectibility of man, or in the ability of the individual to relentlessly pursue the truth, is a reflection of the conviction that it is possible for man, at the individual level and collectively, to proceed non-regressively from a self-regarding to an other-regarding outlook. This pursuit is aided along by the effort to adhere to certain norms of conduct and Gandhi has suggested a number of such referential standards. To that extent, his approach is normative. He also believed that while man's conduct was influenced by the values current in society, man had also the capacity to commit himself to value orientations that lay beyond the sphere of extant social values. Social values emanated from the interaction of man and his social environment and were perforce relative in space and time. However, values which represented a perceived dichotomy between the individual and society, or which were discordant with the essential oneness of all human beings, were falsely reflective of the lower self. True values must, he felt, be relevant to the moral well-being of the individual and society.

But Gandhi was not a positivist, for he did not believe in or prescribe a fixed system of ultimate values and he rejected the concept of progress in a linear fashion. Progress could not be measured on a material scale and had to be related to the extent to which the individual had advanced on the path of self-realization and the extent to which the social order had developed into one which helped, not hindered, this quest. However, Gandhi rejected the utilitarian calculus of the greatest good of the greatest number because it, "in its nakedness, means that in order to achieve the supposed good of 51 per cent, the interest of 49 per cent may be or rather should be sacrificed". He characterized it as "a heartless doctrine which had done harm to humanity". Against the utilitarian ideal, he proposed "the only real dignified, human doctrine" of sarvodaya, or the greatest good of all, which could only be achieved "by uttermost self-sacrifice".[10] To be animated by the spirit of self-sacrifice was to proceed towards self-realization, the goal of which was the achievement of integration between the individual and society. However, this goal could only be reached gradually, for man was subject to a variety of limitations, physical, physiological and intellectual, which retarded his ability to transcend his proximate environs. Gandhi, therefore, prescribed the path of commitment and service to "our immediate surroundings to the exclusion of the more remote",[11] which is articulated by the concept of swadeshi.

The concept of swadeshi was, in Gandhi's theory, inextricably linked with the ideal of the village republic or self-contained, self-sufficient and autonomous communities, which, however, were not self-limited or self-limiting, as they had a network of mutually supportive and sympathetic linkages with their counterparts. These communities were not to be arranged hierarchically, but would be encompassed in "ever-widening, never ascending circles", in which life "will be an oceanic circle whose centre will be the individual always ready to perish for the village, the latter ready to perish for the circle of villages, till at last the whole becomes one life composed of individuals, never aggressive in their arrogance, but ever humble, sharing the majesty of the oceanic circle of which they are integral units".[12] They also represented a social system which was participative in character and was so constituted that it encouraged the cooperative tendency, that is, assisted the individual to break out of the restricted shell of selfish individuality on to the goal of disinterested altruism. In other words, they constituted a social order that enabled man to attempt the transformation of society through self-transformation.

Thus, Gandhi's thinking on social change was in terms of a social revolution in which systemic change was attained through a moral revolution in values. His most important contribution to the general techniques of revolution was the theory of ahimsa (non-violence) and its practice in the form of satyagraha. This included, firstly, the use of moral force by an individual

Talking to a blind villager who contributed to the Bihar Relief Fund on 26 March 1947

Gandhi with Khan Abdul Ghaffar Khan during a tour of Jahanabad, Bihar, on 28 March 1947

dedicated to the service of the people and, secondly, collective pressure and persuasion against the opponents. What was envisaged by Gandhi was a dialectical opposition of values in which the *satyagrahi* pitted the whole of his spiritual strength against the opponent and was prepared to suffer all hardships – physical and emotional – heaped on him. Initially, the opponent might not be moved, but Gandhi believed that no individual was without a divine spark which could, in certain circumstances, be ignited and made to respond to a moral appeal. The *satyagrahi*'s effort was to reach this depth of the individual being and bring out its most noble aspect. Violence, or even a slight compromise in means, could not be considered, as the question concerned human values. Against such an onslaught, the opponent is expected to assert his perception of truth or reality and the struggle might continue, but each stage would be marked by a higher level of truth. In such a moral struggle, however long and protracted, the outcome would perforce be a moral one,[13] for as long as the protagonists of different partial versions of the truth made a constant effort to comprehend the fact of the relativity of their perception, their confrontation initiated the process of its revelation and had the positive outcome of bringing all closer to the absolute truth.

The Modern Non-Violent Social Order

Gandhi was sceptical about drawing up a detailed plan for a modern non-violent social order for several reasons. As the individual was instrumental in transforming society through the extension of his self, social institutions and systems were reflections of his moral and social level. A violent people would obviously create a violent society, while a non-violent people would create a non-violent one. Therefore, Gandhi felt that it was futile to draw up a social scheme before the adequate moral level was attained. In 1929, he wrote: "We do not know our distant goal. It will be determined not by our definitions, but by our acts, voluntary and involuntary. If we are wise, we will take care of the present and the future will take care of itself. God has given us only a limited sphere of action and limited vision. Sufficient unto the day is the good thereof."[14]

Secondly, Gandhi's faith in the principles of renunciation of the fruits of action precluded planning far into the future as that could lead to attachment and desire. It emphasized concentration on immediate duties and problems and reliance on the efficacy of good deeds. If the seeker of truth gave free rein to his imagination and dissipated his energy in an attempt to describe the social order that would emerge after the non-violent revolution, he would encumber himself with irrelevant details and lose his detachment, his thought control and present efficiency.

There was another reason for Gandhi's lack of emphasis on the future social order. Satyagraha was a science in the making. He had not worked it out in its entirety. He was still experimenting with non-violence, trying to apply it to all spheres of life and studying its possibilities. Indeed, he felt that the experiment was not even in an advanced stage.[15] Therefore, he regarded the very effort to determine in detail the institutional forms of the future non-violent society as premature and "unscientific".

Nevertheless, we do find fairly detailed references in his writings to the kind of society Gandhi envisioned as ideal, inasmuch as it had the quality to help man in the pursuit of unfolding his real self. To Gandhi, society provided the framework in which the individual could strive meaningfully and achieve liberation. He had a deep distrust of politics and he refused to assign a significant role to political machinery as the agent of individual or social change. He viewed "an increase in the power of the state with the greatest fear because ... it does the greatest harm by destroying individuality, which is at the root of all progress .... The state represents violence in a concentrated and organized form. The individual has a soul, but as the state is a soulless machine, it can never be weaned from the violence to which it owes its very existence."[16]

He pictured the ideal society as an "enlightened anarchy", where "everyone is his own ruler, and ... there is no political power, because there is no state".[17] However, Gandhi was also a realist and, despite his negative assessment of the political realm, felt called upon to participate in the arena of politics: "If I seem to take part in politics, it is only because politics encircles us today like the coil of the snake from which one cannot get out, no matter how much one tried. I wish therefore to wrestle with the snake."[18] It was the same realism that, in later writings, brings him towards the acceptance of the inevitability of the state in human affairs. However, the state of his conception, the non-violent state, was a distinctive entity, quite different from any other model of the state.

To Gandhi, political power, or the state, was not an end in itself, but "one of the means of enabling people to better their condition in every department of life".[19] Thus, he did not accept the Hegelian view of the state as the final goal of human organization, the ultimate end that has the highest right against the individual and is itself above morality. He was against the theory of absolute sovereignty of the state, which lays upon the individual the duty of absolute, unquestioning obedience to the law of the state. For him, sovereignty was of the people based on pure moral authority.[20] Though Gandhi makes the disobedience of laws that offended the moral sense a right as well as a duty of the citizen and considers such disobedience the key to democracy, he provides ample safeguards against anarchy by making this disobedience civil and non-violent.[21]

Gandhi consistently favoured a democracy, but, for India, based it on a system of indirect election to circumvent the problems of its vast size and its relative backwardness. In his view, all public offices had to be held in the spirit of service without the slightest expectation of personal gain. To ensure that only virtuous persons were elected to represent the people, he postulated the "labour franchise", which meant that political rights would only devolve on those who performed manual labour. To quote him, "The qualifications for franchise should be neither property nor position, but manual work ... [for a] literacy or property test has proved to be elusive. Manual work gives an opportunity to all who wish to take part in the government and the well-being of the state."[22] Labour franchise is the application to politics of the ideal of bread labour, which aims at making life self-sufficient and people self-reliant and fearless. Gandhi wanted to reserve the right to vote only to people aged between 18 and 50. People above 50 would have only moral influence, but no political authority through the vote.[23]

The non-violent state would have to be a secular state. Even if the whole community had only one religion, the state must not patronize it. Everyone living in the state should be entitled to profess his religion without let or hindrance, so long as he obeyed the common law of the land. However, Gandhi held the teaching of fundamental ethics to be a function of the state.[24] The state must not undertake religious education, which must be the sole concern of religious associations. He was also opposed to state aid to religious bodies.

Crime, though diminished, would not disappear from the non-violent state because it would not consist only of ideal men. But Gandhi regarded all crime as the result of social malfunctioning and so prescribed its treatment along different lines. Criminals would be detained, not for punishment or deterrence, but for reform. Prisons would be turned into reformatories and workshops so that their inmates could be rehabilitated and discharged prisoners might become model citizens of the state.[25]

A police force would be necessary, but its ranks would be composed of believers in non-violence. They would be servants, not masters of the people. The force would carry some kind of arms, but they would use them rarely, if at all. In fact, policemen would be reformers and their police work ought to be confined to robbers and dacoits.[26] Gandhi was opposed to the use of the army for the protection of civil liberties, internal peace and even against foreign aggression. In the non-violent state, he would completely decentralize defence against aggression and injustice. However, he was in favour of a non-violent army.[27]

In the sphere of production, the non-violent state would differ from the stateless society in that the indispensable large scale production as well as heavy transport would continue. Gandhi conceded that so-called civilized man had come to regard these as essential for his comfort and convenience. But centralized production, he felt, should be so planned as to subserve and not destroy villages and their crafts.[28] For this purpose, he would permit private ownership of the means of production only if the capitalist raised the worker to the status of co-proprietor of his wealth and both labour and capital worked as mutual trustees and trustees of consumers.[29] Failing this, he would accept state ownership. These nationalized, state owned factories, he said, ought to work under the most attractive and ideal conditions, not for profit, but for the benefit of humanity.[30] In state owned enterprises, workers should have a place in the management through their elected representatives and an equal share in the management with the representatives of the government.

The production of primary necessities such as food and cloth had to be completely decentralized in that it should remain in the control of the masses. Even in this sphere of production, Gandhi said, so long as villages aimed at being self-contained and manufactured mainly for use, he had no objection to villagers using even modern machines and tools that they could make and afford to employ. Only, such machines and tools should not be used as a means of exploitation of others. Thus, if electricity could be made available in villages, he would not mind villagers plying their tools and implements with the help of electricity. But then the village communities or the state would own the power houses just as they did their grazing pastures.[31]

The state would promote small scale industries and would control natural resources such as forests, minerals, power resources and communications in the interest of the people. The state would regulate the rate of commission to be paid to the trustees for the wealth accumulated by them. If landlords and capitalists failed to live up to the ideals of trusteeship and voluntary efforts proved unavailing, the state would have to end the various forms of landlordism and own and manage, jointly with workers' representatives, the unavoidable centralized production.[32] Gandhi was of the view that the role of the state would diminish gradually once the non-violent structure was firmly established and economic life became increasingly self-regulated.

A unique feature of Gandhi's scheme of taxation, however quaint, was the idea of payment in labour, rather than in money. He said, "Payment in labour invigorates the nation. Where people perform labour voluntarily for the service of society, exchange of money becomes unnecessary. The labour of collecting the taxes and keeping accounts is saved and the results are equally good."[33] Payment in this form also implies the use of taxes for the benefit of the area in which they are collected.

Before concluding this section, Gandhi's concepts of nationalism and the related theme of internationalism may be considered as they are the projections of his ideas for laying the foundation of a new social order in the world. Nationalism, in his view, was not confined to the territorial limits of a nation, but transcended them and had universal connotations. It could not be aggressive, exclusive or destructive. One reason why nationalism was constructive in his opinion was that the means it employed to fulfil itself was non-violence, the method of conversion and non-coercion. Besides, it was inspired by the ideal of world unity rooted in the highest truth, the spiritual oneness of mankind and stood for a country learning to live, not by exploiting others, but by serving others and dying for others. As such, he said, non-violent nationalism is the essential precondition of sound internationalism. In 1925, he wrote: "It is impossible for one to be an internationalist without being a nationalist .... It is not nationalism that is an evil, it is the narrowness, selfishness, exclusiveness which is the bane of modern nations .... Indian nationalism ... wants to organize itself or to find full self expression for the benefit and service of humanity at large."[34]

Nationalism to Gandhi did not mean isolated independence, but a state of healthy and dignified interdependence with other nations. Such a condition of peaceful coexistence could only be maintained, he thought, by the world being united under a central governing body composed of the representatives of the component parts.[35] Only such an international organization that was freely established and maintained by non-violence could solve all the problems of the world. The League of Nations failed in its duty because it lacked the necessary sanctions, he felt. This power should be based on satyagraha or non-violent non-cooperation, the efficacy of which had been demonstrated in India.[36] The first necessity was the giving up of armaments and the use of force to defend even proven rights.

"Proven rights," he writes, "should be capable of being vindicated by right means as against the rude, or sanguinary, means."[37] For controlling violent outbreaks between states, he would welcome an international non-violent police force resembling peace brigades or the police force of the non-violent state. Before general disarmament commenced, he said, some nation would have to dare to disarm itself and take large risks. The level of non-violence in that nation would naturally have risen so high as to command universal respect.[38]

Gandhi was clear that all the nations composing the League of Nations would have to be fully independent and there could be no question of superiority or inferiority between them. The smallest nation should feel as the tallest.[39] This state of affairs could only be reached after the establishment of just political and economic international relations and the ending of imperialism. For this purpose, the great nations would have to shed competition and the desire to multiply wants and material possessions.[40] Obviously, a prerequisite of such an international league would be the inculcation of non-violent values by the member nations.

In short, Gandhi's theory of social change would lead to the creation of a society in which the average individual would have attained a high level of moral growth and he would lead a corporate life characterized by approximate social and economic equality, genuine political consciousness, voluntary cooperation and simplicity.

Contemporary Relevance

We finally turn to an examination of the contemporary relevance of Gandhi. "Modern industrial civilization", as Gandhi described it, has crept over most parts of the world and this has led man to seek contentment through the satisfaction of his material needs, concerning himself less and less with discovering his true or inner self. The world has become roughly divided into the very rich countries and the very poor, and within each country, there is social and economic polarization. Exploitation and violence are common phenomena of life. Transcendental values such as honesty, morality, harmony and kindness, which point the way to an integrated and simple life, hold little attraction. Powerful divisive forces are at work in their place, which are leading to an extreme fragmentation of our social and political life. Religion, region and language have become shibboleths under whose cover many crimes are committed. Another major fallout of modern civilization is the very real threat to our ecosystem or biosphere. For example, carbon dioxide emission levels have risen by 29 per cent in the last 150 years, leading to global warming, which is causing glaciers to melt, raising sea levels and drowning coastal lowlands.[41] Our soil, air and water are getting clogged with noxious chemicals from polluting industrial effluents, which, in turn, are dangerously impacting human health, reportedly even causing diseases such as skin cancer, gastrointestinal, eye, dental and bone problems, 'spontaneous' abortions and even altering human DNA.[42]

In such a grim scenario, Gandhi's proposals for social change take on special relevance. Modern writers and thinkers have recognized the fact of the "broken totality"[43] of modern human life lacking a notion of intrinsic good and a holistic approach. Gandhi emphasized the essential oneness of all life with interdependence as the law of life. This was also the supreme truth or God for Gandhi, the realization of which was the goal of all life. Satyagraha was the means he forged for the purpose. The concept was integral to the pursuit of truth and ahimsa. One might question the practicality of the technique of satyagraha for bringing about changes in the modern social and political milieu. If it is accepted that there are and always will be individuals who can rise above themselves and energize radical movements that articulate popular concerns with determination and restraint, satyagraha will assume significance as an effective and relevant modality of popular action. The burgeoning environmental movements in the heartland of modern industrial civilization, and particularly their local and communitarian articulations, represent the core of the technique of satyagraha in their non-violent and mass character. The degree of success they have achieved in forcing governments to institute ecological legislation, compelling industrial units to abide by them and infusing people with ecological consciousness vindicates the practicality and relevance of the concept.

Evidently, there can be no greater indictment of modern civilization than the arms race between the superpowers and the lesser powers, their heavy reliance on the sale of arms to other countries and the increasing sophistication in the production of weapons designed to annihilate large portions of mankind. In this situation, non-violent techniques, which require both moral courage and physical courage, appear to be the only rational way out. As Gandhi suggested, one major power will have to have the courage to begin the process of disarmament by disarming itself, rather than continuing to participate in the arms race.

In this context, it may be noted that a group of Palestinian nationalists had tried to apply Gandhi's philosophy of non-violence to force Israel to end its occupation of West Bank and the Gaza Strip. Leading the movement was Mubarak Awad, director of the Palestinian Centre for the Study of Non-Violence, who was convinced that the Israelis did not know how to handle people who practised non-violence. Awad came to India for six weeks in 1986 and discussed with Gandhians the ways in which he could use Gandhi's philosophy for advancing Palestinian nationalism. He said, "I tell the people no throwing stones, no violent behaviour of any kind. Even if the tanks come, do not run away because you have truth on your side."[44]

Well known people's movements in recent history based on civil disobedience have acknowledged the strong impact of Gandhi on their philosophy and strategy. Martin Luther King, the leader of the civil rights movement in the United States, said: "Gandhi was probably the first person in history to lift the love ethic of Jesus above mere interaction between individuals to a powerful and effective social force on a large scale .... The whole concept of 'satyagraha' was profoundly significant to me."[45]

Gandhi became the symbol of resistance and was acknowledged as such by non-violent revolutionaries in eastern Europe, such as Lech Walesa in Poland and Vaclav Havel in Czechoslovakia in the 1980s.[46] The Dalai Lama has always proclaimed the influence of Gandhi in his non-violent effort to gain autonomy for Tibet.[47] In the 1990s, Nelson Mandela was in a position to publicly acknowledge that "the Gandhian influence dominated freedom struggles on the African continent right up to the 1960s".[48] Very recently, Gandhi's influence appeared to have motivated the Buddhist monks who launched a powerful movement in Lhasa in March 2008 and in Yangon against the authoritarian regime in Myanmar.

In terms of social development, India presents a paradox: While, on the one hand, cultural pluralism is plainly evident, on the other, communalism and communal strife pose a major threat to peace and development. Gandhi's views in this regard assume a great deal of relevance for us. His chief concern was the evolution of human values in the context of truth and morality, and for this reason, he was not dogmatically attached to any religion. In his view, all the principal religions of the world were manifestations of truth, but none was perfect because each was interpreted through human agency. Each religion had to be looked at from the point of view of the adherent as it satisfied a spiritual need in him.[49] Equal regard and mutual tolerance must form the ground rule of life in a multicultural society. What was necessary was to consider the essential and underlying spirit of a religious system, rather than its external and mundane details.[50] Gandhi was uncompromising in one respect. Reason, he said, must form the sole guide for accepting the authenticity of religious texts and, therefore, the irrational and superstitious customs and traditions associated with religion should be rejected.[51]

The state, in Gandhi's opinion, had to be strictly secular and keep aloof from all religious activities and not patronize any denomination at all. Appeal by the government to the religious sentiment in any form was reprehensible. The majority community had a positive role to play in defusing communal tension. Being stronger it must, he said, extend the hand of friendship and try to make the minorities feel secure. In this context, Gandhi always desired that respected leaders of both communities should meet together and discuss contentious issues in a spirit of mutual regard and consideration for the sentiments of each other. Issues that could not be decided in this manner should be referred to arbitration councils composed of eminent persons enjoying a reputation for fairness.

Another suggestion of Gandhi's for defusing communal tension has a good deal of contemporary relevance. At the level of the locality, individuals enjoying the trust of both communities should form peace brigades, the purpose of which would be to iron out differences and form bridges to promote active cooperation between the communities. Women, he felt, had a special role to play here. Gandhi believed women had greater persuasive powers and could effectively mould public opinion. Gandhi died a martyr to the cause of communalism and, in his death, showed the path to communal harmony.

The press and other media have always played a major role in the spread or containment of emotive issues such as communalism. Gandhi was in favour of editors, journalists and reporters following a minimum code of professional morality and reporting with a sense of social responsibility. He was also of the view that scurrilous writing in the press should be submitted for review to the arbitration councils, which would verify the facts and have correct versions published. Such a policy could be followed in our own times with common benefit to all.

Gandhi regarded education as a powerful medium for transmitting secular and humane values to children. He stressed the need to ensure that educational curricula were free from religious bias and designed to promote fundamental ethics common to all religions. He was totally opposed to the ownership and management of educational institutions by religious bodies, as they often propagated communal feelings. However, he did not mind established religious institutions imparting purely religious education, for this was not meant for the general populace or general students. These ideas are quite germane to the present as state sponsored or state aided educational institutions in India are neither able to promote secular ethics or social consciousness among pupils, nor combat overarching communal biases among the young.

Another important value where education could play a positive interventionist role was that of manual labour. It is strange but true that manual labour is looked down upon in an agricultural country like India. This is the reason for the sorry state of the labourers in the country, the undue rush for white collar jobs and the deep social divide so plainly visible between those who labour with their hands and those who function from their desks. Gandhi's doctrine of bread labour made him regard manual labour in the light of a sacred duty laid upon each individual, regardless of his vocation in life. He believed in the equality of all labour and in the corresponding equality of wages. If Indians would alter their attitude towards manual labour and try to approximate Gandhi's approach, many of the economic and social ills in the country could perhaps be resolved. One obvious way would be to include manual labour in the school curriculum, not in a mechanical way, but integrated with the rest of the curriculum, as Gandhi had envisaged.

Gandhi's emphasis on swadeshi, which did not merely denote "belonging to one's country", but also to the immediate neighbourhood, is extremely important for our times. Local institutions and organizations for managing local affairs have either dwindled or become non-existent with the result that we have lost faith in ourselves to do anything and constantly rely on the authorities to solve our local problems. The need of the hour is to arouse popular consciousness about local issues and try to resolve them through voluntary cooperation. People in the field of appropriate and indigenous technology are showing ways in which even a force like electricity can be produced locally, rendering huge dams unnecessary. The indigenous water harvesting technology being tried out in various parts of India would have met with Gandhi's whole hearted approval. Conservation of resources was an article of faith with him.

The doctrine of swadeshi also assumes significance in the face of the economic and cultural imperialism launched by multinational corporations in developing countries. The government and the people need to make concerted efforts to stop the march of the multinationals and launch a simultaneous movement to promote the consumption of indigenous products. With India's manpower and agricultural resources, it must be obvious even to laymen that the emphasis in production should be on small scale and cottage industries, which would do justice to India's resources and bring about substantial uplift of the rural poor, who compose the overwhelming majority of the country's population. Gandhi was wholly in favour of small scale production, it being most beneficial for humanity – man would not be uprooted from his native soil or lose his empathy with nature. This may sound like turning the clock back, but may well become necessary very soon.

Gandhi's persistent emphasis on sound management of agricultural production in India assumes great significance in the context of the current global food and unemployment crises, which have affected India as well. It would be relevant to quote M.S. Swaminathan, the celebrated agricultural scientist and Father of the Green Revolution in India, on the issue: "Carefully planned agricultural progress can help to create simultaneously more food, income and jobs. It is only agriculture, including crop and animal husbandry, fisheries, forestry and agro-processing, which can promote job led economic growth. Modern industry, in contrast, promotes jobless growth, which will lead to joyless growth in population rich nations.[52]

In his quest for the satisfaction of his senses, modern man has indiscriminately exploited his environment, both human and non-human. In the process, he has become spiritually impoverished and alienated from his true self, which demands sharing and giving for its fulfilment. The current danger to life from all kinds of pollution and ecological imbalances is the result of man's thirst for material possessions and personal advancement. This process has had a reaction and led to an upsurge of movements and activities to protect the environment. Some such are mentioned here as they are closely related to Gandhi's ideas.

The Chipko Movement was launched in the Garhwal hills of north India for the preservation of the forests. Inspired by Gandhi and Acharya Vinoba Bhave's Ṣarvodaya Movement, it was led by Sunderlal Bahuguna and first began with the villagers embracing tree trunks to protest the felling of ash trees by a sports goods company. This movement now has global dimensions. Bahuguna is currently engaged in resisting non-violently the threat of enormous destruction to human life and the environment by the giant Tehri Dam Project, which is also in the Garhwal region.

Another strong non-violent movement to save the environment, especially the uprooting of local communities for a giant river project and to prevent the resultant havoc caused by it, is the Narmada Bachao Andolan led by Medha Patkar with the active and committed support of several other members of the intelligentsia. More recently, the satyagraha technique was adopted to protest the construction of big dams across the Bhagirathi river (the upper reaches of the Ganga), as a result of which two of the six projects have been suspended so far. The satyagraha is being undertaken by Professor G.D. Agarwal, a retired professor of the Indian Institute of Technology in Kanpur.[53]

The relevance of Gandhi's ideas in the judicial field is becoming increasingly apparent these days. A lawyer himself, he was well aware of the dilatory tactics and enormous expenditure involved in litigation, which often resulted in the total denial of justice to the common man. He was of the opinion that disputes should not reach the stage of litigation and must be resolved through arbitration and conciliation. He was in favour of reviving the ancient panchayat system of settling disputes in the villages. The modern Lok Adalats exemplify to some extent Gandhi's concept of rendering justice. They were first established in 1982 as part of the legal aid strategy. To quote from the legal journal, *The Lawyers Collective*, "Lok Adalats are informal, flexible, participatory forums which have as their purpose the encouragement of settlements, compromises and the avoidance of litigation."[54]

The parties to a dispute voluntarily utilize their services to avoid the harassment and frustration often met with in ordinary courts of law. Lok Adalats have no adjudicatory authority and their judges are usually retired judges, advocates or social workers, who act only as mediators or conciliators. Lok Adalats have received statutory status and it is hoped that they will be fully integrated into the present judicial structure. This will inspire greater confidence among litigants and advocates and provide access to quick, effective and "inexpensive" justice.

Finally, even on the contentious subject of reservations in jobs and services, Gandhi's views are very relevant today. Gandhi believed in social and economic equality and more`so in equality of opportunity, especially for those he called Harijans. However, he was totally opposed to reservations in jobs and services on the basis of social categories as that was tantamount to compromising the standard of merit in them. Moreover, such reservation removed the incentive for improvement and endeavour in those on whom these benefits were bestowed. He favoured special opportunities for education and training for the underprivileged sections of society, especially the Harijans. This would naturally widen the scope of their employment and betterment. But successive governments have acquired a vested interest in carrying on the policy of reservations and, in the process, fostered a feeling of antagonism towards the reserved categories among the rest of the population. What is required is political courage to phase out the policy of reservations and for the government to follow a comprehensive plan for securing social justice and equal opportunity for all, particularly at the grass-roots level.

It is hoped that the foregoing section has illustrated to some extent the contemporary relevance of Gandhi's theory of social change. Men and women in Gandhi's society would live in close touch with their environment, not wishing to dominate it, but enjoying being part of it. His relevance for all time has been brought out most cogently by Sarojini Naidu, his famous co-worker and India's outstanding poetess, in a passage written a few months before his assassination. The last lines are quoted here: "He was born like other men, he will die like other men, but unlike them, he will live through the beautiful gospel he has enunciated, that hatred cannot be conquered by the sword, the sword cannot be conquered by the sword, that power cannot be exploited over the weak and the fallen, that the gospel of non-violence, which is the most dynamic and the most creative gospel of power in the world, is the only true foundation of a new civilization, yet to be built."[55]

Notes

1. Richard B. Gregg, 'Gandhiji as a Social Scientist and Social Inventor', in S. Radhakrishnan, ed., *Mahatma Gandhi: Essays and Reflections on His Life and Work* (Bombay: Jaico Publishing House, 1957), p. 65. Gregg referred to Gandhi in this essay as 'a great scientist in the realm of social truth'.
2. Ramashray Roy, *Self and Society: A Study in Gandhian Thought* (New Delhi: Sage Publications, 1984), p. 17.
3. *SWMG*, Volume 6, p. 112.
4. Ibid.
5. Ramashray Roy, *Self and Society*, p. 76.
6. *CWMG*, Volume 60, p. 96.
7. *CWMG*, Volume 44, p. 131.
8. *CWMG*, Volume 34, p. 505.
9. Lucien Goldmann, *The Philosophy of the Enlightenment: The Christian Burgess and the Enlightenment*, trans. by Henry Maas (London: Routledge and Kegan Paul, 1968), p. 18, quoted in Ramashray Roy, *Self and Society*, p. 95.
10. *Gandhi's Diary*, Volume I, p. 201.

11. *CWMG*, Volume 13, p. 219.
12. Pyarelal Nayyar, *The Last Phase*, pp. 580–1.
13. *CWMG*, Volume 58, p. 220.
14. *Young India*, Volume III, p. 547, quoted in Dhawan, *Political Philosophy of Mahatma Gandhi*, p. 316.
15. *CWMG*, Volume 71, p. 406.
16. M.K. Gandhi, *Democracy: Real and Deceptive* (Ahmedabad: Navajivan Publishing House, 1961), p. 28.
17. Ibid., pp. 28–9.
18. *CWMG*, Volume 17, p. 406.
19. *CWMG*, Volume 47, p. 91.
20. *Harijan*, 2 January 1937.
21. *CWMG*, Volume 10, pp. 61–2.
22. *Young India*, Volume II, pp. 435–6.
23. *Harijan*, 2 March 1947.
24. *Harijan*, 22 September 1946; 23 March 1947; 31 August 1947.
25. *Harijan*, 31 July 1936, p. 198.
26. Harijan, 1 September 1940.
27. *Harijan*, 12 May 1946.
28. *Harijan*, January 27, 1940.
29. *Young India*, Selections, Volume III, p. 736, quoted in Gopinath Dhawan, *Political Philosophy of Mahatma Gandhi*, p. 353.
30. *CWMG*, Volume 25, p. 251.
31. *CWMG*, Volume 61, p. 187.
32. *CWMG*, Volume 71, pp. 424–5.
33. *CWMG*, Volume 69, p. 53.
34. *Young India*, Selections, Volume II, p. 1292, quoted in Gopinath Dhawan, *Political Philosophy of Mahatma Gandhi*, p. 367.
35. Harijan, 8 June 1947.
36. *CWMG*, Volume 70, p. 245.
37. Ibid., p. 237.
38. *Young India*, Selections, Volume II, p. 863, quoted in Gopinath Dhawan, *Political Philosophy of Mahatma Gandhi*, p. 369.
39. *CWMG*, Volume 68, p. 390.
40. *Harijan*, 16 May 1936.

41. Stephen Hey, 'Gandhi: Guide to a Better Human Future', in Parel, *Gandhi, Freedom and Self-Rule*, p. 14.
42. *The Times of India,* Varanasi, 19 December 2007, Front Page.
43. Phrase coined by Iris Murdoch, quoted in Ramashray Roy, *Self and Society*, p. 24.
44. *Northern India Patrika,* Allahabad, 19 March 1986, p. 7.
45. Martin Luther King, *Stride toward Freedom: The Montgomery Story* (New York: Harper, 1958), p. 45.
46. Rainer Hilderbrandt and Hans-Jurgen Dyck, *From Gandhi to Walesa: Non-Violent Struggle for Human Rights, A Documentation with 181 Photos*. (Berlin: Publishing House at Check Point Charlie, 1987).
47. T. Gyatso, *Freedom in Exile: The Autobiography of the Dalai Lama* (New York: Harper Collins, 1990).
48. *Time,* 31 December 1999, Rudolph and Rudolph, *Postmodern Gandhi,* p. 56.
49. Quoted in S. Maqbul Ahmad, 'Gandhi and Islam', in *Gandhi Theory and Practice: Social Impact and Contemporary Relevance,* ed., S.C. Biswas (Shimla: Indian Institute of Advanced Study, 1969), p. 67.
50. Ibid., p. 72.
51. Ibid., p. 70.
52. *The Hindu,* New Delhi, 2 June 2008, Editorial Page.
53. *The Sunday Times of India,* Varanasi, 29 June 2008, Editorial Page.
54. *The Lawyers' Collective,* January 1990, pp. 10–2.
55. Quoted in Raghavan Iyer, ed., *Moral and Political Writings of Mahatma Gandhi,* Volume I. (Oxford: Clarendon Press, 1986), p. 12.

Bibliography

The Gandhian Oeuvre

Almost all the known writings, speeches, letters and comments of Mahatma Gandhi have been compiled and published in stages, from 1960 to 1994, by the Publications Division of the Government of India, Ministry of Information and Broadcasting, New Delhi, with the permission of the Navajivan Trust, Ahmedabad, in the chronologically arranged 100 volume series, *The Collected Works of Mahatma Gandhi*. All the well-known and widely read works of Gandhi are reproduced in the *Collected Works*. These include, of course, his perennially popular autobiography, *The Story of My Experiments with Truth*, and the fount of Gandhism, *Hind Swaraj*, which has attracted the attention of scholars, disciples and lay people alike since at least 1938, when the theosophical journal, *Aryan Path*, carried a symposium on the book, and it has excited new and almost compulsive interest a century after its first appearance in English. I have read the writings in their various publication avatars, but for ease of citation and tracking, I have sourced most of the references to them in this text to the relevant volumes of the *Collected Works*. As indicated in the Notes, the *Collected Works* have been abbreviated as *CWMG* in the citations.

Several selections, thematic or general, from Gandhi's oeuvre are also available in print. I have occasionally referred to these, mainly for material not chronologically identifiable in the concerned selection. Looking up such selections might also be useful for those seeking specific perspectives that do not require exploration of the massive tomes of the *Collected Works*. A remarkably representative compendium of this kind is *The Selected Works of Mahatma Gandhi*, edited by Shriman Narayan and published in six volumes by the Navajivan Publishing House, Ahmedabad, in 1968, which have collectively been referred to in the Notes as the *SWMG*. Other such selections, including some originally put together by Gandhi himself, or under his guidance, include the following:

1. Gandhi, M.K. *Conquest of Self*, ed., R.K. Prabhu and U.R. Rao (Bombay: Thacker and Co., 1943).
2. *Selections from Gandhi*, ed., N.K. Bose (Ahmedabad: New Publishing House, 1957).
3. *Economic and Industrial Life and Relations*, Volumes 1–3, ed., V.B. Kher (Ahmedabad: Navajivan Publishing House, 1957).
4. *Wit and Wisdom of Mahatma Gandhi*, ed., N.B. Sen (New Delhi: New Book Society of India, 1960).
5. *Democracy: Real and Deceptive*, (Ahmedabad: Navajivan Publishing House, 1961).
6. *The Mind of Mahatma Gandhi*, ed., R.K. Prabhu and U.R. Rao (Ahmedabad: Navajivan Publishing House, 1967).
7. *Gandhi: Essential Writings*, ed., V.V. Ramanna Murti (New Delhi: Gandhi Peace Foundation, 1970).
8. *Moral and Political Writings of Mahatma Gandhi*, Volume I, ed., Raghavan N. Iyer (Oxford: Clarendon Press, 1986).
9. *Gandhi on Women*, ed., Pushpa Joshi (Ahmedabad: Navajivan Publishing House, 1988).
10. *Hind Swaraj and Other Writings*, ed., Anthony J. Parel (Cambridge: Cambridge University Press, 1997).

While Gandhi's writings in *Harijan* and *Young India* feature in the *CWMG*, the following compilations are useful for reading and understanding them in a chronological perspective:

1. *Harijan: A Journal of Applied Gandhism, 1933–55*, Volumes 1–19 (New York and London: Garland, 1973).
2. *Young India, 1919–31*, Volumes 1–13, ed., M.K. Gandhi (Ahmedabad: Navajivan Publishing House, 1981).

Books and Articles

Amin, Shahid. 'Gandhi as Mahatma: Gorakhpur District, Eastern UP, 1921–22', in *Subaltern Studies III: Writings on South Asian History and Society*, ed., Ranajit Guha (Delhi: Oxford University Press, 1984), pp. 1–61.

Andrews, C.F. *Mahatma Gandhi: His Life and Ideas* (Delhi: Anmol Publications, 1987).

Aron, Raymond. *Main Currents in Sociological Thought*, Volumes 1–2 (Harmondsworth: Penguin Books, 1967).

Ashe, Geoffrey. *Gandhi: A Study in Revolution* (London: Asia Publishing House, 1968).

Bakshi, S.R. *Gandhi and His Social Thought* (New Delhi: Criterion Publications, 1986).

Bandyopadhyaya, J. *Social and Political Thought of Gandhi* (Mumbai: Allied Publishers, 1969).

Birla, G.D. *In the Shadow of the Mahatma* (Mumbai: Vakils, Feffer and Simons, 1972).

Biswas, S.C., ed. *Gandhi: Theory and Practice, Social Impact and Contemporary Relevance* (Shimla: Indian Institute of Advanced Study, 1969).

Bierstedt, Robert. *The Social Order* (Mumbai: Tata McGraw Hill, 1970).

Bose, N.K. *Studies in Gandhism*, 2nd Edition (Kolkata: India Associated Publishing Co., 1947).

Bondurant, Joan V. *Conquest of Violence: The Gandhian Philosophy of Conflict* (Berkeley: Oxford University Press, 1969).

Bottomore, T.B. *Sociology: A Guide to Problems and Literature*, 2nd Edition (Mumbai: Blackie and Son, 1971).

Chakravarty, Gargi. *Gandhi: A Challenge to Communalism* (New Delhi: Eastern Book Centre, 1987).

Chatterjee, Partha. 'Gandhi and the Critique of Civil Society', in *Subaltern Studies III: Writings on South Asian History and Society*, ed., Ranajit Guha (Delhi: Oxford University Press, 1984), pp. 153–95.

Chatterjee, Margaret. *Gandhi's Religious Thought* (Hong Kong: The Macmillan Press, 1983).

Dalton, Dennis. 'The Theory of Anarchism in Modern India: An Analysis of the Political Thought of Vivekananda, Aurobindo and Gandhi', in *Tradition and Politics in South Asia*, ed., R.J. Moore (New Delhi: Vikas Publishing House, 1979), pp. 198–227.

Dalton, G.M. *Indian Idea of Freedom: Political Thought of Swami Vivekananda, Aurobindo Ghose, Mahatma Gandhi and Rabindranath Tagore* (Gurgaon: The Academic Press, 1982).

Desai, Mahadev Haribhai. *A Righteous Struggle* (Ahmedabad: Navajivan Publishing House, 1951).

Desai, A.R. *Social Background of Indian Nationalism* (Mumbai: Popular Book Depot, 1954).

Dhawan, Gopinath. *The Political Philosophy of Mahatma Gandhi*, 2nd Revised Edition (Ahmedabad: Navajivan Press, 1951).

Dikshit, G.N. *Gandhi's Challenge to Communism* (New Delhi: S. Chand, 1972).

Eisenstadt, Samuel N. *Tradition, Change, and Modernity* (New York: John Wiley, 1973).

Engels, Frederick and Karl Marx. *Selected Works*, Volumes 1–3 (Moscow: Progress Publishers, 1969).

Erikson, E.H. *Gandhi's Truth: On the Origins of Militant Non-Violence* (London: Faber and Faber, 1970).

Fischer, Louis. *The Life of Mahatma Gandhi* (London: Law and Brydon, 1957).

Ganguli, B.N. *Gandhi's Social Philosophy: Perspective and Relevance* (Delhi: Vikas Publishing House, 1973).

Gangrade, K.D. *Gandhian Ideal: Development and Social Change* (New Delhi: Northern Book Centre, 1991).

Goldmann, Lucien. *The Philosophy of the Enlightenment*, Trans. by Henry Maas (London: Routledge and Kegan Paul, 1968).

Gregg, Richard B. *The Power of Non-Violence* (Ahmedabad: Navajivan Publishing House, 1951).

Gyatso, T. [His Holiness the Dalai Lama]. *Freedom in Exile: The Autobiography of the Dalai Lama* (New York: Harper Collins, 1990).

Haferkamp, Hans and Neil J. Smelser, eds. *Social Change and Modernity* (Berkeley: University of California Press, 1992).

Hilderbrandt, Rainer and Hans-Jurgen Dyck. *From Gandhi to Walesa: Non-Violent Struggle for Human Rights, A Documentation with 181 Photos* (Berlin: Publishing House at Check Point Charlie, 1987).

Hook, Sidney. *The Hero in History: A Study in Limitation and Possibility* (New Delhi: Allied Publishers, 1943).

Iyer, Raghavan N. *The Moral and Political Thought of Mahatma Gandhi* (London: Oxford University Press, 1978).

— *The Gandhian Bridge between Heaven and Earth* (New Delhi: Gandhi Smriti and Darshan Samiti, 1988).

Kalelkar, Kaka. *Stray Glimpses of Bapu* (Ahmedabad: Navajivan Publishing House, 1950).

Kappen, Mercy, ed. *Gandhi and Social Action Today* (New Delhi: Sterling Publishers, 1990).

Karve, Irawati. *Kinship Organization in India* (New Delhi: Munshiram Manoharlal, 1990).

Kripalani, Krishna. *Gandhi: A Life* (Kolkata: Published by the Author, 1968).

Kumar, Ravinder. *Essays on Gandhian Politics: The Rowlatt Satyagraha of 1919* (Oxford: Clarendon Press, 1971).

— *Essays in the Social History of Modern India* (Delhi: Oxford University Press, 1983).

Kuppuswamy, B. *Social Change in India* (Sahibabad: Vikas Publishing House, 1979).

Lyon, David. *Postmodernity* (New Delhi: Viva Books, 2002).

MacIver, R.M. and C.H. Page. *Society: An Introductory Analysis* (New York: Holt, Rinehart and Winston, 1949).

Mannheim, Karl. *Essays on Sociology and Social Psychology* (London: Routledge and Kegan Paul, 1969)

Mashruwala, K.G. *Gandhi and Marx* (Ahmedabad: Navajivan Publishing House, 1956).

Merton, R.K. *Social Theory and Social Structure* (Glencoe: The Free Press, 1964).

Moore, W.E. *Social Change* (New Delhi: Prentice Hall of India Pvt. Ltd, 1978).

Nadel, S.F. *The Theory of Social Structure* (London: Cohen and West, 1965).

Nanda, B.R. *Mahatma Gandhi: A Biography* (Delhi: Oxford University Press, 1982).

Nandy, Ashis. *At the Edge of Psychology: Essays in Politics and Culture* (Delhi: Oxford University Press, 1980).

— *The Intimate Enemy: Loss and Recovery of Self under Colonialism* (Delhi: Oxford University Press, 1983).

Nayyar, Pyarelal. *Mahatma Gandhi: The Last Phase* (Ahmedabad: Navajivan Publishing House, 1956).

— *Mahatma Gandhi: The Early Phase,* Volume I (Ahmedabad: Navajivan Publishing House, 1965).

Nisbet, Robert A. *Social Change and History* (New York: Oxford University Press, 1977).

Ogburn, William F. and Meyer F. Nimkoff. *A Handbook of Sociology* (New Delhi: Eurasia Publishing House, 1979).

Orsini, Francesca. *The Hindi Public Sphere 1920–40: Language and Literature in the Age of Nationalism* (New Delhi: Oxford University Press, 2002).

Paranjape, Makarand. *Decolonization and Development: Hind Svaraj Revisioned* (New Delhi: Sage Publications, 1993).

Parel, Anthony J., ed. *Gandhi, Freedom and Self Rule* (New York and Oxford: Lexington Books, 2000).

Parel, Anthony J. *Gandhi's Philosophy and the Quest for Harmony* (Cambridge: Cambridge University Press, 2006).

Parsons, Talcott. *Social Systems and the Evolution of Action Theory* (New York: The Free Press, 1977).

Pradhan, Benudhar. *The Socialist Thought of Mahatma Gandhi,* Volume II. (Delhi: GDK Publications, 1980).

Prasad, Bimal. *Gandhi, Nehru and J.P.: Studies in Leadership* (Delhi: Chanakya Publications, 1985).

Prasad, Nageshwar, ed. *Hind Swaraj: A Fresh Look* (New Delhi: Gandhi Peace Foundation, 1985).

Radcliffe-Brown, A.R. *A National Science of Society* (New York: The Free Press, 1957).

Radhakrishnan, S., ed. *Mahatma Gandhi: Essays and Reflections on His Life and Work* (Mumbai: Jaico Publishing House, 1957).

— *Mahatma Gandhi: 100 Years* (New Delhi: Gandhi Peace Foundation, 1968).

Roland, Romain. *Mahatma Gandhi* (New Delhi: Publications Division, 1976).

Roy, Ramashray. *Self and Society: A Study in Gandhian Thought* (New Delhi: Sage Publications, 1985).

Rudolph, Lloyd I. and Susanne Hoeber Rudolph. *The Modernity of Tradition* (Chicago: University of Chicago Press, 1967).

— *Postmodern Gandhi and Other Essays: Gandhi in the World and at Home* (New Delhi: Oxford University Press, 2008).

Santayana, George. *The Life of Reason* (New York: Charles Scribners' Sons, 1905–06).

Saran, A.K. 'Gandhi and the Concept of Politics: Towards a Normal Civilization', in *Gandhi Marg* Volume I, No. 11 (February 1998), pp. 675–727.

Sarkar, Sumit. *Modern India 1885–1947* (Delhi: Macmillan India, 1984).

Sills, David L., ed. *International Encyclopedia of the Social Sciences*, Volumes 13 and 14 (New York: The Macmillan Company and the Free Press, 1972).

Sim, Stuart. *Post-Marxism: An Intellectual History* (New York: Routledge, 2000).

Singh, Yogendra. *Modernization of Indian Tradition* (Faridabad: Thomson Press, 1977).

— *Social Stratification and Change in India* (New Delhi: Manohar, 1980).

Sinha, M.P., ed. *Contemporary Relevance of Gandhi* (Mumbai: Nachiket Publications, 1970).

Sztompka, Piotr. *The Sociology of Social Change* (Oxford: Blackwell, 1993).

Tendulkar, D.G. *Mahatma: Life of Mohandas Karamchand Gandhi*, Volumes 1–8 (New Delhi: Publications Division, 1969).

Unnithan, T.K. *Gandhi and Social Change* (Jaipur: Rawat Publications, 1979).

Weber, Max. *The Protestant Ethic and the Spirit of Capitalism*, Trans. by Talcott Parsons (London: George Allen and Unwin Ltd, 1930).

Journals and Newspapers

The Lawyers Collective, Mumbai.

The Times of India, New Delhi.

Northern India Patrika, Allahabad.

Index

ahimsa (non-violence)
  principle of, 20-25
Ajmal Khan, Hakim Saheb, 126
Alexander, Horace, 19
All India Village Industries Association (AIVIA), 58, 147
anti-untouchability movement, 171-78
Arnold, Edwin, Sir, 22

Bapa, Thakkar, 153
Bardoli Satyagraha, 153
Basham, A.L., 18
Basic Education Scheme, 169
basic education, 165-71
Bhatt, Shamal, 19, 20, 22
Bhave, Vinoba Acharya, 234
Bierstedt, Richard, 5
Birla, G.D., 123
Blavatsky, 22
Boer War, 28
Bose, J.C., Sir, 123
Bose, Subhash Chandra, 123
Boudrillard, Jean, 7, 8
bread labour
  doctrine of, 48-49, 56

capital-labour relations, 101-2
Carpenter, Edward, 39
caste system, 80-91
Child Marriage Restraint Bill, 141
child wives/widows, 140-45
citizenship, 71
civil disobedience, 31
communal tension, 93-97

decentralization of the economy, 198-201
democracy, 69-70

economic equality, 61
economy of resources, 149-50
education, 71, 109-14
  physical, 166
equality of labour, 147-49
equality of the sexes, 33-36
Escombe, Harry, 28

Gandhi, Mahatma
as a postmodernist, 9-10
economic ideas of, 46-48
social ideas of, 13 evolution of, 13-17; impact of Hindu religious philosophy on, 36-38; impact of Indian social philosophy on, 40-42
socio-economic ideas of, impact of western civilization on, 38
Gandhi-Irwin Pact of 1931, 38
Gokhale, Gopal Krishna, 110
Green Pamphlet, 27
Gujarat (Kheda) Satyagraha, 162-63
Gujarat Vidyapith, 167

Haferkamp, Hans and Neil J. Smelser, 6
Harijan Sevak Sangh, 173, 175
Harijan, 148, 152, 174, 200
Hind Swaraj, 2, 9, 39, 47, 50, 55, 60, 62, 68, 73, 76, 94
Hindi
as the national language, 121-25
Hindu-Muslim relations, 125-29, 185-88

ideal ruler, 68-69
ideal society
vision of, 55-62, 64; plan for, 66-68;
"ideal village", 66
Indian Ambulance Corps, 28, 31
Indian civilization, 56, 97-101
Indian education system, 91-93
Indian National Congress, remodelling of, 191-95
Indian Opinion, 30, 109
Indian social structure, 84

justice
concept of, 61

Kalekar, Kaka Saheb, 124
Kallenbach Herman, 32
Kantak, Premabehn, 138
Kumar, Ravinder, 2, 39
Kuppuswamy, B., 5

Lyotard, Foucault, 7

marriage, 42
Mehta, Rajchandra, 23
modern non-violent social order, 222-28
Mueller, Max, 23

Naidu, Sarojini, 144
Nandy, Ashis, 9
Nayyar, Pyarelal, 14
Nehru, Jawaharlal, 66
Non-Cooperation Movement, 166

Paranjpe, Makrand, 9
Parel, Anthony J., 3
Phoenix Trust Deed, 56
Poona or Yeravda Pact, 172
postmodern debate, 9
postmodernism, 6
postmodernist writers, 7
Prasad, Nageshwar, 9
public service/worker, 45-46

Ram Rajya, 68
Rajagopalachari, C., 196
Removal of Civil Disability Act, 176
Roy, Ramashray, 60
Rudolph, Lloyd I. and Susanne Hoeber Rudolph, 9, 10
rural regeneration, 195-98
Ruskin, John, 29, 39

Sanatana Dharma, 129
satyagraha, 25-30, 159-65
  as means for creating ideal society, 58-60
Seeker's Club, 29
self-esteem, 114-16
self-sacrifice, 166-18
Shraddhanand, Swami, 128
shuddhi movement, 96
social change, 5
  basic issues of, 206-14
  concept of, 5-6
  Gandhi's theory of, 214-22, contemporary relevance of, 228-36
  instruments of, 159-201
social equality, 61
sovereignty, 8
svadharma, 40
Swadeshi Movement, 178-85
Swaminathan, M.S., 233
swaraj
  concept of, 62-65
Sztompka, Piotr., 6

Tata, R.J., 32
The Lawyers Collective, 235
Thoreau, Henry David, 31, 67
Tikekar, Indu, 150
Tolstoy Farm, 32, 45
Tolstoy, Leo, 23
trusteeship, 49-50, 150-54
truth
  ideology of, 17-20; 60

untouchability, 83-91, 129-34, 134-36

varnadharma, 41-42
varna system, 42-43
varna vyavastha, 41
village life, 119-21

Walker, R.B.J., 8
Wardha Scheme of Education, 168
women
  as catalysts, 189-91
  Gandhi's perception of, 13, 137-40
women's status, 102-5
work ethic, 145-47

Young India, 126, 146, 171